INSIDE THE UNDERGRADUATE TEACHING EXPERIENCE

INSIDE THE UNDERGRADUATE TEACHING EXPERIENCE

*The University of Washington's
Growth in Faculty Teaching Study*

Catharine Hoffman Beyer
Edward Taylor
Gerald M. Gillmore

Published by State University of New York Press, Albany

© 2013 State University of New York

For information, contact State University of New York Press, Albany, NY
www.sunypress.edu

Production by Diane Ganeles
Marketing by Michael Campochiaro

Library of Congress Cataloging-in-Publication Data

Beyer, Catharine Hoffman, author.
 Inside the undergraduate teaching experience : the University of
Washington's growth in faculty teaching study / Catharine Hoffman Beyer,
Edward Taylor, and Gerald M. Gillmore.
    pages   cm
Includes bibliographical references and index.
ISBN 978-1-4384-4605-9 (hardcover : alk. paper)
ISBN 978-1-4384-4604-2 (pbk. : alk. paper)
 1. University of Washington. 2. Education, Higher—Washington
(State)—Longitudinal studies. 3. College teaching—Washington
(State)—Longitudinal studies. I. Taylor, Edward, 1959– author. II.
Gillmore, Gerald M. (Gerald Millard), 1941– author. III. Title.
 LD5753.B495 2013
 378.797'772—dc23

                                                    2012017558

10 9 8 7 6 5 4 3 2 1

I kind of began to believe that you have to introduce [students] to this world of ideas, the life of the mind, that ideas have value for their own sakes. . . . [That] world has a door, and you need a pass.
—Faculty participant in the University of Washington's Growth in Faculty Teaching Study (UW GIFTS)

This book is dedicated to all those college teachers who are helping students find that door and get the pass that opens it—and especially to our participants in the UW GIFTS.

CONTENTS

TABLES AND FIGURES

ACKNOWLEDGMENTS

We are grateful to our colleagues in Undergraduate Academic Affairs at the University of Washington for providing us with encouragement, love, and ideas. In particular, we thank Nana Lowell, director of the UW's Office of Educational Assessment, who gave the University of Washington Growth in Faculty Teaching Study (UW GIFTS) significant financial and moral support and who served as a generous listener and caring guide throughout the life of the study. We also thank Jennifer Dow Walls in the Dean's Office for graciously making it possible for us to conduct research and write together, as well as for her significant administrative help.

We also thank Dr. Richard P. Beyer for his statistical analysis of our results and his thoughtful review of our manuscript. His work gave us new ways to view our results—both quantitative and editorial—and his personal response to the faculty stories in the book was gratifying.

In addition, we gratefully acknowledge the help of our families and friends. Catharine Beyer acknowledges with gratitude her husband, Richard, for his considerable help in the study and, more important, for continuing to be the amazing light that he is in her life. In addition, she is grateful to her daughters, Jessica and Emily, for their ideas about study results, their willingness to read drafts, and, most of all, for their examples as remarkable teachers in their own rights. She thanks her parents, Arthur and Lucia Hoffman, for celebrating question-asking and for making her feel cherished. She thanks her sisters, Mickey Grooters and Dorothy Schlientz, and her friends, who listened to stories about faculty and to the agonies and ecstasies of the research process. Finally, she thanks her students for all they have taught her.

Ed Taylor wishes to express his gratitude to the countless dedicated educators at the university. Many of our finest and most dedicated teachers do so with little public recognition. Yet their work is manifest in the good work of their students and the lives well lived many years after their students have left their classrooms. In addition, he is also grateful to Sharon Parks, Arthur Zajonc, Angeles Arrien, and Rachel Remen who have spent a lifetime educating so many willing students like him.

Gerald Gillmore wishes to express his gratitude to the faculty and staff of the University of Washington who directly and indirectly supported him and his work over a long and satisfying career. In particular, he is deeply honored to have been associated with an institution that willingly encourages and supports open, self-reflective research on and assessment of the effectiveness of its teaching and learning mission, as illustrated by the research both underlying this publication and the earlier publication of *Inside the Undergraduate Experience*.

Finally, the authors thank each other for making this study a journey of the heart as well as the mind.

1

GIFTS

I had to practice learning how to be at ease, consciously thinking about the words "flexible," "relaxed," "open," instead of about what I know. I had to remind myself to pay attention to what is happening, to just be a little bit more in there—outside of myself.

—Faculty member in the humanities[1]

B y every measure of success, Professor Murray Mann's work as a faculty member at a large, R1, public university has been stunning. Dr. Mann is one of the world's most highly regarded scholars in the study of law and legal systems, publishing numerous books, articles, book chapters, and reviews in his field and giving talks all over the world. In addition, Dr. Mann has received strong evaluations for the large lecture and small seminar classes that he has taught to undergraduates for more than a quarter of a century. When he was an assistant professor—only five years out of a prestigious graduate school program in which he received no teaching training—the university recognized Dr. Mann's exceptional undergraduate teaching with a distinguished teaching award. His reputation as an excellent teacher extends to his work with graduate students, who speak of him as a generous mentor capable of both nurturing their creativity and critiquing their work in ways that push them to deeper intellectual engagement with their own and others' ideas.

Little external pressure is imposed on most faculty members at large universities to make changes in their teaching, but for faculty members with Dr. Mann's level of success, there is no pressure at all. Now a full professor whose reputation draws brilliant young scholars to the university, Dr. Mann could easily pull his yellowed notes from his battered briefcase, give the same lectures he gave 15 years ago, and focus

100% of his time on his research—an image of professors that many people believe represents the reality at large U.S. universities. However, Dr. Mann's story takes him in a very different direction from that image of college faculty. Dr. Mann describes his direction as "increasing frustration and insecurity about my capacity to teach effectively—the opposite trajectory of what should be."

For years, Dr. Mann focused his teaching on his lectures. In his words: "In the lecture format, it was all about putting out a great performance and teaching relevant, important materials so the students really felt they learned something. And it worked. So I never thought much about teaching." But after he won a distinguished teaching award, Dr. Mann began to "deconstruct" his own teaching. As he described it, "That led me to a whole lot of experiments." Currently, Dr. Mann spends much of the 80 minutes in his large lecture classes getting his students to participate actively in constructing the class. Although he still does some lecturing, he describes it as "less traditional lecturing," adding:

> I try to get the students to do that for me, so I start with an outline—"Here's what we have been talking about so far. Here's where we got to last time." And then I say, "But it's more complicated than that and here's why." Then I ask them what they think about that. Or I might say, "Here's the concept of legal mobilization—can someone talk about that?" I introduce a segment of the class and conclude a segment of the class to bring some greater order to the class. The class averages about 150 students. I walk around when I ask them for their ideas. I am not as skilled at this kind of format as I was as a lecturer. Once I wrote my lecture, I could spend a half hour looking at it before walking in and giving the lecture without looking at the notes very much. What I find in this new format is that I spend far more time on it.

Dr. Mann said that integrating active learning strategies such as these takes more time because he feels he has to prepare for a wide range of possible directions the class may take on any given day. In his words:

> I try to change the reading material on a regular basis, if for no other reason than to keep [students] from being able to copy

papers from another class, for instance. I spend a lot of time dealing with those instrumental problems. But even when I'm using material I've used before, I have a terrible problem of over-preparing—over-preparing in such a way that I tend to paralyze myself. I don't know where discussion is going to go, so I feel that I have to be prepared to answer all possible turns of discussion and re-familiarize myself with all the literature in a way I didn't have to do in the lecture format. And in being over-prepared, my head is often too full of knowledge. I haven't really worked that out yet. At this point I shouldn't be preparing like that for a class I've taught 20 times. I also think that level of preparation makes me less light on my feet than I should be.

Although research on best practices in college teaching (Bain, 2004), on assessing classroom learning (Angelo & Cross, 1993), and on student engagement (Barkley, 2010) suggests that Dr. Mann's shift from a focus on lecturing to a focus on engaging active student learning in his class is the right direction, it is not a direction that he has always felt comfortable with. As he puts it: "Trying to make the communication between students work is much more uncertain, much more episodic than a lecture class is. It does make you more vulnerable. So strangely I feel more insecure all the time, especially in the large class."

Why would faculty members with Dr. Mann's considerable success continue to make changes to their teaching, especially when such changes require them to devote hours of extra time to the teaching aspects of their work, take them outside their comfort zones and away from the practices that have been successful in the past, and are rarely noticed or rewarded by the institutions in which they work? Why would any faculty member—not just those with Dr. Mann's stature—do that?

College Teaching Realities

It isn't as though faculty have been trained to make changes in their teaching. As Dr. Mann's experience illustrates, new PhDs often have had little teaching experience, and their graduate programs have not encouraged them to think about teaching before they become faculty members (Nyquist et al., 1999). Instead, their graduate school experience has trained them to be thoughtful researchers—to use the methods and practices of their respective disciplines effectively and to have faith in the values in their fields. This work is neither small nor unimportant. Indeed, top quality research is critical to our society. It is the work of discovery, of creating knowledge, of generating solutions. It is complex, difficult work, requiring imagination and full understanding of what came before it, as well as a sense of new pathways into an invisible future. That graduate study can prepare students to continue the work of knowledge creation is miraculous.

But while graduate school has prepared students to discover new knowledge, in most cases it has not prepared them to teach or to think about changes in their teaching work. Even those who have worked as teaching assistants (TAs) in graduate school are likely to have had few opportunities to teach a class of their own or to have taught the same class more than once. Instead, most TAs lead small discussion sections attached to large classes; the main purpose of their work is to help the students meet *someone else's* goals for student learning. Sometimes professors give their TAs detailed "playbooks" about how to conduct sections, and sometimes they provide loose guidelines. However, in most cases, the work that the graduate student TAs are doing in sections is the result of decisions made by the faculty members who are teaching the class to which the TAs are assigned.

Often that experience is rich and profound. Graduate students can learn a great deal by working with professors who are well-respected scholars and teachers and by interacting with undergraduates in a number of ways. Graduate student TAs also often make significant contributions to the faculty member's learning and to the course's success. In contrast, the experience of being a TA can sometimes be challenging, particularly when faculty members are unclear about course expectations and are not open to their TAs' experience in sections or ideas about the course.

However, no matter whether the TA experience is good or bad, in most cases there are limits to what graduate students can learn about teaching in their roles as TAs who are leading discussion sections for faculty members' classes. Working as a TA does not give graduate students the difficult experience of winnowing a gigantic subject area into the small packages necessary for a 10- or 12-week class. It does not require them to identify goals for up to 700 students' learning or the experience of sifting through a wealth of possible readings and other media to arrive at the few that can be covered in a short space of time. Unless they are teaching their own classes, TAs usually do not have to create assignments that address the learning goals they have identified or to shape and deliver class time day after day that is both instructive and engaging for all 700 students. The TA experience usually does not require them to think about the outcomes, both daily and over the course of the quarter or semester, in order to determine what to change tomorrow or next year to make the class better. Furthermore, TAs usually do not have to walk into the classroom a year later, meet an entirely different population of students, and try it again. Without such experiences, it is difficult for graduate students to know themselves as teachers, to reflect on their teaching work, and to put new practices into play in order to improve that work.

Furthermore, in most cases, the teaching graduate students do is not structured to help them develop into good teachers, but, rather, to help their academic institutions fulfill their undergraduate teaching missions (Austin, 2002; Deresiewicz, 2011). Often, the more highly ranked the institution is, the fewer opportunities faculty had as graduate students for teaching or teaching instruction. In the words of two University of Washington (UW) faculty members:

> I didn't even think about [teaching in graduate school]. I thought about the graduate courses that I took and why I liked them and why I didn't like them. But I didn't think about undergraduate teaching at all. A lot of us didn't TA. Nobody talked about teaching; the faculty didn't talk about teaching. And when I called my advisor when I realized that I was going to have to start teaching, it was like, "Stan, what do I do?" And he said, "Don't work on your classes over the summer. You won't get your own research done. Just wait till the semester starts." I was teaching two large undergraduate classes, and it was the worst advice I have gotten—and followed—in my life. (Faculty member in the social sciences)

> I was in the College of Engineering there, and it was pretty classic, as far as my understanding of a classic engineering PhD goes, where the focus was solely on research. I actually did TA work, where I had to do just one-on-one office hours and grading, so I didn't actually teach a section. I only substituted for

my professor once, and that was a frightening experience. (Faculty member in engineering)

Furthermore, examining one's teaching and making changes to it often require that faculty step out of the position of authority, or in the words of the humanities faculty member whose quotation begins this book, out of what they "know." Learning to step away from what they know is not likely to have been part of most graduate students' experience. Programs may differ dramatically across the country, but nearly all are marked by a hierarchy with faculty advisors at the top holding complete power over the futures of the graduate students under them. According to many new faculty members, this structure, however kind the people in it may be, often makes graduate students feel compelled to display what they know at all times. In this structure, graduate students often feel that they are being judged—and usually found wanting— as the wonderful comic strip *Piled Higher and Deeper*, by Jorge Cham (1997–2012), frequently illustrates.

For these reasons, the graduate school structure does not foster in students the sense that it is safe to admit weakness or wise to yield authority to others (Kramer, 1998). Therefore, just as the graduate experience often has not provided new faculty with much training in teaching or in the kinds of experience that might lead to teaching improvement, neither has it typically given new PhDs the "flexibility" and "openness"—in the words that begin this chapter—required to teach well and to examine one's teaching work.

Yet after graduate school, these new PhDs are the people who create and sustain the best learning system in the world—the U.S. system of higher education (Times Higher Education, 2011). These are the people who find themselves asked to speak to, engage, and foster the learning of between two and 800 students in classes day after day. These are the people who are asked to ensure that all students in the room learn the same content, such as theories of crime, introductory biology, beginning acting techniques, Shakespeare's comedies, calculus, international political and economic interaction since 1945, how to build a bridge, and the medieval world.

In addition, these are the people who will help students develop a pack of skills—how to read scholarly and technical articles; how to write arguments and reports; how to think critically, creatively, and scientifically; how to speak effectively about what they know; how to define and solve problems; how to find and use information—in ways that those students could not do before. These are the people who will literally change the structure of their students' brains; who will open interests, abilities, and passions in students that those students never imagined they had; who will profoundly move students whom they'll never meet; and who will set students on paths into academic and professional futures that they will love. The teaching work of faculty is so complex and demanding it sometimes seems as though we are asking them to write, conduct, and perform a symphony that will make 400 people laugh in the same place, cry in the same place, and leave the room with a shared understanding of the intricacies of the tune and with the ability to hum it perfectly, adding their own clever variations, for the rest of their lives.

Faculty members are asked to give this kind of performance not only with little previous experience and training in doing it; they have to do this work no matter who they are. If they are shy, as many faculty report they are, they still must face those many eyes, 30 to 50 times a term. In the words of one faculty member:

> When I started, I wasn't an outgoing person. I liked to be in an observatory all night long staring at stars, so lecturing time after time with 250 students and being able to make that work— I think my [own] growth has played a significant role. (Faculty member in the sciences/math)

If they have a fear of public speaking, as more than three-quarters of the U.S. population do (Lilienfeld, 2010), that fear does not excuse them from speaking to classes of students every day and then getting up and doing it again the next day. For example, the faculty member who made the following comment speaks to more than 100 students for four hours every week:

> Well, to be honest, I have a phobia about public speaking. I think my fear of public speaking is greater than most people's, so to get up in front of the class was one of the hardest things for me to do. (Faculty member in architecture/built environments, 300 level, 111 students)

Finally, there is little external pressure on faculty to do well at their teaching. It is true that emphasis on teaching has increased dramatically over the past few decades in higher education, with many faculty members having to demonstrate effective teaching in order to get tenure or promotions. However, particularly at large public research institutions, the measures of effective teaching that administrators review are often confined to a few questions on a few course evaluations. Also, at most institutions, faculty who are remarkable researchers will not be booted out by a few mediocre teaching evaluations. In fact, at most institutions of higher education, if there are no complaints from students, college administrators have little knowledge of what faculty are doing in their classrooms. In the words of Derek Bok (2006):

> However much professors care about their teaching, nothing forces them or their academic leaders to go beyond normal conscientiousness in fulfilling their classroom duties. There is no compelling necessity to reexamine familiar forms of instruction and experiment with new pedagogic methods in an effort to help their students accomplish more. (p. 32)

Yet in spite of these realities—little or no training to teach, a graduate school experience that does not encourage exploration of failure, ridiculously challenging teaching demands, and no external pressure to be great at teaching—faculty continually seek and explore ways to improve their teaching. As a nationally renowned scholar and UW faculty member for more than 35 years said, when asked if she were still making changes to her teaching:

> Yeah—it's hopeless. I keep making little changes and bigger ones. I keep thinking I'm going to be done, but, just like invasive species, teaching is never done! (Faculty member in the sciences/math)

Purpose of the Study and Key Findings

The purpose of the UW Growth in Faculty Teaching Study (UW GIFTS) was to determine how pervasive change was in faculty teaching, what kinds of changes faculty made, and why they made them. Our study intentionally did not address "good teaching." In fact, although we are big fans of Ken Bain's book, *What the Best College Teachers Do* (2004), as well as of John Bransford et al.'s book, *How People Learn* (2000), we did not set out to discover whether the changes that faculty members were making led them to what others considered "best practices." Our interest was on what caused faculty to make changes in their teaching and what the directions of those changes might be. We believed it was possible, and even likely, that such change might lead faculty to *less* effective teaching as well as to better teaching, and we wanted to be open to all kinds of change.

Furthermore, we believe that "best practices" are defined, at least in part, by pedagogical contexts, as Shulman (1988) argued decades ago and as Bransford et al.'s (2000) work has supported. In the words of David C. Berliner (1991): "For many years pedagogical knowledge was studied as if there were generic teaching skills, as if such knowledge existed independent of the subject matter being taught. . . . But pedagogy and content are linked, and to separate them is to miss something about the intimacy of that relationship" (p. 147). If good teaching strategies are disciplinary, then generic "best practices" do not always make sense. Also, if good teaching strategies are disciplinary, then researchers from outside those disciplines—researchers like us—can hardly judge whether faculty members teaching classes in disciplines outside their own are engaging in the pedagogical practices best suited to their fields.

Perhaps our key finding in the UW GIFTS is that change in teaching was pervasive. For distinguished teaching award winners, brand new teachers, world-famous scholars, faculty with and without tenure, faculty teaching math and faculty teaching art classes—for all of them—change in teaching was a constant. This result buries the image of university professors lecturing from notes that have yellowed from 15 years of use. It challenges Derek Bok's (2006) argument that because they are not required to do so by college leadership, faculty do not move "beyond normal conscientiousness in fulfilling their classroom duties" (p. 32). Furthermore, it suggests that those who characterize faculty as dragging their feet in the face of change (Tagg, 2012) may be missing something important—especially the provosts at the institutions where faculty are teaching who characterize faculty as "resistant" to change (Kuh & Ikenberry, 2009). Given the finding that all faculty made changes to their teaching, what do we know about those changes?

What were they and why did faculty make them? Our study aimed to answer those questions.

A second key finding from the UW GIFTS is that reasons for change most often emerge from the interaction between the faculty member and the particular students and course she is teaching, rather than from sources external to the classroom. In other words, mandates for change are likely to have far less effect on teaching practice than are the faculty members' observations of their own students' behavior and performances in the classroom.

The purpose of this book is to present what we learned about change and growth in teaching from the UW GIFTS. This is a book of stories of change, of overlapping goals, of growth in and away from confidence. Primarily a qualitative study, the UW GIFTS can help new faculty think about their teaching work. Perhaps more important, our findings can help other institutions understand the ways their faculty are thinking about and changing their teaching, so that we can honor that work, as well as celebrate and nurture the analytical power and personal courage it takes to create, conduct, and perform the thousands of symphonies that faculty across the country are engaged in right at this moment.

Literatures

The UW GIFTS was an exploratory study, rather than a study that set out to validate theory or support hypotheses. We had some preconceptions about why faculty might make changes to their teaching, and most of those were structural. For example, we anticipated that faculty members might make changes to their teaching because they had been told to increase the size of the classes they were teaching. Beyond that kind of speculation, we had no hypotheses for change. Therefore, we needed to design a study that helped us understand the nature and full range of faculty experiences, as well as the meanings that change had for faculty (Merriam, 2001).

Although our study was not shaped prominently by a body of theoretical literature, we found a variety of literatures helpful to our thinking. For example, although the UW GIFTS was focused on change in teaching rather than on the relationship between belief, intention, and classroom practice, we read with interest the literature on those relationships. Norton et al.'s (2005) study of 638 faculty members' responses to a survey on beliefs and intentions presented interesting results about the role of context in shaping intentions. Kane et al. (2002) provided an excellent critique of the research on faculty beliefs, intentions, and practices, which we address in chapter 2.

Studies, such as those of Hativa et al. (2001) and McAlpine et al. (2006), provide thoughtful attention to contexts and perspectives; however, while providing rich details on how faculty think about their teaching, their small sample sizes (four and two, respectively) make it difficult to draw conclusions about faculty at large. The UW GIFTS sought to provide a close, primarily qualitative look at a larger sample in the hope that the level of details sacrificed by increasing the scale would be balanced by our ability to make some general statements about change in teaching.

We found David Leslie's (2002) study on the relative value faculty place on research and teaching particularly important. Leslie analyzed data from 517,954 full-time faculty respondents to the 1992–1993 National Survey of Postsecondary Faculty (NSPF) on the importance of teaching and research. He found that "research university faculty . . . agree on average that both teaching effectiveness and research and publication should be the primary criteria for promotion" (p. 64).

In addition, Leslie noted that disciplinary differences in how faculty view criteria for promotion were stronger at research universities than they were at other institutions. Leslie also found that faculty in the fine arts placed the highest value on teaching in promotion decisions and faculty in the natural sciences rated teaching the lowest of the disciplinary groups. This is no surprise since the extensive research that faculty in the fine arts might engage in to prepare for the work they create is often "invisible" in the projects they produce, while the research that faculty in the natural sciences do is often highly visible and well funded.

Leslie's study is important to our work because it suggests that faculty at research universities make changes to their teaching for the same reason that faculty at more teaching-focused institutions make changes—because they think teaching matters. In the words of one of our faculty interviewees:

> My job is to help students learn. My job is to be an instructor, and I want to do a good job. If they don't learn, I haven't done a good job. (Faculty member in the sciences/math)

In fact, Leslie found that faculty at research institutions place as much value on teaching as they place on research, even though their institutions may privilege research over teaching in promotion decisions.

However valuable Leslie's work, great changes have occurred at R1s in the 18 years since the NSPF collected the data that Leslie analyzed in 2002. These changes raise the question of how accurate Leslie's findings are in relation to today's faculty. The NSPF data were taken before Barr and Tagg's (1995) article shifted the assessment focus from teaching to learning. They were taken before 9/11 and before No Child Left Behind changed the face of K–12 in the United States and knocked at the door of higher education in the guise of the Spellings Commission Report (U.S. Department of Education, 2006). They were taken before the U.S. economy collapsed, freezing faculty salaries, reducing the number of faculty at every state college and university in the country who were teaching the same or increasing numbers of students, and damaging faculty morale. They were taken before state threats to tenure and collective bargaining gained a foothold in the Midwest, further deepening faculty concern about their profession and its future. Obviously, although Leslie's important work helped guide our thinking, we need current research that takes up Leslie's question about the value university faculty place on teaching.

In this regard, the Faculty Survey of Student Engagement (Indiana University Center for Postsecondary Research, 2010) offers some help. The Faculty Survey of Student Engagement (FSSE) is the partner of the National Survey of Student Engagement (NSSE). The FSSE measures faculty members' estimates of students' participation in a number of educational practices and compares those estimates with student reports of their own participation. In addition, the FSSE surveys faculty members about how they spend their time. In 2010, 19,399 faculty responded from 154 baccalaureate-granting colleges and universities to the FSSE; 232 (about 12%) of those faculty members were from doctoral/research universities. Their responses to questions about how they spent their time confirm the importance of teaching that Leslie noted in the 2002 data he analyzed.

Table 1.1 shows those results. As the table shows, faculty member FSSE respondents from "all doctoral/research universities" reported spending an average of 34.8 hours on classroom teaching activities per week and about 10 hours on research. In other words, the time that faculty members at research institutions spent on teaching activities

Table 1.1. 2010 FSSE results on faculty time

Activity	Hours Spent per Week
Teaching undergraduate students in class	8.8
Grading papers and exams	6.5
Giving other forms of written and oral feedback to students	5.8
Preparing for class	8.7
Reflecting on ways to improve my teaching	5.0
Research and scholarly activities	10.2
TOTAL	45

was, on average, more than three times the amount of time they reported spending on research.[2] Certainly, this level of time commitment indicates that faculty members at research institutions care about their undergraduate teaching.

Robert Menges' (2000) article on shortcomings of the research on teaching in higher education was also important to our study. Menges identified four areas in educational research that need to be more useful in answering critical questions about teaching. The UW GIFTS falls into the first of those questions, which asks why faculty teach the way they do and how theories and research on teaching inform what faculty do. Menges notes that the research conducted on faculty teaching in the 1990s was mainly quantitative, and that recently, research is beginning to recognize the importance of context in teaching. Menges felt that attention to contexts and perspectives "requires moving beyond surveys" (p. 8), which the UW GIFTS sought to do.

In addition to studies of how faculty think about and value teaching, we found the literature on how faculty were trained to teach—or rather *not* trained to teach—valuable. Fairweather and Rhoads (1995), for example, raised the question of how faculty are socialized into their roles as teachers, a subject discussed by Austin (2002) and Nyquist et al. (1999) as well. Nyquist et al. (1999) was also valuable for clarifying the emotional path of graduate study.

We also looked at literature on incentives and change. The work of Alfie Kohn (1999) was instructive, and the study by Ariely et al. (2009) on whether increased monetary rewards bring about improved performance was fascinating. Ariely and his colleagues tested the arguments that monetary incentives improve motivation and effort and that those improvements result in improved performance with residents of a rural town in India, MIT undergraduates, and students at the University of

Chicago. In all three cases, the highest rewards produced lower performance on all tasks, which included tasks that depended primarily on motor skills, tasks that focused on concentration, and those that required creativity. Ariely et al.'s results offer some insight into our finding that faculty members continue to think about and change their teaching even though they are not rewarded for doing so.

Finally, although the UW GIFTS was exploratory rather than theory driven, constructivist perspectives that argue that learning and knowledge are created in social contexts make the most sense to us in relation to our findings. As Peter Ewell (1997) noted, learners—whether students, faculty, or staff—are not merely "receptacles" of knowledge; they shape their own learning in individual ways. Also, as Shepard (2000) notes, "an important aspect of individual learning is developing experience with and being inducted into the ways of thinking and working in a community of practice" (p. 1074).

At institutions such as ours, it is easy to observe knowledge being constructed in social contexts. Every day, teams of researchers from our institution learn from each other and work together to create robotic contact lenses, knowledge about the effects of global warning on marine life in Puget Sound, and new insights into Jane Austen. This work is built on the work of others and often includes the participation of colleagues from institutions across the world. Furthermore, this process of socially constructing meaning does not exclude undergraduates. Research at our own institution, for example, has examined some of the ways that undergraduates enter disciplinary communities of learners, become acculturated to their practices and values, and participate in the construction of new knowledge—a process that begins very early for some students (Beyer et al., 2007; Beyer and Graham, 1990, 1992, 1994). The disciplinary communities that undergraduates join include participants from across and outside the U. S., and involve "conversations"—real-time and delayed—with earlier thinkers, learners, and knowledge creators.

While we embrace social constructivist theories, we would not place ourselves in the "sect"—in D. C. Phillips' (1995) words—that would argue that all knowledge is "entirely a matter of sociopolitical processes or consensus" (p. 11) and that neither nature nor individuals outside social groups offer opportunities for or impose constraints on knowledge creation. In Phillips' continuum, we are closer to the center.

However, although we see evidence of social constructivist theories around us and although our study findings, in some ways, may serve as evidence for these theories, we did not set out to validate them, nor do we examine our findings through that lens. Even so, we believe that it is important to note that we have that lens and have likely been influenced by it.

Our Paths

When we began this study, we had a fairly good idea that many faculty members would say that they had made changes to their teaching. In spite of persistent public images of tweed-coated, sleeve-patched professors giving the same lectures year after year, our own experience as faculty members has been marked by change in our teaching and by conversations with colleagues about changes in theirs. Furthermore, our research on graduate students and underrepresented minority students (Taylor et al., 2009; Taylor & Antony, 2000), on undergraduate learning (Beyer et al., 2007), and on students' ratings of their academic experience (Gillmore & Greenwald, 1998; Greenwald & Gillmore, 1997), as well as our years of working closely with faculty, gave us evidence that change in faculty teaching was fairly constant.

However, while we knew that faculty members were likely to report changes to their teaching, we did not know the extent of those changes, nor did we have any certainty about why they made such changes. Therefore, our own paths through the UW GIFTS were marked by surprise and gratitude.

Organization

This book includes the following four major sections and chapters:

I. Overview
   Chapter 1—GIFTS—provides a summary of the study's rationale, purpose, key findings, and academic context.
   Chapter 2—How Was the Study Conducted?—presents information on our study sample, methods, and the generalizability of the study.
II. Summary of Findings
   Chapter 3—What Courses Did Faculty Describe?—presents a numerical picture of the courses that faculty interviewees described.

Chapter 4—What Changes Did Faculty Make to Their Courses?—presents results of the changes faculty members described making to their classes, as well as findings regarding "big directions" of change in their teaching.

Chapter 5—Why Did Faculty Make Changes to Their Courses?—discusses reasons for the changes faculty made and presents an image of the change process.

III. Themes

Chapter 6—What Allowed Faculty to Teach "from the Self"?—addresses one of the major themes of change in the study, the movement away from content and toward bringing the self into the classroom.

Chapter 7—What Did Faculty Say about Students?—addresses a theme of change that crossed faculty responses to many questions—the move to seeing students as new learners.

Chapter 8—What "Research" Methods Did Faculty Use?—discusses the many kinds of informal research faculty members engaged in to identify whether students were learning what faculty members hoped they were learning.

Chapter 9—Were There Differences across Groups?—reports analysis of differences in the responses of several subgroups in the faculty that comprised the UW GIFTS and includes differences between the responses of faculty of color and white faculty, between faculty in three disciplines, and between faculty members and graduate students.

IV. Conclusions

Chapter 10—Learning in the Act of Teaching—summarizes the findings in the UW GIFTS

In addition, the book's appendices include interview and focus group protocols for adaptation or use by other institutions of higher education.

Throughout these chapters, we make extensive use of quotations from faculty interviewees to illustrate and clarify our findings. Faculty quotations also show the complexities of our findings, the blurred lines between our categories and themes, and give voice to the unique experiences and remarkable hearts and minds of college teachers.

2

How Was the Study Conducted?

> I tell them research is about being curious and having questions that are
> researchable.
> —Faculty member in the social sciences

As we noted in chapter 1, the UW GIFTS was an exploratory study rather than a study that set out to validate theory or support hypotheses. Our research questions were simple:

Without external pressure to do so, do faculty make changes to their teaching?

If so, what kinds of changes do they tend to make?

Why do they make those changes? What sources of information trigger or inspire the changes faculty make?

Faculty Sample

Our sample of 55 faculty members came from three sources. First, we contacted department chairs, described our proposed study, and asked them to recommend faculty members we might interview who were known in the department to be "thoughtful about teaching." We invited 67 chairs, representing all departments that offered undergraduate majors, to submit names, and 30 chairs (45%) did so, sending us the names of 91 faculty members. We invited 50 faculty members from this group, a randomized sample stratified by department, professional level (full, associate, and assistant professors; senior lecturers and lecturers), gender, and ethnicity. We stratified the sample in order to increase diversity in those areas. In our email message inviting this

17

group of faculty to participate in the UW GIFTS, we told faculty members that they had been identified by their chairs as thoughtful teachers. Twenty-five (50%) of the chair-selected faculty whom we contacted agreed to be interviewed. These 25 faculty members comprised 45.5% of our sample, as figure 2.1 shows.

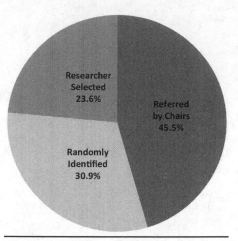

Figure 2.1. Sample composition

Second, we invited the participation of 140 faculty whom we randomly selected from a list of all UW faculty but stratified in the same ways as our chair-selected group. We told this group that they had been randomly selected for participation in the study. Seventeen (12.1%) of those faculty members agreed to be interviewed, comprising 30.9% of our final sample. As the difference in volunteer rates of these two groups makes clear, having been identified as "thoughtful about teaching" by one's chair appeared to make faculty members more willing to be interviewed than did random selection.

Third, as figure 2.1 shows, researchers directly invited 13 (23.6% of the sample) faculty members to participate. Some, but not all, of these participants had reputations as effective teachers. We selected these faculty members based on a number of factors, such as increasing the number of faculty of color or the number of faculty in the humanities participating in the study. However, the main factor in our selection of this group was that we knew them from previous experiences, and we found them interesting.

Nine (16.4%) of the faculty members in the study had won distinguished teaching awards from the university, one during the course of the study. Of those nine, seven were faculty members whose names had been given to us by department chairs; one was a faculty member who was randomly selected from the complete list of UW faculty; and one was a faculty member whom we had selected to interview.

Demographics and Departments

In terms of gender, 29 (52.7%) of the participants were female and 26 (47.3%) were male. The sample of interviewees in UW GIFTS was comprised of the following ethnic groups:

> Four African American faculty members (7.3%)
> Three Asian faculty members (5.4%)
> 48 Caucasian faculty members (87.3%)

In addition, these faculty members represented the following kinds of academic appointments:

> 14 professors (25.5%)
> 12 associate professors (21.8%)
> 16 assistant professors (29.1%)
> 8 senior lecturers[1] (14.5%)
> 5 lecturers (9.1%)

The disciplinary areas represented by this group of faculty included the following:

> Arts (4 faculty members, 7.2%)
> Architecture/built environments (3 faculty members, 5.5%)
> Business (3 faculty members, 5.5%)
> Engineering (3 faculty members, 5.5%)
> Humanities (11 faculty members, 20.0%)
> Sciences (11 faculty members, 20.0%)
> Social sciences (16 faculty members, 29.1%)
> Other, including forest resources, informatics, and oceanography (4 faculty members, 7.2%)[2]

Teaching Training in Graduate School and Experience Teaching

In terms of teaching training, we asked 54 of the 55 faculty participants whether they had received any direct instruction in teaching while they were in graduate school, and, if so, to describe the kinds of training they had received. We defined teaching training as deliberate instruction. We did not include general observation of others' teaching as teaching training, and, in fact, faculty members in the study often had both good and bad things to say about such observations, as this faculty member's comment illustrates:

> I grew up in the days when faculty didn't care about lectures, especially in physics at [the university where I studied]. I mean the undergraduate lectures in physics were just horrible, unbelievably bad. These people would drone on and walk into a classroom with a textbook and without saying a word, spend 20 minutes of student time, copying a table from the textbook onto the blackboard. Twenty minutes of silence while they copy something that we already had, and they point at it as if revelation is now occurring. Now, chemistry at [this same institution] had a very different tradition. A fellow named [Professor X] who founded something called the College of Chemistry [there], really thought teaching undergraduates was important and in the sixties the quality of undergraduate teaching of chemistry was very high, partly because of a tradition [he] started. (Faculty member in the sciences/math)

Using our definition of "deliberate" instruction in teaching, 63% of the faculty in the UW GIFTS said that they had received no instruction in teaching as graduate students. (Two faculty members said they had no training as graduate students but noted that they had taken classes on teaching as undergraduates.) When institutions were funded so well that they could fully support all graduate students with fellowships, or when students were given individual fellowships because they were considered more promising than other graduate students, they neither received instruction in teaching nor had teaching experience—not even experience serving as teaching assistants for faculty members in their fields. Two faculty members' comments illustrate the group of "no" responses to this question.

> No—my advisor was completely negligent in teaching and in giving teaching advice, and they were the worst teachers I've ever seen. This was at [X University], and they are the best

seismologists in the world and the least interested in teaching. One instructor I had had these yellowing overheads that were full of equations. He'd put the page on the overhead and say, "Any questions?" And then he'd take that one off and put the next one down, "Any questions?" We didn't even know what he was talking about. He'd made the transparencies 20 years before, anyway, so if someone asked a question, he'd get confused. At [X University] the ethic was that it was the students' responsibilities to learn and the teachers just made themselves available for questions. Some faculty members were easy to communicate with, and some were just impossible. But most didn't put much effort into teaching. (Faculty member in the sciences/math)

No. In fact, I got a couple of fellowships that took me completely out of teaching. (Faculty member in the social sciences)

The remaining 37% of our sample said that they had experienced some kind of teaching instruction while in graduate school. Some (16.7%) said that they had taken seminars that emphasized pedagogy. For example:

Actually, at [X University], I TAed for the first three years, a few courses, all physiologically based. There was a faculty member, TL—I can't believe I remembered his name—who was somewhat atypical for 1985 in that his emphasis in his research was education. All the grad student TAs at [X University] had to take a seminar course from him. (Faculty member in the sciences/math)

Others (9.2%) said that they had attended meetings with the faculty for whom they were TAs, and those meetings sometimes included conversations about teaching. These conversations were not always fully informative, as this faculty member's comment illustrates:

I did. [X University] makes everybody teach and they give you one big lecture class with 20 TAs and then you also had a chance to teach your own sections of beginning Latin. The instruction in supervision was exclusively in the form of meetings about your class. Nobody came to your class and told you to do better; we just went to the TAs meetings. They talked about teaching but it wasn't pedagogical methods. (Faculty member in the humanities)

In addition, some faculty members (9.2%) said that they had attended orientations for all graduate students that did not emphasize teaching but at which teaching may have been discussed, as this faculty member remembered:

Yes. All TAs at [X University] have to go through a brief training programming. We met three or four times. It was useful, but it was also challenging because you have TAs sitting next to you from all different disciplines—chemistry, English, and so on. It talked about basic dos and don'ts, ethics about teaching. I don't remember the details. (Faculty member in the sciences/math)

Finally, one of our faculty members (1.9%) remembered being observed as a TA by two faculty members when she was in graduate school.

Regarding their experience teaching, 10 (18.1%) of the faculty members in our sample had done no teaching before they came to the UW; others had taught in a range of places including Harvard, Rutgers, Sheffield College, UC Santa Cruz, Tel Aviv University, Lane Community College, and University of Sydney. In addition, the faculty members we interviewed had worked at the UW between two and 40 years, with the average time at the UW at 13.4 years.

Classes

In interviews, we asked faculty members to speak about changes in two of the courses that they had taught, although one faculty member described three courses and four spoke about only one class. Altogether, we gathered information about change in 107 courses. Figure 2.2 shows how those courses were distributed across disciplinary areas. As the figure shows, about 76% of the classes came from the College of Arts and Sciences (social sciences, science/math, humanities, and arts), which is a bit higher than the percent (70%) of overall UW student credit hours taken in the College. The remaining 24% came from various other schools and colleges, as the figure shows. Details about the courses faculty members described are discussed in chapter 3.

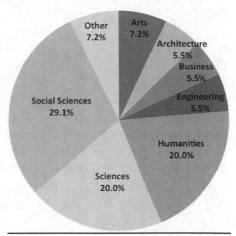

Figure 2.2. Classes in UW GIFTS by disciplinary area

Graduate Student Sample

In addition to interviews with faculty members, we conducted two focus groups with eight graduate students who had been identified by their department chairs as "thoughtful about their teaching." Our hope in including graduate students in the UW GIFTS was that they might provide a comparison with the more experienced faculty group. Chairs sent us the names of 78 graduate students, but we could schedule only eight (10.3%) of them for focus group meetings. Graduate students in these groups included five females and three males from departments in the sciences, social sciences, humanities, and business. All of them had teaching experience, seven of them prior to their entry into graduate school. During graduate school, all eight had served as teaching assistants in courses in their disciplines, most of them multiple times in the same course, as well as in others. Furthermore, four of them had taught their own courses, and two of them had led teaching training seminars for new graduate students in their departments. We ensured anonymity to participants, so we did not track any additional information about them other than what was readily apparent by observation.

Study Design

The UW GIFTS was primarily an interview study of UW faculty. However, our interview questions included a survey portion, and we conducted two focus groups with a small number of graduate students for purposes of comparison.

Preliminary Considerations

In designing our methodology for UW GIFTS, we began with the assumption that changes in teaching are not easily tracked with surveys, because definitions for kinds of pedagogy and meanings for words that describe motivations can differ dramatically among individuals. A conversation we had with a faculty member illustrates this point. We were conducting interviews for a different study on our campus, and our interviews included a conversation with a faculty member who taught large lecture classes in the humanities and who had won a distinguished teaching award for her work. During the interview, the professor said that she knew that other faculty found "active learning strategies" helpful, but that she could not fit them into her class. She said that her class time was already overfilled with lecture material and interactions with students about that material, and there was just no time to incorporate other activities into the hour. The lecture pieces were important for clarifying the challenging and dense reading she assigned, she said. Furthermore, she added that asking students to voice their ideas and reasoning about others' ideas, which took up a great deal of her class time in the large lecture hall, was an essential learning goal in her discipline, so she could not cut that back to make room for "active learning strategies."

Although it seemed obvious to us that students in her large lecture class were engaged in active learning strategies both to prepare for and to participate in the "interactions with students" parts of her class, the professor did not see it that way. Her definition of "active learning" included only certain kinds of activities, such as the use of clickers. Therefore, on a survey, she would have selected "no" if asked if she used active learning.

In addition to our own observations, we noted questions about use of questionnaires to gather information about faculty teaching behaviors and beliefs in the research (Norton et al., 2005; Kane et al., 2002). Therefore, because of definitional and other identified problems with surveys and because we hoped to understand both faculty experiences and their meanings to the faculty members who were living them, we decided to conduct an interview study with faculty, even though that decision limited the number of faculty from whom we might gather information. In addition, we decided to attach a survey piece to our interview questions, which would allow us to compare qualitative with quantitative data.

Kane et al. (2002) argue that direct observation must be part of any study examining faculty teaching beliefs and practices. Our study was not examining consistency across belief and action, and although we were interested in the theoretical beliefs that faculty felt informed their teaching if faculty offered such beliefs, we did not set out to explore theory. Our focus was on practice and on what caused faculty members to make changes in that practice. Furthermore, we asked faculty to root their discussion of change in two courses, which they had also described, because in our experience working with both faculty and students, we have found that asking participants to speak about specific experiences produces more reliable and interesting information than when they speak abstractly about all experiences. For example, asking a student to talk about what two papers show about her writing and where in the papers those aspects of her writing are in evidence produces better information than asking a student to talk about her writing, in general—such as "what are your strengths and weaknesses as a writer?"

Furthermore, although Kane et al.'s point about the value of classroom observation makes sense, we believe that research has demonstrated that pedagogy is shaped by the disciplines in which it occurs (Donald, 2002; Pace & Middendorf, 2004; Wineburg, 2001, 1991; Neumann et al., 2002; Shulman, 1988). Therefore, individual observers who are not participants in the disciplines they are observing may not be expert judges of the classroom conduct of faculty. In our case, faculty represented 38 academic fields, and collectively, we were well versed in only three of them. If we had observed faculty teaching, there was a good chance that we would not know what we were seeing.

We limited participants to our own campus for two reasons. First, when we began the UW GIFTS, we thought that it would be helpful to new faculty and graduate students at our own institution to learn about the experiences of other faculty members here. Our faculty come from all over the world, representing a rich diversity of experience that we believed would be interesting to others. Furthermore, we felt that faculty and administrators planning faculty development experiences would find it helpful to know how faculty members arrived at ideas about change in their teaching. However, after analyzing our results, we felt that they were likely to be useful to faculty and graduate students at other institutions, as well as at our own.

A second reason we confined interviews to our own campus was because the economic issues of our time confined us. Travel money for professional staff and administrators was not available during the years of the study, making face-to-face interviews with faculty at other institutions problematic. Therefore, we decided to interview faculty at our own institution, trying to include a diverse population that might encompass experiences at other institutions as well as at our own.

Structured Interviews with Faculty

We conducted 60- to 90-minute structured interviews with 56 faculty members, one of whom asked to be removed from the study a few months after the interview. The complete set of interview questions is included as appendix A. We sent faculty members copies of the interview questions in advance and gave them a copy of the questions at the time of the interview, as well. Interview questions asked faculty members to describe two classes and one or two changes they had made to those classes, in addition to asking them about big directions of change in their teaching, about their teaching training, and about the causes of change in their teaching.

At the end of a set of 12 open-ended interview questions, we asked faculty interviewees to rate (on a 4-point scale) the contributions to change in their teaching of 17 potential sources of change. As previously noted, we added this quantitative feature into the qualitative questions so that we could compare ratings with qualitative results. In addition, we gave faculty members opportunities to explain their ratings of those 17 items, which helped us avoid definitional problems and deeply expanded our understanding of the sources that we had come up with.

Some of the interviews were audiotaped and transcribed; however, one researcher was able to take notes verbatim, so that researcher entered notes directly into a Word document at the time of the interview. Mechanical errors for both transcribed notes and those taken at the time of the interviews were cleaned up, and the full interview transcript was sent to the interviewee for comments and editing. Once the faculty interviewee returned the transcript with changes, researchers entered the changes, created aliases for the participant, and the interview process was then considered completed. Researchers saved the final transcripts under faculty aliases, with only one of the researchers maintaining the alias key.

We analyzed interview responses to each question with a constant comparison method of analysis, an inductive process that allows themes to emerge from the participants' words rather than imposing categories of response on the analysis at the beginning (Merriam, 2001). Interview responses were transferred to Excel, and we coded responses, using an iterative process that required reading and rereading the interviews, summarizing responses, coding and often recoding them, identifying major themes, merging some of them, and redefining others. The use of Excel spreadsheets allowed us to build an audit trail for ourselves and others (Kane et al., 2002). Researchers eventually arrived at categories of responses for any given question, while still preserving responses that were idiosyncratic. As we coded, we also identified quotations that illuminated emergent categories of response.

As any qualitative researcher knows, this process of reducing full interviews to codes and themes is both scary and unsatisfying. The full interviews are so much bigger than the sum of their parts that it always feels as though we are pulling the petals off flowers and hoping that those in the pile labeled "pink" say something meaningful about an array of sizes and scents, of openness and tightness, of pale pinks and fuchsias without the complete loss of all the diversity and grace the petals represented before they were pulled apart. Nevertheless, the piling and re-piling of pieces of interviews is exactly the coding process for qualitative data.

Quantitative Analysis

In addition to qualitative analysis, we conducted statistical comparisons of the changes and reasons for change reported by faculty subgroups. We used a Welch (1951) two sample t-test as implemented in R (R Development Core Team, 2011), a computer language and software environment for statistical computing and graphics. We identified statistically significant differences in the changes and reasons for change in the following faculty groups:

Selection method. We compared the responses of faculty who were referred to us by chairs, randomly selected, or selected by researchers.

Gender. Faculty members were identified by the UW as male or female, and we compared their responses.

Ethnicity. Because we had so few faculty members of color, we divided our sample into two groups—white (87.3%) and faculty of color (12.7%) and compared responses of the two groups.

Academic rank. We compared the responses of faculty in the UW GIFTS who were professors, associate professors, assistant professors, senior lecturers, and lecturers.

Years at the UW. As a way of determining the impact of the UW climate on changes faculty members made to their teaching and their reasons for change, we compared faculty who had been at the UW for a short time (1–6 years), those who had been here an average amount of time (7–13 years), and those who had been working at the UW for a long time (14–40 years).

Disciplinary area. In order to increase statistical power, we grouped like disciplinary areas together, creating four major disciplinary categories, as follows: 1) arts and humanities; 2) social sciences; 3) science (including faculty in forestry and oceanography), math, and engineering; and 4) "other" (business, architecture/built environments, and informatics faculty).

In addition to these faculty characteristics, we compared changes faculty made in teaching and their reasons for change by size of the classes they were teaching. For this analysis, we grouped classes into three categories, based on the breaks in the class sizes faculty reported: large (61 students or more), medium (30–60 students), and small (4–29 students).

Finally, we used SPSS to analyze faculty ratings of the 17 sources of change that we provided at the end of the interviews.

Structured Focus Groups with Graduate Students

We also conducted two focus groups with eight graduate students whom department chairs had identified as "thoughtful about their teaching." Our purpose in conducting the focus groups was to compare the experience of new teachers with that of more experienced teachers. The questions they answered were similar to those used in the faculty interviews and are included as appendix B. Focus groups lasted 90 minutes and were conducted by two researchers, with one primarily posing questions and following them up and the other taking notes. The note-taker was able to capture most of what students said verbatim. Researchers then analyzed the notes, using the constant comparison method described previously to identify recurring themes and paying careful attention to agreement among focus group participants within and across the two groups.

Generalizability and Usefulness

Qualitative studies, such as the UW GIFTS, usually do not attempt to generalize findings to large populations because of their smaller sample size in relation to large-N studies. Nevertheless, we believe that consideration of generalizability is important enough for us to address the study's limitations in that regard. In examining these limitations, we make a distinction between generalizability, which we cannot claim in any strong way, and usefulness, which we believe we can claim.

One issue that limits generalizability is that our sample, although randomized in the ways described previously, were volunteers. This raises the question of whether faculty who have not given much thought to their teaching would volunteer to spend 90 minutes talking about it with strangers. Although not caring about teaching may be one reason why faculty would not volunteer for the UW GIFTS, there are other reasons for not volunteering for the study, as well. One obvious reason is the time pressure most faculty experience. Indeed, scheduling interviews and the timely moving of interview transcripts back and forth literally doubled the length of time of the study. In our original estimate of study time, we did not anticipate the full impact that the complex demands of faculty schedules might have on our planning.

Another reason a faculty member may not volunteer to speak with us is that—thoughtful about teaching or not—such conversation has little to offer the interviewee, who already is aware of what she is doing in her classrooms. We did not offer faculty members any compensation for their time, so they had little stake in participation. Finally, some faculty members may have been concerned about being identifiable by their quotations; indeed, some of our participants asked us about the ways we had designed to protect their identities with at least two of them asking for additional measures.

Thus, while we can assume that the voluntary nature of our study may not have attracted faculty participants who had not made changes to their teaching over time, we cannot assume that is the only reason faculty may not have volunteered to participate. In addition, regarding voluntary studies, it is good to remember that nearly all educational research, whether it is a nationally respected quantitative study such as the NSSE or a qualitative study such as ours, is dependent on voluntary samples; therefore, some level of selection bias plagues all of the research we do.

Another problem with the voluntary sample is that although our sample was drawn from UW teaching faculty, it was in fact drawn from three overlapping but distinct subpopulations: a random set, a chair-nominated set, and a researcher-selected set. Thus, there is no one population to which we can satisfactorily generalize. However, as our statistical analysis in chapter 9 shows, these three groups were remarkably similar in their responses. Furthermore, the broadness of the sample and its range of origins do not detract from the potential usefulness that one faculty member might find in speaking to others—no matter how those others entered the conversation.

Two additional challenges to the generalizability of UW GIFTS are the single-institution nature of the study and the research-oriented purpose of the UW itself. Although it is true that single-institution studies raise questions about generalization, many useful studies (for example, Light, 2001; Baxter Magolda, 1992; Beyer et al., 2007) have been limited to one kind of institution, and, therefore, one kind of culture. While we feel safest, of course, in claiming that our study results are useful to other urban, research universities and acknowledge that faculty at the UW's Seattle campus may not be perfectly generalizable to those at other institutions, we believe that faculty at institutions of any size can learn from our results. We feel that our results will be particularly useful to new faculty just out of their graduate school experiences. Those experiences have nearly all occurred at large research institutions, even though the teaching experiences that they will have afterward will occur in many types of institutions. We believe that our results may speed the transition of new faculty from the particular demands of their graduate school experiences to the new demands of teaching in college as professors and instructors, wherever they find themselves doing that work. Therefore, we would argue that the study results are broadly useful, if not generalizable.

In addition, some might argue that institutions, like ours, where the pressure to publish is strong, do not have much to teach institutions about teaching. Indeed, since 1974, the University of Washington in Seattle, a large (37,000 students), public, "Research 1" institution, has received more funding in federal support for research than any other public university in America. For tenure-track faculty at the UW—a group represented by 76.4% of our UW GIFTS sample—research plays the most significant role in decisions about tenure and promotion, although teaching effectiveness and community service are also factors in those decisions, as Leslie's (2002) research demonstrated.

Furthermore, although public perception and researchers on higher education such as Astin (1993) may argue that it is "virtually impossible" to maintain strong focuses on research *and* on students in the same institution, the UW has tried to do so. For example, the UW's dean and vice provost of undergraduate academic affairs (one of this book's authors) and his office advocate for undergraduate education, and the unit offers a wide range of experiential learning opportunities for undergraduates. The UW also supports several undergraduate study/tutorial centers, including math and writing centers, a study center that is open five nights a week (Center for Learning Undergraduate Education—CLUE) and the Instructional Center, an award-winning multidisciplinary tutoring center primarily for underrepresented students.

As well as sites for student learning, the UW offers teaching training opportunities to faculty members, which involve the participation of distinguished teaching award winners and which address pedagogical matters, such as integrating active learning techniques and learning technologies into teaching. These have included the Provost's Fall Workshops, the Large Class Collegium, the Institute for Teaching Excellence, and the Faculty Fellows Program, a faculty-led program for all new UW faculty members that provides a week-long program of teaching training and information about university resources. The UW also supports several centers whose purposes are to improve teaching, including the university-wide Center for Teaching and Learning, the Center for Engineering Learning and Teaching, and the Physics Education Group.

While the UW provides support for effective teaching, it is still true that research is the primary force in tenure and promotion decisions about faculty. However, in spite of that priority, all of our 55 interviewees, most of whom were working hard on demanding research projects at the same time they were teaching, made changes to their teaching, and all of them considered teaching a serious part of their work. It seems to us that faculty who value teaching, but who are working in institutions that emphasize research, may have important things to say to faculty operating in structures that make it easier to work on teaching, as well as to others teaching in institutions like ours. Caring about students' learning connects our sample to other faculty members who care, in spite of their individual campus cultures. Therefore, we believe that the results of the UW GIFTS will be useful to most faculty.

Finally, although the UW GIFTS is not perfectly generalizable to other institutions, the study included methods, detailed in this chapter, that strengthen external validity. For example, we used standard sampling procedures, multiple cases to study the same issues, a range of types of cases so that we could compare groups, predetermined questions that repeated from person to person, inclusion of "survey data" in the interviews so that multiple methods were used for gathering similar data, and specific procedures for coding qualitative data. In addition, we frequently treated qualitative data quantitatively (Merriam, 2001).

For these reasons, we believe that readers from other colleges and universities can find similarities between their and our faculty members' experience that may help illuminate their own paths, whatever their particular environments may be.

3

What Courses Did Faculty Describe?

[Once] one kid jumped up—one of 120 kids in a senior quantum mechanics course, about the fourth lecture into the quarter—and just burst out: "Professor Williamson, this is just absolutely impossible. This is out of the question! You're expecting us to be thinking about quantum mechanics every single day of the week." And I jumped up and said, "Yes! You've got it! You've got it! And it's going to keep coming. And if you are not thinking about quantum mechanics, at least some of every single day of the week, you are not going to be successful in this course."

        —Faculty member in the sciences/math, 400 level, 120 students

We asked faculty interviewees to describe two courses that they had taught more than once, so that their conversation about change in their teaching would be grounded in specific classes. Most faculty members described two undergraduate courses they had taught. Altogether, our 55 faculty members described their work in 107 classes from 38 academic departments in 10 disciplinary areas (e.g., arts, social sciences, and so on, shown previously in figure 2.1). As one might expect, the courses faculty described represented an impressively wide range of courses, from instruction in Latin to construction management. This chapter summarizes our findings with respect to various aspects of those courses.

As we report the aspects of the courses that faculty described, it is important to keep two things in mind. First, these aspects emerged from faculty descriptions; we did not explicitly ask faculty members whether their courses asked students to engage in each of the course aspects we tracked—to think critically, write, or conduct research, for example. Second, the numbers and percentages we report refer only to the courses that faculty described; they are not averages of all university courses.

Key Findings: Disciplinary Practice, Content, and Critical Thinking

Three aspects of the courses were visible in every class that faculty members described. First, each course clearly carried the practices, values, theories, and approaches of the academic discipline in which it was situated. An understanding of disciplinary practice was often explicitly stated as a learning goal for majors taking senior-level courses, as we might expect and as this quotation illustrates:

> By the end of this course, they know what it's like to be a field ecologist. (Faculty member in the sciences/math, 400 level, 16 students)

But understanding of disciplinary practice was a goal that was also embedded in classes for freshmen, as these two examples suggest:

> The course introduces students to the idea that history is really a set of arguments that historians make about the past, and that there aren't very many agreed-upon ideas about the past, but that it is possible to have more satisfactory and less satisfactory explanations for it—those that account for more of the evidence than those that take a piece of evidence and ignore the rest, for example. So the class is really a model of historical argument. (Faculty member in the social sciences, 100 level, 350 students)

> We are trying to have them imitate in these exercises as much as possible what an astronomer would do. (Faculty member in the sciences/math, 100 level, 250 students)

· Even when the content could be said to be similar across the courses faculty described, those courses were filtered through the lenses of the disciplines offering them. Consider how language is thought of in classes in the following three disciplines. In the first example, a foreign language faculty member described asking students to consider what parts of language were universal and what were cultural. In her words:

> I hope they learn that if you speak a foreign language that means that you perceive the world differently. We should not

assume that because the world speaks English that everyone all over the world thinks as we do. What about languages is universal and what is culture-specific? We look at politeness and rudenesses across language. We look at speech acts—apologies, thanks, and things like that. And then we look at gender—the way that men and women speak. Are there universal aspects to that or is it all culture-bound? (Faculty member in the humanities, 400 level, 27 students)

Another faculty member, this one in the Communication Department, described a class that focused on language and culture as follows:

One of the things I really try to focus on in this class is changing their assumptions about how nonverbal communication works. Like this idea of "body language"—people have this idea that nonverbal communication is the "universal language," and we all mean the same things by it. I try to teach students how much nonverbal communication is tied to culture. There's a repertoire of meanings that can be given to you by your culture, but then we decide what that means based on our context and our own assumptions. We don't realize how much interpretation we are putting into what we think something means. (Faculty member in the social sciences, 300 level, 35 students)

In contrast, a faculty member in speech and hearing sciences described a class on language that had a different focus:

. . . my goal is to introduce students to the concept of thinking about language as a scientific field. . . . so I focus a little bit on each of the main areas of linguistics—the sounds of the language, word formation, structure of sentences, and then using language in context. (Faculty member in the sciences/math, 300 level, 80 students)

Research on student learning has presented ample evidence of the disciplinary nature of learning, as well as of pedagogy (Beecher & Trowler, 2001; Bransford et al., 2000; Beyer et al., 2007; Donald, 2002; Pace & Middendorf, 2004; Wineburg, 2001, 1991; Neumann et al., 2002; Menges & Austin, 2001; Shulman, 1988; Biglan, 1973), so the finding that university courses carry with them the perspectives and practices of their academic disciplines should not be surprising. However, as the quotations throughout this chapter (and others) show, even the earliest courses are fully shaped by their disciplinary contexts—a reality confirmed by previous research on student learning conducted at our institution (Beyer et al., 2007).[1] Furthermore, topics that may appear similar, such as the study of language, differ in different disciplinary contexts.

Our second key finding was that faculty descriptions of all courses included knowledge-based or content goals, as well as thinking goals for students. These two goals were foundational for all classes, in that they appeared to serve jointly as the reasons for pedagogical choices and for all other course requirements. Writing assignments, instruction in the use of certain technologies, and active learning strategies—to name a few components—were all aimed at getting students to learn, think about, deepen their understanding of, challenge, and use course content and practices.

Third, the content knowledge and thinking in the discipline goals that we found in all courses were difficult to pull apart, as the quotation that begins this chapter illustrates. No faculty member seemed interested in transmitting a memorizable body of knowledge to students who would then merely be able to repeat it on an exam. Instead, the content simultaneously presented students with something to think about and, usually, with specific (i.e., disciplinary) ways to think about it. For example, a faculty member in philosophy was not just trying to present differing arguments about the nature of freedom; she required students to use philosophical reasoning to compare those viewpoints in class. A faculty member in engineering was not merely telling students about how gas molecules behaved in certain circumstances; he required them to discover such behavior through experimentation. An example of the close relationship between conveying content knowledge and pushing students to think in the discipline is provided by a faculty in mathematics who describes a course about techniques and "trying" things:

> In integral calculus you learn how to compute integrals and how to apply that. The techniques that they learn are somewhat challenging, and a large part of the class is devoted to learning these computations. It's a bit of an art to compute an integral. You have to guess. You have to try things. I like the class because it introduces a type of thinking that maybe is unfamiliar to the students. They are used to having the teaching in a math

class give them a recipe for doing some computation, and they learn to regurgitate these methods without much thought. Many of them think it's magic; they have no idea why these things work. They can reproduce the technique they learned and get a good grade. But this is really more of an art form. We can present a certain number of techniques that may be useful, but any time you confront an integral for the first time, you look at it and think, "I don't have a clue." Then you think, "Why don't I try this?" And it doesn't work. But then there are other things to try, and you realize that if you do this technique for a while, it leads into this other technique, which may lead you to something else. It's really a kind of problem solving, and it is also more what real math is like. (Faculty member in the sciences/math, 100 level, 120 students)

In addition to describing the importance of getting students to think critically, creatively, scientifically, or synthetically in the classes they described, many faculty members had developed specific ways to encourage, help students develop, or ask for a demonstration of such thinking. For example, one faculty member described special quizzes to stimulate "a different way of thinking" about course material. In his words:

The "think-about-it" quizzes appeal to a different sort of student experience than do the weekly assignments or the more comprehensive exams. For the quizzes, they have to draw a picture, draw a basic chart, show with a diagram how this relates to that. There are minimal equations or computations involved. This is a different way of thinking than opening the book and bringing out the calculator and solving a detailed problem. It's a different kind of intellectual work. (Faculty member in engineering, 300 level, 45 students)

Similarly, a faculty member in philosophy described asking seniors to write a paper about their thinking in each area of her course on ethics:

I have them write a paper on each of the sections of the course, and that gives them some space to reflect on the meta-ethical theories, to understand them, take a stand, say which they think is the right one, to explore these debates on the nature

of reasons and take a stand on that. In the end I am very interested in what they say about the aims of ethical theory—what
we should be trying to do. (Faculty member in the humanities,
400 level, 32 students)

A faculty member in landscape architecture asked students from a variety of majors taking his design class to take content learning out of the
classroom and into their daily lives every week, and then to report back
on their observations:

> There's a weekly assignment in this class—three pages of ob-
> servations a week. We may be talking about different layers of
> plants and they do observations about plants above them or at
> eye level. We may be talking about the diversity of plants. I
> want them to discover that there are hundreds, possibly thou-
> sands, of kinds of plants around us, and then spatially I want
> them to look at that diversity. Another week we may be look-
> ing at color and texture. The observations I tell them need to be
> notes and diagrams. The Da Vinci sketchbook is a good model,
> except they shouldn't write backwards. (Faculty member in ar-
> chitecture/built environments, 300 level, 80 students)

In addition, a faculty member in biology described asking students to
write challenging papers based on their observations, because:

> I'm teaching them rigorous standards of scientific thinking
> and reasoning. I think the reason why paradigms don't shift
> very well in science is that we overlook things we don't expect
> to see. You have to examine alternative hypotheses—that's a
> critical thinking skill. And if they don't pay attention to their
> data, they won't see the things they don't expect. So I want
> them to learn to write scientific papers but mostly I'm trying
> to teach them to think. (Faculty member in the sciences/math,
> 400 level, 16 students)

Finally, a faculty member teaching finance not only used a variety of
methods to teach students to think in the discipline, she also gave them
a rationale for doing so. In her words:

The class has two major teaching components. One is understanding the theory and the second component is being able to apply the theory. I don't want them to think that this accounting stuff is just learning formulas and plugging in numbers and—bam! bam! bam! You have to think about things, realize the shortcomings, know when you can do it, and when you can't. I want them to start thinking. And many of them have not experienced that before—actual thinking. They are used to memorizing things, spitting it back, and thinking they're good. I tell them that this is their comparative advantage over the machine. Machines don't think like this; you can. (Faculty member in business, 200 level, 120 students)

The key findings our analysis produced about the classes faculty described included disciplinary practices and a focus on content and thinking. In most cases, learning about content and learning to think formed a kind of double helix, where each strand was inseparable from the other. The additional course components we were able to identify from faculty descriptions usually related to helping students move forward along the two strands.

Class Size, TA Help, and Course Levels

The sizes of the classes faculty discussed ranged from very small (fewer than 14 students) to very large (more than 200), as figure 3.1 shows, with the average number of students per class at 94. Faculty had the help of graduate student teaching assistants in about half of the classes they described, as figure 3.2 shows.[2]

Regarding the course levels of the classes faculty members described, the only guidelines we gave them for selecting courses was to suggest that they discuss two they had taught more than once to undergraduates, focusing perhaps on one they typically taught and one that was their favorite to teach. Two-thirds of the classes faculty members chose to describe were 300- and 400-level courses—those typically taught to juniors and seniors in the majors. Of the 107 courses faculty described, 12.1% were 100-level; 19.6% were 200-level; 29% were 300-level; 37.4% were 400-level; and 1.9% were 500-level courses, primarily graduate level.

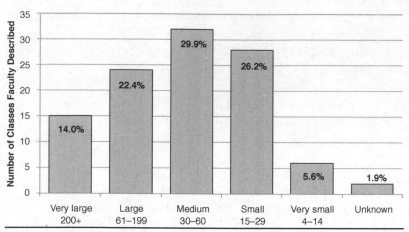

Figure 3.1. Class sizes

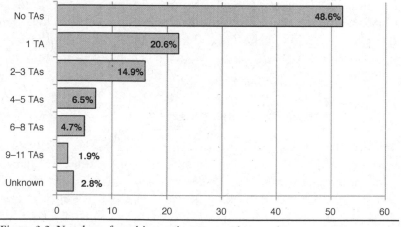

Figure 3.2. Number of teaching assistants per class

Pedagogy

In addition to noting that some degree of lecturing was present in near-ly all classes, we tracked two aspects of pedagogy: use of active learning strategies and use of classroom technology. As stated earlier we looked in faculty descriptions for the presence or absence of active learning strategies, rather than asking faculty members if they used them. We did, however, often ask faculty members if they used any kind of classroom technology, although, as that section shows, we were not consistent in asking that question.

Use of Active Learning Strategies

Active learning strategies have been said to increase learning, keep students engaged in class, and help faculty assess what students are "getting" from lecture so that faculty can make changes on the spot or later (Bonwell & Sutherland, 1996; Angelo & Cross, 1993). Such strategies are often considered superior to "lectures" as ways to foster learning, even though they are also acknowledged to be more time consuming and challenging to teachers than straight lecturing (Bok, 2006), as the example of Dr. Mann, which opened this book, illustrated.

Although we consider active learning strategies to be valuable, we would not argue that such strategies are always better than others. In that regard, we agree with Ken Bain (2004), who noted that "some professors stimulate learning using what others would regard as outmoded pedagogies while others fail miserably with the latest rage, and still others do the opposite" (p. 192). In other words, the use of active learning strategies does not necessarily guarantee learning, nor does failure to use them guarantee *not* learning. Furthermore, we note that the use of specific active learning strategies, like all pedagogy, is linked to disciplinary practice and convention. Demonstrations conducted in front of class, for example, are often used in physics and chemistry classes but rarely in others.

Even though we believe some caveats are in order regarding active learning strategies, we were able to track the use of such strategies in the courses described by faculty in the UW GIFTS. In defining active learning strategies, we did not include the use of sections led by teaching assistants but confined our definition to what the faculty member whom we were interviewing did or assigned in his or her classroom. We counted a class as using active learning strategies when the faculty member described facilitating in-class discussion, asking or seeking questions, using small group work, requiring the use of clickers or similar forms of response, giving students time to do in-class problem solving or writing, and other activities that called on students to think and respond as part of their time in class. We also counted assigning projects, presentations, performances, and written assignments that might be completed outside class as active learning.

Using this definition, we found that the vast majority (83.2%) of the courses that faculty members in UW GIFTS described made use of at least one active learning strategy. This finding was not surprising because of the desire that faculty expressed to ensure that students think critically or analytically about course material. Faculty descriptions of nine (8.4%) of the courses appeared not to use active learning, and we were unable to determine if nine (8.4%) other courses used them or not.

One simple example of the use of active learning is asking questions in class. One faculty member described how she began to use questions in a large class, as well as why that felt risky:

> When [my mentor] started talking about questioning my students, I thought, "Why would I do that? I'm doing very well in the classroom." To make that first jump is the hard part—to let go of the side of the pool. I don't know why I was ready. I think that part of it was that I do feel confident in front of the classroom. So maybe the fact that the classroom was really comfortable for me made it possible to change. I remember saying to myself, "I will ask ONE question in class today; I don't have to do more than one." And after about two weeks I had to stop myself from asking so many questions. And having never seen this model before in my own education, I didn't know what it would look like. (Faculty member in the sciences/math, 200 level, 250 students)

Another form of question-asking as an active learning strategy is Socratic dialogue. It should probably not be surprising that a philosophy faculty member described the use of Socratic dialogue in her class of 150 freshmen and sophomores:

> I have to have Socratic dialogue—even in my 150-student class. And they do that. I think to get that kind of participation, you have to be really encouraging—and I think I've learned better how to do that over the years. You have to respond in a way so that the classroom feels like it is a welcome and warm environment, and you have to make it clear that you are really

interested in what they have to say. I think philosophy is conducive to that because it really is a discipline that is an ongoing conversation over the years. The issues we are discussing are still live issues, so I am interested in what they want to say and I try to make them realize that I'm not just looking for THE answer. That helps foster that sort of participation—helping students feel like they can have a dialogue in that class. (Faculty member in the humanities, 200 level, 150 students)

Active learning strategies are not only face-to-face activities. Several faculty members described using online forums as ways to engage students in thinking about their classes, as this faculty member described:

I added an online forum, which is totally awesome, and they love it. I put out one question on the forum about every week and a half to tee-up what we are doing in class. I tell them that what I will base their grade on in the forum is whether they participate—they have to participate at least once for each question. They love it though. The first one, I expected maybe 70 posts, two for each of them, but it was 400 posts for 35 kids in class. Students who are good or really thoughtful on the posts might not be as vocal in class, so it gives them a different way to participate. It's also a check for me to see what's going on in class. (Faculty member in the social sciences, 100 level, 35 students)

Faculty reported that developing effective active learning strategies took time and willingness to take a risk. They also noted that such activities required them to cut back on what they felt they should be "covering" in class. But many of them said that the learning gains were worth the payment of time before and during class. In the words of one faculty member:

I find that where people's creativity touches down on the ground is the place where most things happen, even though that is a place that is often outside people's comfort zones. Somehow I'm always trying to change the "I'm sitting at the desk and you are sitting out there" feeling of the classroom. We need to change that, even though it sounds scary and is risky. (Faculty member in the social sciences, 200 level, 90 students)

Classroom Technology

About 70% of the faculty members we interviewed mentioned the use of classroom technology when describing their courses. Twenty percent of this group said that they used no technology. A little more than a third of that group (34.5%) spoke of using one kind of teaching technology, such as a course webpage or PowerPoint. Close to 15% said that they used two kinds of technology—PowerPoint and discussion boards, for example, and another 15% mentioned use of three kinds of classroom technology, such as PowerPoint, a course webpage, and online activities or discussion boards. Finally, another 15% spoke of courses that made frequent use of a range of technology, including disciplinary software, so that their courses were infused with technology. The most frequently mentioned kinds of technology were use of course webpages that allowed students to download or view a variety of materials, PowerPoint as a lecture tool, online quizzes or activities that were machine scored, online discussion boards, and clickers. The following quotations illustrate faculty use of technology:

> I do some PowerPoint but more movie and video clips. I show movies of examples of kinds of systems operating in the real world—anything that blows up. I get a lot of stuff off YouTube—for example, cornstarch on a speaker that dances around because the sound waves make the cornstarch move. These examples are pretty applied. They like the one about shaking the helicopter until it breaks. (Faculty member in engineering, 300 level, 52 students)

> I have a website where they can access the WebQs [online quizzes] and all the course information. I also have an open discussion board, where they pose questions about course material or course issues. I tell them that if they have a question, someone else does too, so put it online. They have been really good about asking each other questions. I have rules about appropriate behavior and only once did I have to talk to someone. Sometimes I bring their questions from the board into class and sometimes, if I felt there was confusion about a point, I'll post a clarification to the board. (Faculty member in the social sciences, 200 level, 440 students)

Our results suggest that most faculty, and especially those teaching large lecture classes, used some kind of technology in their classes. However, faculty members' attitudes about technology were not always positive. About one out of four of the faculty members we interviewed had some negative things to say about the use of technology, with most of those comments focused on the use of PowerPoint. One common complaint about using PowerPoint to facilitate lectures was that the technology often felt as though it were driving the class, rather than the opposite. One faculty member in a large, 100-level science class stopped using PowerPoint and started using a Toshiba tablet for that reason. Another faculty member noted:

> With PowerPoint you are locked into a path and you don't feel you can deviate from that path. (Faculty member in the sciences/math, 200 level, 55 students)

Another objection to PowerPoint that faculty members voiced was that, because the slides are prepared in advance, faculty members can no longer "think along" with the students in the class. Two faculty members' comments illustrate this concern about PowerPoint:

> I think I am able to create better dialogue, better conversation in class by appearing to be less prepared and less focused behind a set of slides or a set of topics. My observation is that sometimes PowerPoint can be a filter that structures things in not quite the right way. (Faculty member in the social sciences, 400 level, 35 students)

> I use technology not so much in the class. I am a big believer in the overhead projector. I like to write with the students. I don't use pre-made slides or PowerPoint. I've gone back and forth on that. When I chose this new book for last year, I spent hours making these PowerPoint presentations. I worked all these presentations out, and then I deleted them all. Then I went back to my pens. In a class that big, I want to try to maintain contact, and one of the ways I do that is by working through the concepts with them. I think it helps me keep better pace with them if I'm writing [too]. (Faculty member in the social sciences, 200 level, 440 students)

Finally, other faculty members spoke of concern about student learning and new problems they had experienced with the advent of the technology they were using, as this faculty member described:

> I use PowerPoint now largely because the students expect it, not because I think it's better. In fact, I think it is so structured that it sometimes is limiting. I'm not convinced that it improves student learning. I have no concrete evidence either way about that. But as a consequence of the use of technology, I have to be a whole lot more prepared, which adds to my stress levels. You go into your classroom room wondering, "Will the projector work?" "Will the Ethernet be down?" (Faculty member in the social sciences, 200 level, 200 students)

Although faculty clearly were using technology in their courses, their reservations about the use of PowerPoint show that for many faculty, class time is an interactive experience, where the faculty member and the students move along a path together. One faculty member we interviewed said that in the most effective classes, the students feel as though they are creating the class with the professor in the moment. For many faculty members, the use of PowerPoint interferes with that sense of shared thinking.

On the other hand, technology also had its virtues. For example, PowerPoint allowed many faculty members to bring audible and visual material to class, along with printed texts and their own outlines. Online discussion boards extended the classroom into the time outside it. The internet, and particularly YouTube, allowed language learners to hear languages not frequently heard in Seattle, such as Urdu and Polish. Course webpages allowed students to access deadlines and class materials without the faculty member having to repeat due dates and carry extra materials around. As is true of everyone's experience with technology, faculty described both pleasure and pain in its use in the classroom.

Course Requirements

We tracked the mention of six kinds of requirements through faculty descriptions of their courses: exams and quizzes, writing, research, projects/presentations/performances, quantitative reasoning, and disciplinary technology. As noted previously, we did not ask faculty to identify which of these requirements were present; we analyzed faculty members' descriptions of their classes in order to identify categories of requirements and to note how often they were mentioned. Our "tally" of these requirements is likely, therefore, to underestimate how often each one may have been present in a class.

Exams and Quizzes

About two-thirds (64.5%) of the classes faculty described included explicit reference to quizzes or exams. The exams that some faculty members described were machine-gradable, multiple-choice exams. Others were completely short answer or essay exams. Several faculty members spoke about giving students a list of possible essay exam questions before exams as a way of using the exam to foster learning. For example:

> The final exam is in-class and all essays, but I hand out 10 or 12 essay questions in advance, telling them I will put four or five questions on the exam, and they will be able to choose two. I get much better exams by giving them the 10 or 12 possible questions ahead of time and letting them choose the two out of the five I give them. It sends them off with a sense of having learned something. (Faculty member in the social sciences, 100 level, 325 students)

One faculty member said that she had stopped giving students exams and, instead, had started giving them "big quizzes." In her words:

> I had exams for awhile; then I got rid of those. Now we have big quizzes and we have clicker questions every day. What I've found and why I do this is that students are lazy, just like I am, and if you tell them that everything's on a final exam they don't do things until then. So if I have these questions I ask them every day, they will do their readings, open their books, or know what's coming up, because they have a reason to know the right answer. Their learning didn't improve with the clickers, but I continue to do it because they like it. That matters in terms

of how they value the class. It's kind of like why I got rid of exams—they don't like exams. It was too much of a hurdle. It scared a lot of them. The quizzes are not as scary, but they still accomplish the same thing. (Faculty member in the sciences/math, 400 level, 90 students)

Another faculty member spoke of helping her students reflect on their exams and improve their study habits by using Bloom's Taxonomy[3] (Bloom & Krathwohl, 1956):

I've started introducing Bloom's Taxonomy the first day of class, and explaining that we are moving more and more into more sophisticated and higher levels of Bloom's. So in class, when I ask a question, I will tell them what level of Bloom's it is—"This is a knowledge question." "This is an application question.". . . And when they get their exams back, they not only get their scores, they get their Bloom's scores, too. The answer key gives them not only the answer, but the general model the question represents and what level of Bloom's the question is. I actually—for every question—enter individual exam question scores, and I can just generate Bloom's scores for all of them from that. Students can get their exam score back and their Bloom's score back. Also [two of my colleagues and] I came up with a Bloom's study chart for students that directs them. "If you scored badly in this [area], what can you do by yourself and what can you do in a group to improve this score?" I tell them that if they got 70% or less in any area of the Bloom's, they have to go to this chart and figure out how to change the way they are studying. (Faculty member in the sciences/math, 200 level, 250 students)

About one in five (21.5%) of the courses faculty members described did not include exams or quizzes. In a few cases, faculty spoke of exams being inconsistent with their course goals, as this example illustrates:

I know that the students who don't do as well as they want often think that writing papers is inherently more arbitrary, subjective, and less consistent [than exams], and I wrestle with that a lot myself. But I think of the class as learning how to think and analyze. It's not a knowledge-based class. There's no knowledge I expect them to come out with, so knowledge-based examining techniques don't really fit the pedagogy of what I'm trying to do. (Faculty member in the social sciences, 300 level, 150 students)

Most of the time, faculty members did not explain why they did not include exams in their courses. However, we noted a pattern in the courses that did not include exams, which was that often they required three or more formal papers (sometimes in draft form before final revisions). It is likely that in cases where students completed several papers or projects, faculty members felt that exams were unnecessary. Finally, it was unclear whether exams or quizzes were aspects of about 14% of the courses faculty members described.

Writing

Writing was an explicitly reported component in close to two-thirds (62.6%) of the courses faculty described. Some faculty members spoke of assigning students short pieces of writing, often referred to as "low-stakes" writing because it is either not graded or "graded" with a system of checks. Such assignments are designed to help students engage with, learn, and think about class material without penalty (Elbow, 1997). The following two quotations illustrate this kind of "low-stakes" writing:

About once a week, we'll use the last 10–15 minutes of class for them to address a question in writing. The question might come from the *Wall Street Journal* or it might be theoretical. Often, they respond to the question in small teams. I take four answers—a good one, a not-so-good one, a half-hearted one, and one that is off the correct path—and I put them as they are in a file and put it on the website. Each paper has four names on it, but I take the names off before I put it up online. So I end up picking out the work of a good number of people. Then I add my own answer or I add a lot of comments to the others, so they understand what a good answer would be. (Faculty member in social sciences, 200 level, 375 students)

They have a portfolio where they have to pick a quotation from one of the pieces of theory for the class and do some free-writing about that—to bump into what it's like to talk about awkward language. They turn in the portfolio to me and I've experimented with different styles of that—turning it in three times during the quarter, for instance, and then turning it in twice. There's an end assignment where they have to reread all their entries and reflect on whether and how they think their way of engaging with the theory has changed. Many of them are surprised by how much they didn't understand the theory at first but do now. (Faculty member in the humanities, 300 level, 40 students)

In addition to short writing activities, many faculty members gave students more formal writing assignments. Formal assignments also help students engage with and learn class material, but, in addition, they allow students to grapple with larger questions, write researched arguments in a discipline, and practice and improve their writing skills in the disciplines. For example, a faculty member in the sciences spoke about using writing to help students learn the work of astronomers:

It's a skills-based course, in that I help them learn how to use a telescope, how to use an astronomical camera, how to observe, how to get data, how to reduce the data—get rid of noise—and then how to analyze that data to produce a pretty darn good final rough draft of an article. The article is based on some of the astronomy journals' formats for writing. They are doing things—and these are their own choices—like measuring the fall off of the brightness of an elliptical galaxy as a function of distance from the center of the galaxy. They check the period of a variable star or the warping of the disk of a spiral galaxy. They are looking at colors of stars in huge clusters or calculating the orbit of a comet. This work they are doing is serious. It's not publishable data because we are looking at really familiar objects, but they are checking their results against what is known about that object. (Faculty member in the sciences/math, 400 level, 20 students)

Another faculty member spoke of a writing assignment designed to help freshmen and sophomores begin to think about historical evidence. In his words:

> I have a very early paper assignment, in which I give them a short account of the conversion of an Anglo-Saxon king to Christianity, and I ask them to tell me everything they can about Anglo-Saxon pre-Christian traditions from that account. They have to allow for the bias of the source, recognizing, for example, that the monk who wrote it had his own reasons for saying things the way he did and finding a method to separate what the monk said for his own reasons from those things he said that he had no particular reason for saying so that they could identify the things that were probably true. I ask them to write about two and a half typed pages about the text, which is about a page long and this gives them an introduction to how to use primary documents in a historical argument. (Faculty member in the social sciences, 100 level, 325 students)

Also in the social sciences, another faculty member described two different writing assignments she gave in her class—one to students who had chosen to complete a service learning component in the class and another to the students who had not—both of them including the application of theory to a case:

> They write a proposal for the paper, which the TAs review, and then they write a final paper where they identify one specific social problem and examine that problem through a theoretical lens they have selected. Students who are doing the service learning component write a different paper. They highlight how the organization they have been working in views the social problem it addresses—how does the program describe it and how does it try to address it. And they highlight one interaction they have that was an eye-opening experience for them. Maybe it made them notice something inaccurate or not highlighted as important in our class, for instance. (Faculty member in the social sciences, 200 level, 275 students)

Faculty members often described using both short pieces of writing and longer, formal assignments, with the short assignments building up to the longer, as this faculty member describes:

> We adopted the response papers as a way to force them to read and also the pop quizzes for the same reason. In [this class], you could see that they weren't reading in the exams, and the TAs would tell me that students would come to section and not have done the reading. And then I kind of fell in love with the response papers. And students have the hardest time with them. What they do in these response papers—even though I warn them ahead of time—they don't write on the text, they write on the topic. So I have to tell them, "I don't want you to write on globalization but on Stiglitz." I want them to begin to see texts as not just trippers to their own thinking but intrinsically important in themselves—where there are internal contradictions, the hermeneutics. So at first I gave this utilitarian reason: I wanted them to read. But then I saw this as an approach to writing the research paper [assigned in the class]. This was writing about Smith, who might be used in the research paper. (Faculty member in the social sciences, 200 level, 300 students)

In addition, faculty members whose courses included formal writing often incorporated writing instruction into class time. For example:

> One of the things that has evolved in my teaching is explaining what's involved in a philosophy paper. The first few years of teaching this class, I didn't do that, and we got really bad papers. I think it's a real art to write a good philosophy paper, and I spend almost a whole class session now explaining how to do that—what the premises are, what the conclusions can be. I give them examples, too, of what a good paper would look like. I also try now to post things on my electronic website—links to good explanations for how to write a philosophy paper. I try to give the students a whole lot of information on how to write a good paper. (Faculty member in the humanities, 200 level, 150 students)

As noted at the beginning of this chapter and as the quotations about writing assignments indicate, formal writing assignments carried disciplinary practices within them. Furthermore, all writing assignments, both "low-stakes" and more formal assignments, required that students think about the course material. In thinking about it, they learned it; in learning it, they thought about it. The two acts were difficult to separate.

Research

Close to 29% of the faculty members spoke about asking students to conduct research for their classes, usually as a part of a writing assignment or project. We should note that often students conduct research related to coursework, particularly online, when it is not required (Beyer et al., 2007), and that engineering, fine arts, and creative writing majors speak about research as a continuous aspect of their learning that takes place in and outside the classroom (Peterson et al., 2009). However, the following three examples suggest the range in the kinds of research and research purposes found in the courses where faculty noted that they required research.

At the university, research with both a large "R" and small "r" is a normal part of daily life. Similarly, the research faculty required for their courses was not always formal, nor did it always end in a written document. For example, this faculty member described students working together on topics related to the Puget Sound area:

> Another cool thing we do in that class is that the students write a wiki on specific topics. The students self-organize into the topics, which are salmon, Puget Sound, Maury Island, the aquarium fish trade, and coral reefs. The students in that class wrote the whole Wikipedia site for Maury Island, and they heavily referenced it at the bottom of the wiki entry where you add citations. (Faculty member in the sciences/math, 100 level, 150 students)

Another faculty member described a group project that ended in a "product fair" for construction management projects:

We do a group project where they work in teams of four and they do in-depth research to develop a product. I'm always trying to figure out how to go deep in the class, because it is such a survey class. They go deep in this product research project, where they research one product and it can be an exterior or interior product. I have them look at the whole life cycle. Let's trace it out. We just have a great time. We take over Gould Court [for a product fair] and they all get to be there for the afternoon. (Faculty member in architecture/built environments, 300 level, 111 students)

Finally, another faculty member described assigning a project that asked students to combine individual and group research in an upper-level science class:

At the beginning of the quarter, I tell them to pick a disease they are really interested in. Usually it's a disease that's in their family—that their grandmother has or something they have a personal connection with. I put them in groups of four based on their choices. Then each individual has to find two primary research papers on their aspect of the topic and analyze those—compare them and write me a paper on it. They meet in groups, help each other, and put together a story on this disease. Sometimes there is so much information on a disease, they have to narrow it down. One group decided on gene therapies for Parkinson's for example. (Faculty member in the sciences/math, 400 level, 60 students)

Projects, Presentations, and Performances

Although we often assume that most students demonstrate understanding and critical thought through written work, faculty members also frequently require projects, oral presentations, and performances that require little or no writing but a great deal of thinking, as well as research. Faculty members described requiring such projects, presentations, and performances in about 25% of the classes they described. For example, one forest resources faculty member spoke of requiring students to conduct research and put together posters of their results. As she described it:

They go out, collect some soils, ask a question, try to answer it, and then they do a poster presentation. We have a poster session, where they put their posters up, and I have soils graduate students and faculty come in and give them some feedback. The second presentation is just for the students in the class, where they give an oral presentation with their posters to each other. It's fun, and I think they really love doing it. And I get a kick out of it too. Some of them are so creative. (Faculty member in the sciences/math, 200 level, 55 students)

Faculty members in the arts nearly always require performances or pieces that students must produce as part of their course requirements. For example, one faculty member in art spoke of a class she taught that centered on installation art in Seattle's major medical trauma center, Harborview Medical Center:

Installation is also part of the art world, where you create your work to interpret a particular three-dimensional space. . . . This class has done a project at Harborview Medical Center. Each student goes to the hospital, gets a tour, and goes back and designs something that's appropriate for that context. The project asks them to take into account a lot of considerations that they may not take into account as students. For example, the installation can't cause stress. It can't be offensive. It has to appeal to many cultures and ages. A couple of students have done some things that are interesting with patients—long-term care patients for example, where the students are asked to do work that is really quite sensitive and is done in collaboration with someone there. Other students might physically create a piece about the hospital. But they all have to take things into account they don't usually have to think about. They all do an installation there and we have a show. (Faculty member in the arts, 300 level, 20 students)

In addition, a faculty member in the Dance Department spoke of grading choreography projects at the end of the quarter:

Sometimes I've had them do group choreography projects at the end. They perform them for each other, and I grade those. And sometimes I have had performance exams at the end. It is not hard to see differences in students' performances. You can see the differences in dance bodies. Those differences are not subtle. (Faculty member in the arts, 200 level, 42 students)

Finally, a faculty member described the observation exercises and performances his students completed to demonstrate learning in a beginning acting class:

> In this class, students do an observation exercise, in which they go sit somewhere out in the world, engage all five senses, and come back and talk about it. "I sat on a bench; the bench was cold on my skin; I saw a couple walk by they were having an argument; I smelled the cigarette smoke from him; I heard their voices"—that kind of thing. They do a monologue, and then they do a scene. They do these in sections in front of others, and at the end of the quarter I sometimes get them up to demonstrate something in front of the whole lecture. I get volunteers. And also, during the last week of class, everyone performs a little bit of their final scene for the whole lecture class. (Faculty member in the arts, 200 level, 145 students)

Like the writing assignments we noted earlier, faculty required students to complete projects, presentations, and performances to demonstrate that they understood, had thought about, and were able to apply the knowledge conveyed in the classroom. Faculty descriptions of the courses requiring these types of assignments underscored the importance of remembering that asking students to demonstrate that they have learned to apply concepts and think critically should not be confined to written work.

Quantitative Reasoning

About 17% of the courses that faculty described included quantitative reasoning as a component in their classes. Two of these courses were in the social sciences, and the rest were science, mathematics, or engineering classes. Two faculty members' quotations illustrate this course component:

In the class, they need to learn some fundamental math and how to apply it to control theory problems. So it's like an applied math class; a lot of what I do is applied math. They need to come out of the course being able to apply particular types of tools to systems to get information out of them. (Faculty member in engineering, 400 level, 30 students)

What I wanted was for the students to be able to do derivative and integral problems—have those skills down pat—and also be able to apply them to other certain types of problems like optimization problems. So the first course is aimed at getting the students up to speed on skills in the first part and then how to use them to solve various types of problems in the latter part. (Faculty member in the sciences/math, 200 level, 50 students)

In both cases, faculty speak of the importance of students applying the mathematical skills and tools they have learned to specific kinds of problems, demonstrating once again that thinking is intimately connected with content in quantitative reasoning, as well as in the other course components.

Disciplinary Technology

Students are required to use some form of technology in all of their courses, if only being able to access a webpage. However, a few of the courses faculty described—9.3%—taught students to use technology that was important to the disciplines in which their courses were situated. Technology as a course component served either as the central focus of these courses or as a smaller part of the class. Examples from two disciplinary areas follow:

This is three-dimensional (3D) modeling and rendering—a class in how computing is used to do those tasks in the context of architecture—so it has a certain amount of content related to computer graphics in 3D and a certain amount that's architecture-specific. It's a hands-on class, where students are doing projects as well as mastering a certain amount of academic content. (Faculty member in architecture/built environments, 400 level, 17 students)

We do a computer simulation where they run a business on the web in teams outside of class for a simulated time of four years. (Faculty member in business, 400 level, 45 students)

Learning beyond the Classroom

In addition to the traditional aspects of instruction that we tracked through faculty descriptions of their classes, many faculty members described one or more aspects of their courses that felt intangible, difficult to measure, yet important. We had no way to classify these aspects, except to say that they represented faculty members' desire to give something to their students that went beyond the boundaries of the particular courses they were teaching or that, perhaps, they wanted to lead their students to the same sense of wonder that they themselves felt about their subject areas. The following eight examples illustrate this "something else":

I can close my eyes and imagine being in the body, and I hope that they'll be able to do that too at some point. (Faculty member in the sciences/math, 200 level, 250 students)

The main thing I want them to learn in this class is the thing that I learned at some point—that working in science and math is the most fun you can have with your pants on. I want to lift the curtain a little bit, to help them get a glimmering that there is something big behind it all, something they might be interested in doing. (Faculty member in the sciences/math, 100 level, 120 students)

I kind of began to believe that you have to introduce them to this world of ideas, the life of the mind, that ideas have value for their own sakes. I also want to give them the impression that they aren't there yet, but that they have to do some things to get into this world of ideas. The world has a door, and you need a pass. (Faculty member in the social sciences, 200 level, 300 students)

Another thing I've taken to doing over the years. I take part of a class session and give them a 15-minute presentation on what inspired me to get into aerospace. It starts with the Apollo moon landings and all that. Also, I ask them what it was for them. Did you see a space shuttle launch? Did you see a helicopter go over? Was it your first ride on an airplane, or your first air show? I tell them here's what it was for me—the Apollo 8 mission in 1968. And the closing challenge is "Don't ever forget this. There's a reason you are doing all these difficult things at this point in your lives. It's because you have a vision. Cherish that, enjoy it, and do your best to live it." (Faculty member in engineering, 300 level, 45 students)

My whole philosophy for this class is what can I teach them that they can take out of the university with them? It's about skills and confidence, awareness that they are scientists, that they are the experts. I've started thinking of them as young ambassadors to educate the public in science literacy. They can get at the truth of things, rather than what you see on the TV or in the newspapers. I want to help them use their education in a way that they can help educate other people. (Faculty member in the sciences/math, 400 level, 60 students)

I want them to leave class with an interest in war and with a framework to think about it. But most important, I want them intrigued by it, puzzled by it, and wanting to learn more about it. I want their ears to perk up if a program about war is on TV; I want them to see paintings in museums in new ways—to see how certain paintings reflect certain attitudes about war or transformations in warfare for example. I want them to seek out battlefields when they travel. I want them to come away with a fascination with the topic [and] knowing about how to ethically evaluate wars. (Faculty member in social sciences, 400 level, 100 students)

And one thing that I sort of specialize in, my little niche among my colleagues, is that I'm very good at teaching people how to read a Latin text they've never seen before without a dictionary. It's a different skill than learning to read with a dictionary. So, when they've gone through a class with me, they are never frightened of that ever again. (Faculty member in the humanities, 400 level, 15 students)

The whole course is about that—being attentive to their own lives. (Faculty member in the humanities, 400 level, 20 students)

Summary: Courses

Faculty descriptions of their courses showed that all courses were deeply embedded in the disciplinary content and practices of the fields in which they were situated. Furthermore, faculty descriptions of the knowledge and thinking goals they had for students were so closely intertwined that it was difficult to distinguish one from the other. Perhaps for that reason, the majority of faculty included active learning strategies of some kind in their courses and asked students to demonstrate learning through exams, writing, research, and a range of projects and performances. In addition, faculty often hoped for learning that went beyond the boundaries of the classroom, learning that affected students' broad intellectual development and sense of their own direction and lives years after they were out of college.

These findings do not argue that the faculty members in our study were excellent teachers, nor do they provide evidence that students learned what faculty members hoped they would learn. They speak to intentions rather than outcomes. As such, they are inconsistent with public narratives that portray college faculty as speechifying machines with little thought or concern about what their students are learning. The descriptions of their courses that faculty members in the UW GIFTS gave us challenge such narratives.

4

What Changes Did Faculty Make to Their Courses?

What I do, every time I've taught the course—and sometimes I think my teaching career is like *Groundhog Day*, the movie—I have to keep doing this over and over until I get it right—the fundamental change is that I keep on pulling content out. The first time I taught it—you know, the first time you teach something you're trying to learn the stuff ahead of your students, it's all white noise, and you're thinking, "Did I say that right?" But you are much more concerned about information with a capital "I." I tell my students that my job is to prepare them to be successful in this major—so that means in the subsequent courses in the intro series and then in the 300- and 400-level courses. And so the more experience that I get, the more confident I am that this is not the last time you're going to see this topic called "sexual selection" or "genetic drift," because I know you are going into these other courses. I don't have to tell you everything we know about sexual selection. So I just strip the content out and keep to the essence and really train them how to think.

—Faculty member in the sciences/math, 100 level, 440 students

After faculty members described two courses they had taught, we asked them to talk about one or two changes they had made in those courses, if any, over the time that they had taught them. We felt that it was important to ask faculty members about actual changes in their real classes, before they spoke abstractly about change. Later in the interview, we asked faculty to describe the "big directions of change" in their teaching. This chapter reports on both kinds of changes: some of the changes faculty made that were grounded in the courses they described and those they described more abstractly as big directions of change in their teaching work. In addition, we asked faculty members if they were still making changes to their teaching, and this chapter reports their responses to that question, as well.

Analyzing changes was a challenging process, because an explicitly stated change might clearly necessitate another kind of change. For example, adding scaffolding to an assignment—such as adding supporting assignments and instruction to a writing assignment—might lead to covering less content in order to focus time on the writing assignment. Thus, one change often involved others. The quotation that opens this chapter is an excellent example of this phenomenon, where a stated change—covering less content—likely led to an unstated change—integrating active learning, for example, or revision of the whole class. Similarly, the most explicitly stated reason for the repeated changes in the opening quotation was knowledge of what subsequent courses in the major would teach. However, the quotation reveals a less prominently stated reason for that choice, as well: the faculty member wants to "really train them how to think" in biology.

Although stepping into one kind of change often took faculty into a place where other changes were necessary and a given reason for change may have other reasons embedded in it, we noted changes and reasons only when faculty members explicitly stated what those changes and reasons were. However, the footprints of implied or suggested changes and reasons are often visible in the quotations we include.

Changes to Courses

Faculty members described 211 changes, approximately four changes per interviewee and two per course, which we were able to group into 10 categories, as shown in figure 4.1. Those 10 categories included changes to assignments, full class revision, the addition of active learning strategies, changes in classroom technology, a move to more explicitness, less coverage of content, changes in the self, logistical changes, and the infusion of real-life examples into the class. In addition, six faculty members identified idiosyncratic changes that we grouped into a "miscellaneous" category.

Changed Assignments

More than one in four (27%) of the changes that faculty described were changes in assignments, which were noted in more than half of the

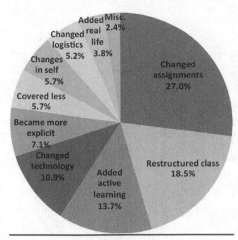

Figure 4.1. Kinds of changes faculty described

courses faculty described. In this category, we included changes that faculty made to writing, projects, performances, homework, and exams. Obviously, changes in assignments can mark other kinds of changes, including shifts in the learning goals faculty members have for their courses, increases in the active learning strategies that faculty members use, changes in grading policies, and others. Faculty members sometimes included these other changes in their descriptions, but often they did not.

In describing the changes they made to assignments, faculty spoke of adding and deleting assignments, as well as of changing existing assignments, particularly by adding "scaffolding" or sequencing for those assignments. Adding assignments and including scaffolding for existing assignments constituted about half of the changes in this category. When faculty spoke of scaffolding or sequencing assignments, they did not describe breaking assignments into smaller pieces—into "atomized bits of knowledge," in the words of Lorrie Shepard (2000, p.1070). Rather, they described assignments that allowed students to try something new, get feedback that might advance their understanding of the task and their performance of it, and, with that new knowledge, try again. For example, the following two faculty members described changing writing assignments by adding a series of draft and revision stages to them:

> I used to have them just hand in their papers, and I would grade them. Now I have them hand in a draft. Everyone reads the draft and comments on it, including me. I changed that because I hated having student papers in my office. When they hand them in at the end of class and you comment on them, they never come to get them. So this way, they read the comments and then, it's a more complete transaction. And plus, I

feel like it's much easier to grade. I hate the feeling that my grades may seem arbitrary, so once I give the comments, then it's clear—either you did what I said or you didn't. Also, I like the intellectual risk-taking that people are willing to do in a draft. I'll say, "You might not be sure this is going to fly; you might think that it's kind of a crazy idea, but I'll always pull you back from the brink if I think you've gotten too far." So the papers got more interesting when I graded the drafts. (Faculty member in the humanities, 400 level, 14 students)

And then the other thing that changed was the peer study groups. These are study groups that also serve as peer review groups for the research papers. The Catalyst [web tool] where they can comment on each other's papers electronically helped us a lot. I don't think in the beginning I had the multiple [versions of] papers. I think that may have come from working with [Interdisciplinary Writing Program instructors]—having them write a number of versions. I do that all the time myself when I write, but I never asked students to do that. (Faculty member in the social sciences, 200 level, 275 students)

Another example of a change in assignments came from a faculty member who multiplied and shortened the number of assignments he gave his students, so that they would have more frequent opportunities to practice skills:

The big change here is moving from four projects—one large project and three smaller ones—to having them do a new mini-research assignment every week. There are now 10 little projects each quarter. This change was the most responsible and effective thing to do for a methods class. They were constantly having to do something, do some discourse analysis, collecting a little bit of data, and doing an analysis. I know they found it intensive, but I know they also found it very enjoyable. That change was partly motivated by the fact that discourse analysis has lots of different methods or modes of analysis; it's a very broad church. If I want to expose them to many different kinds of analysis, I have to increase the number of tasks that they do. Also it allowed me to work with lots of different types of data, not just different types of analysis—and that's a skilling thing too. There's spoken data, visual data, media data, and they were going to have to collect some graffiti data. (Faculty member in the social sciences, 400 level course, 70 students)

Finally, a faculty member in the arts describes changes she made to her students' final exams:

> For awhile, I was doing take-home essay exams, asking them to synthesize material and compare this with that, and I liked that model. But the students rebelled at [some] point. I felt they were going to hang me out the window. They said there was too much work up to that point, and they weren't going to do the final exam. So I came up with this compromise. I said they could do the take-home final or do it as an oral exam. They had the option of taking the questions home, then coming in and answering the questions orally. Many of them did it, and they were happy with it, and we all got to synthesize the material together. So now I make that an option every time. More do the oral than the written. Each group has the same questions, and they all can hear each other's answers. They don't all have to speak on every question, but they all have to speak and say something significant to the conversation or they will fail. (Faculty member in the arts, 200 level, 35 students)

Restructuring the Class

Reorganizing or restructuring all or a large part of a course represented 18.5% of the changes faculty described. Faculty identified such changes in about a third of the courses they described. We included changes faculty made to a significant part of their classes as well as changing the whole class structure in this category of response. The following extended example illustrates this group of responses. In the interview, the faculty member described a multiyear revision to a course taught to 111 majors:

> That first class was just so hard and so not good! I blush just because of the preparation from zero to 60, with three lectures.

I mean the preparation was enormous and coming up with all this material from scratch was pretty daunting, and I probably don't do things the easy way either. I was given a textbook that has a set of slides that come with it, and I had really big Zs in a bubble above my head on some of those slides. The slide deck was just not doing it for me, and I thought, "If it's not going to do it for me, it's really not going to do it for them."

I found, too, that working with someone else's slide deck—I don't know the stories behind those slides. I can talk about "Here's a nail, and here's a two by four." I can talk about those concepts, but I didn't have my personal stories to go behind them. So, there was a lot of trying to bring in my consulting and putting in my own experience, to explain it to them, and find good examples. And, so that first year was just about sur-viving—surviving three lectures a week and getting prepped for them, getting all of the images and things prepared.

In my first year, we had a field trip. I just had this idea because we lived in Seattle. From the West Seattle Bridge, you can see both the concrete and the Nucor Steel sites, so I thought, "They're right there. Let's see if we can get tours." I contacted Nucor, and they were willing to host this tour of 111 students, and we pulled it off.

Nucor takes scrap, recycled steel, and they melt it down in their furnace and out comes molten metal. And then they make these billets. They put it through this rolling process, and it's just an awesome process to see. Really, anybody would love it.

Watching the students come off that tour is like watching people get off the roller coaster. It's really fun. It's noisy, and you can't hear what anyone is saying, but yet they still love it. So we did that the first year, and the feedback I got in their evaluation forms, when I asked a question about what surprised them or what did they think was good, they said the field trip was what this class should be.

So I said okay. The next year, I think I actually had six tours scheduled. We didn't have a hands-on lab, but we took them out into the city. We went to Woodinville Lumber, Olympian Precast, Nucor Steel, the International Masonry In-stitute, Western Clearview, and I had set up a tour on campus where they toured buildings with the architect and the builder.

We did all these tours, and it was too much; I went too much the other way. I overdid it. But I really liked the balance of that. So, in my third year I got more organized, and I did only five tours.

What I was able to do then in subsequent years was find more of the focus, the learning objective focus, and then add videos to the class. So, that was last year's project—finding some video content that helped with the class, because with construction methods, my first year—it was so sad—I would just say, "Okay, step one, dig a hole; step two, place a rebar; step three, put a pipe in the hole." Everybody was bored. The overhead projector was not a great way to present things, so it was really hard with only words and in a lecture format to explain the construction process.

But now, I can pop in a clip of a video and they can see these huge machines pulling dirt, and pipes being placed. They can see the guys with the boots, up to their hips in the concrete, pulling it back and forth. That says so much more than I could possibly ever say with an overhead projector.

For each lecture I have four or five learning objectives that I use to frame the class. I've defined those. And that helps me then organize the lecture; I can revisit my problem sets with those objectives in mind making that correlation much more strong. And then I try to take those learning objectives and build the exam off them too. So, they are an organizing force through the course.

That's one of the reasons I like the class, because I put so much into it. (Faculty member in architecture/built environments, 300 level, 111 students)

Course revision in the second example of this category of responses began with the arrival of a new textbook with a new approach for foreign language instruction. The faculty member who described this change was in charge of all French 101 courses, so after piloting the course change, she helped others teaching first-year French do the same. In her words:

When I first started, we followed a traditional communicative approach. Most textbooks are similar, so we took one that we thought was okay and then we followed it. The learning pattern was still very much the instructor-to-students paradigm. I would ask a question, and the student would answer. The speaking time each student had in the class was still very minimal. When you have 24 students and a 50-minute class, you have maybe one or two minutes of speaking time for each student per class, which is not enough to develop communication skills.

About five years ago, I was growing a bit frustrated with what I saw happening. The best students would learn but there was a big chunk of students who were not really learning well. I started looking at other textbooks and other approaches, and out of the blue I received a textbook by a publisher from France asking if I could take a look at it and give the publisher some feedback on it.

The textbook was totally different from anything I had seen before. It was a task-based method. And it was love at first sight almost. It looked different. The activities were totally different. The publisher was asking if I would like to try it, so I said yes. They gave me samples and I piloted the methods in two sections.

What happened in those classes was like magic. It required a lot of work on my part, but it was refreshing, and I loved it. The activities were more exciting than in the traditional textbooks. In the traditional textbook, learning is exercise-based. There is something that is not natural about it. It's not authentic, and it can be plain boring.

In this new approach, in chapter 1 you are told that you are going to make yourself a new address book with the addresses of all the people around you in French. So you have to find out all this information about them in French—their names, addresses that include numbers and street names, cities, and so on. So from day two or three of learning French, they already have to learn how to function in a natural way.

All of the activities in that book were things you might have to do in actual life. In actual life you are never told, "This person is going to say this and you need to say that," as you are in a traditional textbook. That's the prevalent method out there, and people think that because they are going through the motions in this way, that when they are in an autonomous mode they will remember how to do things from Exercise B. But they won't.

In this new approach, they have to use their own strategies. They are thrown into the pool, and they have to find their way, and you can give them help as they do that. The role of the instructor becomes that of a coach and not of pouring this knowledge into someone else's mind. You are there, and you guide them along. Each learner learns at his or her own pace.

They are investing their whole selves, and they are learning in a social pattern. They are constantly having to go to another group and negotiate meaning—"I'm not sure what you are trying to say, can you clarify?" They help each other. The paradigm of learning from teacher to student shouldn't always be the case—you should also have student-to-student teaching and learning, with the teacher there to be a guide. The students are much more comfortable trying to say something in French to their peers than they are having to say something in front of everyone else to their teacher. We try to avoid that situation.

It's a decentralized way of teaching. You are not the ultimate authority anymore, and that's what some instructors are not always willing to give away. That's very scary for some people. At the same time I feel that as instructors, we are there to teach people to become life-long learners and to survive on their own, so teaching them those skills from the beginning is the best thing we can give them. (Faculty member in the humanities, 100 level, 27 students)

As these two examples show, whole-course changes often involve many of the other kinds of changes that faculty described. In the first example on changes in a construction methods course, the faculty member added technology and assignments and integrated active learning strategies in the form of tours of local construction-related sites into the course. Later in that class, the faculty member added labs. In the second example, the faculty member added active learning strategies to the course, as well as new assignments. Sometimes, however, whole-course change meant starting over, as this faculty member said:

After the first year, I threw that [course design] out and started over. (Faculty member in the social sciences, 300 level, 150 students)

Added Active Learning Strategies to the Class

In the previous chapter, we noted that most of the faculty members described using pedagogical strategies and/or assignments that could be defined as active learning strategies. In analyzing those aspects of the courses faculty described, we included writing assignments and projects in our definition of active learning strategies.

In contrast, in analyzing specific changes that faculty made to their classes, we separated writing assignments from other active learning strategies, counting the addition of writing assignments and other types of projects that might be considered "active learning" in the previously discussed category of "changed assignments." Therefore, the number of changes in active learning strategies is smaller than our parsing of the classes that faculty described might suggest. This is particularly true in those cases where the change that faculty described included adding writing assignments or projects to classes or added scaffolding for existing writing assignments.

In analyzing active learning changes that faculty described making to their classes, we focused primarily on the addition of in-class techniques, such as small group work, asking questions in class, use of clickers, and so on. With this definition, 13.7% of the changes faculty described centered on integrating active learning strategies into their courses. Faculty members made such changes to about one out of every four courses they described. The following three examples, all involving faculty members in the social sciences, illustrate this category of response. In the first example, an anthropology faculty member spoke of continuing to add active learning strategies to her class as part of a longtime commitment to using active learning:

> I'm working all the time to more and more put it in the students' hands, so I would say these changes are affecting their learning. In my experience, every lesson has a piece that is theirs, that they are hopefully out of their seats working on in a big class. I learned in a teaching institute at [X University] to work individually with students, get them to work together in pairs and large groups, work with the two sides of the classroom, and with the whole room. I use every combination of level of discussion to work on something—having people come up, having people perform, having people go back and elicit

responses, having people work together and apart. I guess that always feels like a certain risk. (Faculty member in the social sciences, 100 level, 90 students)

The second example is from a faculty member speaking of an honors seminar:

I've made the class much more student-centered and hands-on. So before I was teaching them about the research process— telling them about it the way you would in a methods class. But now any material I tell them about is immediately turned around to them: "So okay, how are you going to do this?" So it's almost a workshop. I'm giving it back to them and having them really work with it. (Faculty member in the social sciences, 400 level, 10 students)

Finally, this example from a faculty member in sociology describes an active learning strategy that the faculty member learned by observing a colleague:

We have something called learning enhancements that I stole from another colleague. I say "learning enhancement" and the rules are that they have to turn around and talk to everyone around them. They have to design a study, for example, based on the lecture about HIV AIDs. If I see anyone who is not engaged in that conversation, I take points away from the people around them. I ask groups to share when we come back to the full class. Also, in general in lectures, I'll throw questions out to hear their responses. I usually do the learning enhancements the first day, so that I can turn things back on them right away. I use it to see what they are thinking. But I will also do it sometimes if they are just bored and seem not engaged in the class to get them engaged in the material or to check in and see where they are with the material. (Faculty member in the social sciences, 200 level, 275 students)

In almost every case, faculty members who described integrating active learning strategies into their courses did so as ways to foster and elicit thinking from students.

Changed Technology

Close to 11% of the changes faculty mentioned were changes in technology. Such changes were made in about one in every five classes that faculty described. The largest group within this category was composed of faculty who added technology to their courses or increased their use of class technology, as this quotation illustrates:

> The improvement I've made is that I started out on overheads a long time ago, and now I've gone to PowerPoint. I put it all on the web before class, and I encourage them to print it all out so they aren't writing down every word I say as I'm talking. They sit there, and I encourage them to ask questions as much as they are willing to. I tell them that I'm just going to get more and more boring [and] talk faster and faster, unless they ask questions. I like to be interrupted. (Faculty member in the sciences/math, 200 level, 80 students)

Another example of adding technology comes from a faculty member who replaced the active learning strategies he was using in the classroom with technology when the size of the class increased:

> The biggest change in this class is the use of technology in teaching. I went from it being a whiteboard and my notes to a more interactive style, but as the class got bigger, I couldn't do that very well. After you get to 150 or above, it just gets very hard. I tried to do it in a kind of interactional style with 150—breaking them into groups, and it didn't work. We covered so little material that way, it wasn't good. So I switched to PowerPoint and integrated movies into the PowerPoint, and I like that. It really means there's very little time for Q and A but it does stimulate stuff when students go into their sections to discuss. (Faculty member in the social sciences, 200 level, 200 students)

This category of responses includes those who changed the technology that was taught as part of the content in the discipline, such as this faculty member described:

In my favorite class, I introduced MATLAB and taught them how to use it. It was an expected skill that was used in subsequent classes, but it was a difficult program for them to master. The students always asked for a separate course—learning Excel, learning MATLAB, and learning Word—and I thought that was too dumbed down, so instead of having them use MATLAB as a trial by fire, I developed a tutorial, which was subsequently used by my colleagues and the TAs. (Faculty member in engineering, 400 level, 35 students)

This category of change also includes those who eliminated or cut back on their use of technology, in most cases for reasons discussed in chapter 3, as this quotation illustrates:

I began being quite structured in class with PowerPoint and so on, and as I've taught more, I've used PowerPoint less and less; I use the whiteboard more and more. (Faculty member in the social sciences, 300 level, 35 students)

Became More Explicit about Expectations and Practices

About 7% of the changes faculty mentioned concerned becoming more explicit in class about their expectations, including about aspects of disciplinary practice. One faculty member spoke of being explicit about the ways his discipline operated compared with those of others. In his words:

My job is to get them to understand how my discipline thinks, and they can transfer that later to a discipline they will call their own. With [the Interdisciplinary Writing Link instructor], we try to put that right out in the open. It is very explicit. When you talk about inequality, for example, you have these light bulbs go off—"Oh, school may not be the great leveler." I want them to come to the conclusions as sociologists. Philosophical beliefs or ideology—there's a place for that—but that is not what this class is looking for. They can come to conclusions in different ways, but for this class, they need to understand how

sociologist would do that. So we added [information on] how
to do sociology. (Faculty member in social sciences, 300 level
honors course, 35 students)

Similarly, another faculty member, quoted in more detail in chapter 3,
spoke of making disciplinary practice more explicit to students, but, in
her case, with a focus on writing. As she put it:

One of the things that has evolved in my teaching is explaining
what's involved in a philosophy paper. (Faculty member in the
humanities, 200 level, 150 students)

Finally, another faculty member spoke of being explicit in relation to
modeling what she wanted her students to do:

But I learned that unless I modeled my expectations to them,
it wasn't fair to ask them to perform something. I realized that
if I hadn't demonstrated overtly, passively, and then in repeat
models, I shouldn't ask them to have learned it. I learned a lot
in the six years teaching here, like learning that you can't just
tell them to do something; you can't just give them a paper
asking them to do something or lecture on it once. It has to be
the pedagogical practice of the whole class. If I want them to
read a historical text and fathom that that text has something
to say about their reading of the literature, I'm going to have
to spend some time in class to talk about why they have to do
that, how to do that, what it looks like when it's done, and
then to model moments of enthusiasm in the class when we
have learned something by doing things. I've learned how to
enhance a sense of why and how to do things, instead of setting
up my objectives, asking them to meet them, and then having
to clean up confusion and self-doubt later. (Faculty member in
the humanities, 200 level, 53 students)

Like other categories of change, when faculty members become
more explicit about their expectations and disciplinary practices, sometimes other changes become necessary. For example, the faculty member
describing changes to his honors sociology course spoke of a process of

becoming more explicit to himself about his goals and intentions, as well as being more explicit with his students. This step caused him to cut content out of his course, as well as readings. As he put it:

> I keep trying to cull out things that don't push forward to what we're trying to get to. (Faculty member in the social sciences, 300 level, 35 students)

In addition, the faculty member describing modeling what she wanted her students to learn to do is also describing a move to more explicit teaching, and both changes suggest a revision of the whole class.

Covered Less Content to Increase Instruction in Key Areas

The quotation that opens this chapter is an example of this category of change. As noted previously, the need to cover less material in order to increase learning in one area or another was sometimes the *effect* of other changes faculty mentioned. For instance, integrating active learning strategies into class time often required faculty to cut back on course content. In addition, this particular category of change was also the *cause* of other changes. For example, intentionally covering less material often brought about a major revision of a class.

We counted responses in this category when faculty members explicitly mentioned that they were covering less content in order to go into more depth or provide instruction in other areas. About 6% of the changes faculty members described were included, and "covering less in order to focus on key areas" was a change made in about one out of every 10 courses that faculty described. The example that follows reiterates one of the considerations noted in the quotation that opened this chapter—consideration of what comes next in the major:

> I'd say the biggest change I made in that class was last year, after I taught it the first time. I decided to cover less material. I had originally included more topics, and I found that we weren't getting to the level of complexity of the problems that I'd hoped we would. If we'd had another day or two on each topic, we'd be able to tackle more complex problems. So I cut

out topics based on two criteria. One was I thought about the majors. It's a required class for the majors, so even though there were lots of non-majors in there, I thought about class topics that students would cover in other classes in the department. For example, I thought that they would be getting information about child language development in future courses—majors take a whole class in child language development—so I kind of cut that out. That opened up about two weeks of time, and I was able to redistribute that. (Faculty member in the sciences/math, 300 level, 80 students)

The second example of this category of responses shows a second consideration—a focus on what is possible for the students to learn:

What has changed is my thinking about how much material I can effectively cover in the 50-minute, three-days-a-week time that I teach—especially with someone like Kant, recognizing just how difficult that material is for someone who has never taken any philosophy, let alone someone who has never read something written in the 18th century. So cutting down the material and walking them through that material more carefully—doing some more work with the texts—reading the texts and presenting the argument in them—that's what I try to do now. I still go in sometimes thinking I can cover a certain amount, and the time goes by and I still couldn't cover it and I think, "I should have known!" It's an ongoing challenge, but I have a better sense now of knowing what is reasonable to get through. (Faculty member in the humanities, 200 level 150 students)

Responded to Changes in Oneself

In some ways, most of the changes that faculty make are linked with changes in themselves, a topic we will take up in more detail in chapter 6. However, in describing changes they had made to their courses, sometimes faculty members explicitly described changes in their beliefs about teaching and learning, changes in their own expertise, and changes in how they thought about or interacted with students. These changes represented about 6% of the changes faculty described and were linked to about one in 10 of the courses that faculty discussed. As would be expected, these changes were highly individual. For example, one faculty member described coming to understand his own shift in how he taught his design courses:

> Many years ago I started thinking that I don't do facts any-more. I keep trying to get to the point of learning to steward things, to being part of the things we are creating as opposed to being "in charge." Another thing I've realized is that when you're teaching, your whole personality is wrapped up in it. In Scottish history, which is the most bloody, bigoted, stupid, vicious, ignorant history you can imagine, we argued over religion for centuries. The Presbyterians would not accept the English Book of Common Prayer because they believed that prayer should be extemporaneous, rather than rehearsed. So they fought the English and massacred each other for centuries. But I realize that I now believe that. One should come into class like that—open. Class is not an information dump; it's a way of looking at things. It's tied up in values. (Faculty member in architecture/built environments, 300 level, 80 students)

Another faculty member—one who won a distinguished teaching award at least in part for how he treats undergraduates in his courses—spoke of changes in how he interacts with students:

> I do have an acerbic style in some ways with students, with a lot of irony and sarcasm. Once a student got very offended and told me off when I was teaching at [X University]. The other students came to my defense. But I really thought about it, and I thought, "I have to temper that." I can't become someone I'm not, but I can really temper that and be very sensitive to that. So that's changed. The way I treat them—I think it has evolved over time. I think I treat them with a lot of respect. I think that they get that. They get that they are not being talked down to, that they are being taken very seriously. (Faculty member in the social sciences, 200 level, 275 students)

Made Logistical Changes

About 5% of the changes that faculty described were logistical changes, such as changes in grading policies or class size. Faculty members made these kinds of changes in about one in every 10 of the classes they described in their interviews. One example of this kind of change is described by a faculty member in humanities:

> One thing I've learned in the process of teaching that particular class is that I never put on a syllabus that late assignments are not accepted. And the reason is that I was ready to give the final one day, the second time I taught the class, and a girl came up to me and she said, "I'm going to take the final." I said, "Well great." And she said, "I just want you to know that if I do badly, it's not your fault. I'm ready to take it as far as I can be, but I was working at my job in a convenience store last night and I was robbed at gunpoint and the police had my bag until 3 in the morning." I was like, "Please go away and come back when you are ready." But, it struck me that she was very nervous about talking to me. One of the things I'm always telling the TAs [in the teaching training seminar I teach] is that story. You just never know what else is going on with someone. Don't make a policy that will penalize someone in that kind of situation. If you were teaching in a teeny tiny liberal arts college, where everybody is living in the dorm and eating in the cafeteria, that's a different thing. This is a different place. (Faculty member in the humanities, 300 level, 35 students)

Added Real-life Examples to Class

Some faculty members spoke of starting to integrate real-life examples into their course content, including examples that students volunteered from their own lives. These changes were noted in just under 4% of the changes faculty described. This change pertains to faculty members' bringing their own experience into the classroom, as this example indicates:

> It just occurred to me after a few years that I had all the juniors there, so I should do that. I always bring in my industrial

experience into the class, and I thought why not formalize it for the course. (Faculty member in engineering, 300 level, 45 students)

It also includes faculty bringing the "real" examples of others into the classroom, as this faculty member described:

I point out the way we think in marketing—here's how Google actually uses marketing; here's how Microsoft actually uses marketing—and to use examples like that and drill down into some of those details without getting too detailed—to make it short examples. (Faculty member in business, 400 level, 25 students)

Finally, it includes bringing the students' experience into the class-room, as this faculty member noted:

I think the biggest change I've made over time is getting students to apply the concepts to their own experiences. And this is a shift I go back and forth on. I often have them write research papers or analyze a research article—so the class is very transparently research-based. That's the "serious academic area" side to the class. And the whole thing about applying it to one's life—that sounds softer, but I've grown much more comfortable about doing that. (Faculty member in the social sciences, 300 level, 35 students)

Miscellaneous Changes

A small group of changes were noted by individual faculty members, including that the faculty member:

Started teaching courses in a new field of study
Opened the course to honors students
Stopped continuously revising the course
Changed the name of an activity

A faculty member described the last item in this list of singletons—changing the name of an activity:

When I first introduced these [active learning] exercises, I separated them from the rest of the class, standing by themselves. I
called them "discovery-based learning exercises" or something
like that. And students complained about it. They said they felt
it was just extra work they had to do—busy work. So the next
year, I just called it homework and said the questions would
end up in exams—whatever I asked them to do in the homework might appear in exams. So my emphasis that this would
be important to their futures, alongside using them in exams
and calling them homework have made students complain less
about them than they did at first. (Faculty member in the social
sciences, 200 level, 375 students)

Few Changes

All but one of the faculty members in UW GIFTS reported making significant changes to their teaching. The one exception reported making
small changes in the use of teaching technology—the move from overheads to PowerPoint, for example. Other than reporting minor changes,
there was little to distinguish this faculty member from others in the
sample. She appeared to care about and respect her students and to be
thoughtfully considering whether students were learning or not. She
had participated in teaching training, and she preferred and took steps
to achieve an interactive classroom, rather than one in which students
were passive listeners. Nothing in her interview suggested that she was
different in any way from the faculty members who had made more
substantive changes to their courses.

Big Directions of Change

After faculty had discussed the changes they had made to their classes
and their reasons for those changes, we asked them to describe one or
two big directions of change in their teaching. The 55 faculty described
87 major directions, and we were able to categorize those into 10 broad
directions of change. Table 4.1 shows those 10 areas and the percentage
of faculty identifying each direction. The table displays the "big directions" categories adjacent to the categories of change that faculty noted

Table 4.1. Big directions of change in teaching and changes to courses

Big Directions of Change in Teaching (% of Faculty Identifying the Direction*)	Changes to Courses
Developed a stronger focus on students' learning (52.7%)	Changed assignments
Responded to changes in oneself (21.8%)	Reorganized/revised whole class
Added active learning strategies (18.2%)	Added active learning strategies
Covered less content to focus more in depth (12.7%)	Changed technology
Had no big directions of change (9.6%)	Became more explicit
Changed how I thought about/taught discipline (7.3%)	Covered less content to focus more in depth
Integrated more diversity into class (7.3%)	Responded to changes in oneself
Changed the way I treat students (7.3%)	Made logistical changes
Became more explicit (5.4%)	Added real-life examples to class
Used technology in new ways (5.4%)	
Made logistical changes (3.6%)	
Misc. (7.3%)	

* Numbers do not add to 100% because faculty sometimes identified more than one direction of change

when speaking about their specific classes. As the table shows, there is overlap in the two lists, particularly in the areas of adding active learning, responding in the classroom to changes in oneself, covering less content in order to go deeper into key areas, logistical changes, and changes in technology. This section briefly addresses the four most frequently mentioned big directions of change listed in table 4.1.

A Focus on Students as Learners

The direction of change mentioned most frequently—developing a stronger focus on student learning and students as learners—is a change that faculty did not mention when discussing the changes they had made to their courses. We speculate that they may not have mentioned it because it likely signals a change in attitude that can underlie many of the actions faculty took to change their courses. Indeed, when faculty spoke about a shift in their focus on students as learners, that shift required them to change what they were doing in the classroom, as this faculty member's comment suggests:

> I feel like I have gained an understanding of how people learn language best, and this has totally changed how I teach and how my students are learning. (Faculty member in the humanities)

Therefore, a change in awareness of students as learners invariably brought other changes in its wake. For example, one engineering faculty member described his shift in thinking of his students as learners, a change that motivated him to include discussion with students on where their particular places might be in the engineering world of work after graduation. As he described it:

> The major theme is that the technical content is important, but connecting it with the people is vital. The people *are* the process, and it's important to connect the individuals with the material and help them grow both in terms of their technical knowledge and as young engineers, appreciating themselves in relation to this engineering world they are preparing for. When I taught a couple of classes here at the UW as an adjunct professor, I think my focus then was just on the content. [My own experience in] industry—having to think about what about that job worked for me and what didn't work—was a big growing experience for me. If I help people find what works and doesn't at this stage, it might help save them from doing those long and varied tours of duty I did along the way." (Faculty member in engineering)

Another faculty member described this shift as causing her to slow down and recognize that learning is a process that takes time:

> Teaching to learning—that actually helped me. Also the concept of the "time for understanding" from Jacques Lacan. He breaks logic into these three parts: the instant of seeing, the time for understanding, and the moment of concluding. I like

thinking about that for teaching. They encounter it; they think they get it; but actually the time for understanding and drawing conclusions about it is much longer. The "aha!" phase of it—I need to have much more patience around. (Faculty member in the humanities)

In addition to describing the class changes they implemented based on this shift to an awareness of students as learners, faculty members also spoke of triggers for this change. For example, a faculty member in the social sciences spoke of this change in thinking about students as learners and what it caused her to do in her course as coming from external sources. In her words:

Something I've been doing that's a big shift is that as often as I can, I try to create a range of different forms of assessment for students, so that they can show their knowledge in a way that works for them. Sometimes I've had every assignment, including exams, come with an array of ways they could do it and count it, including not taking the exam if they wanted and doing more papers instead. I think some of this is because of the learning workshops or books I've read. I did the [teaching training retreat] out in Forks and that was one place where I got a lot of that concept about finding ways to let students show what they know in the ways they best know how to do that. (Faculty member in the social sciences)

Similarly, a faculty member in the sciences talked about the shift in thinking about students as learners being triggered by a valued mentor. As she described it:

[My mentor] is the person who made the change in my life from teaching as something you do to your students to helping the learner to learn. You don't impart, you don't transmit. You can't do any of those things. All you can do is help them learn. He got me to see them as learners, as opposed to empty vessels to fill. Once you see that you are more a coach or a facilitator of learning you might see that you've got one person who is the professional dancer in *Dancing with the Stars* and one who would like to learn how to dance. Both people have to work very hard; both have a role. You don't just stand and show them the dance; it becomes much more interactive. That makes the classroom so much more alive and interesting. My job is to be more organized, to know where I am taking my students, to question them so I know where they are and then to respond to that, to help them get to where they need to be. So it is very, very fluid, as opposed to lock-stepping through biology. (Faculty member in the sciences)

Thinking of students as learners caused some faculty members to begin their course planning with where they hoped the students would be at the end of the course. For example:

I don't start thinking about what I will do in the class now until I know what I want the students to know when they leave. I think it becomes more focused on what the student should be able to do rather than on what I'm going to cover. That was not an easily won lesson, because there's all this stuff they should know. But I realized that covering it doesn't mean that they've learned it. So my biggest lesson is just to back off, figure out what I want to accomplish, and then help them do that. Everything goes back to those learning objectives.

I'm just starting to develop a class for next year about communication approaches to the study of war. I have one approach, but there is so much we can learn from other approaches that I have to stop and ask: so what do I want students to know at the end of the quarter? what do I want them to be able to think about that may be useful to them? That's where I am right now. I think in the past I built off what someone else had done in the class. I think these are the biggest changes in my teaching. They influence everything. Focusing on what I want them to know at the end—that means I have to think about not only what's expedient for me to do in the classroom, but how I'm going to help them. How am I going to give them opportunities to do things even though that may not be what I'm most comfortable doing? Those are the big things that have influenced everything else. (Faculty member in the social sciences)

As this faculty member noted, this direction of change was "not an easily won lesson." When faculty members first embrace the idea of the student as learner and of making their teaching more "learning centered," what that means they should be doing in class is confusing. Also, faculty members sometimes have the sense that they are not doing their jobs if they turn over too much of their courses to student-centered practices, as this comment illustrates:

> In terms of student learning, I just don't know. I'm still oriented toward me as the focal point of learning as opposed to having discussion groups. I have tried more student-centered learning in terms of students' doing projects that allow them to explore things with less supervision from me or TAs—in that sense, less structured—but I'm not sure about the value of that. In the end, if I'm not involved, I kind of feel like I'm ripping them off. I feel like I'm not doing my job. (Faculty member in the social sciences)

The shift in perception of students was a pronounced change for faculty, as they noted when asked about big directions of change in their teaching. However, this change also can be identified in responses to other questions we asked faculty in UW GIFTS. We will return to this kind of change in chapter 7.

Responded to Changes in Oneself

About one in five (21.8%) of the faculty members responding to the question of big directions of change in their teaching mentioned changes in themselves. For example, faculty members often noted that they had become more confident in the classroom and that they had become more compassionate over time. Several faculty members spoke of being able to teach more from who they were than from what they thought they ought to be. In the words of one faculty member:

> Feeling more comfortable about my teaching is a direction of change. I have a better understanding of what motivates me as an artist, and that will be reflected in how you teach it. I think early on you teach out of obligation about what you think is

important content to learn. I think it's better not to teach all that content but to teach an aspect of it that you feel comfortable with and engaged in. (Faculty member in the arts)

This shift from teaching what one believes one "should" to teaching from the self is a change that crosses faculty responses to a number of questions. We discuss faculty members' response to changes in themselves in more detail in chapter 6.

Added Active Learning Strategies

We have discussed the move to incorporate active learning strategies into the classroom earlier in this chapter when identifying the changes that faculty described making in their specific courses. Not surprisingly, about 18% of the faculty also mentioned the use of active learning strategies as a big direction of change in their teaching. In the words of one of the faculty members:

One [of my basic teaching premises] is that students learn best in philosophy if they are active participants. In philosophy, they have to be engaged; they have to be actively working through the arguments. (Faculty member in the humanities)

Covered Less Content to Focus in-Depth

Close to 13% of the faculty noted that a major direction of change in their teaching was that they were covering less content in order to focus more in-depth on some areas. This was also a change that many faculty noted they had made to the specific courses they described, and we have discussed these changes earlier in this chapter. In describing this change as a major change in her teaching, one faculty member said:

The quarter is short; students are busy; and I want to get through as much significant stuff as possible—the stuff that is really important. . . . The first year I had a whole set of stuff I wanted to do. It went okay but I got some criticism that there was too much to do. The next year I would ask myself what it was important to focus on, what is the biggest bang for the time I have. (Faculty member in the social sciences)

Are You Still Making Changes to Your Teaching?

We asked 53 of our 55 interviewees if they were still making changes to their teaching, and all of them said that they were. Many faculty members said that they were changing their courses all the time, as these two examples illustrate:

Yeah, always innovating, always looking for ways to improve experiences, improve students' access to material. Looking for better sources, better things for students to read, better clips, better assignments. Always, always thinking about it. (Faculty member in the social sciences)

Always. Always. I certainly hope there's not a time when I think I've got it down now, because then I shouldn't teach anymore. There has to be that moment of regret afterwards when I think, "I should have gotten that student to say more than she said." I've learned that often my classes, after that kind of thinking, end up being the best I've ever had. (Faculty member in the humanities)

In addition, several faculty members commented that after a certain point with a class, changes were more modest than they were at the start. As one faculty member said:

I hope so! But not of the same magnitude. Now it's more of an issue of changing the readings, doing different lectures, and covering different topics. (Faculty member in the social sciences)

Finally, some faculty members indicated that they were working on changing specific aspects of their classes. For example, one faculty member spoke about trying to make stellar evolution clearer and described her approach to this problem:

The students are still not getting the basic physical facts of why stars evolve, and it's not that difficult, so I'm still working on how to help them understand that process. I've put together a stellar evolution game—marking the progress of the sun. They have markers and each step has questions about what is going on in the sun. That helped, but one TA said that the students who did well on the exams that tested that concept were students who memorized the answers to the game and not necessarily the students who understood the processes that were going on. I think the wording was poor on the midterm, so I will modify the game to get them deeper into the concepts. About 25% of the students still miss one of these questions, and they chose an answer that they had just memorized based on a word they recognized, even though it was totally the wrong word. But when 25% miss it, it's just not satisfying. I'm wondering if maybe this is not a multiple choice concept. Right now all my questions are multiple choice, but I'm thinking that I could have a series of short essay questions. (Faculty member in the sciences)

Summary: Changes

In his book on college teaching (2004), Ken Bain describes faculty who are experts in their fields and who also have become expert at creating positive and effective learning climates for students. Bain found that the faculty he studied had "at least an intuitive understanding of human learning akin to the ideas that have been emerging from research in the learning sciences" (p. 16). Our study does not claim that the faculty we interviewed are "the best," nor can we tell if the changes they have made to their classrooms have improved student learning there. However, we can say that the changes that faculty described mirror much of what Bain describes his "best teachers" doing and suggest an awareness of and focus on how students learn.

The changes that faculty members said they had made in the specific courses they described signal that awareness and focus. The most frequently mentioned changes related to a shift to a focus on student learning. These included changes in assignments (and especially when faculty members spoke about including scaffolding and improving sequencing for assignments); changes made to reorganize the whole class;

changes involving adding active learning strategies to class; changes in how explicitly faculty members communicated expectations and disciplinary practice to students; and changes centered on covering less content in order to focus on key areas of knowledge and skills.

Furthermore, a focus on students as learners was the most prominent of the changes that faculty members noted when asked to describe the one or two big directions of change in their teaching. More than half of the faculty in our study described this shift to a focus on student learning. Other big directions of change that faculty mentioned echoed the changes they had described making to their courses and included a big directional change to active learning approaches, to reducing the amount of content covered in order to focus more deeply on learning, and to becoming more explicit about expectations and disciplinary practices. Finally, all faculty members described themselves as continuing to make changes to their teaching—no matter what they taught or how long they had been teaching in colleges and universities.

In their famous article on the shift in higher education from a focus on teaching to a focus on student learning (1995), Barr and Tagg quoted Buckminster Fuller describing how such change might begin:

> Buckminster Fuller used to say that you should never try to change the course of a great ship by applying force to the bow. You shouldn't even try it by applying force to the rudder. Rather you should apply force to the trim-tab. A trim-tab is a little rudder attached to the end of the rudder. A very small force will turn it left, thus moving the big rudder to the right, and the huge ship to the left. The shift to the Learning Paradigm is the trim-tab of the great ship of higher education. It is a shift that changes everything. (p. 24)

The information we gathered on the changes that faculty made to their courses strongly suggests that the ship is, indeed, turning.

5

WHY DID FACULTY MAKE CHANGES
TO THEIR COURSES?

I've always been a good teacher, I think, because to be a good teacher, you
have to love teaching. If you don't love teaching all those other bets are off;
you are never going to be a good teacher. That is a necessary condition. But
you also have to know your topic well—well enough to explain it—and you
have to love your subject. And if you have those two, then you are going to
get the maturity.

> —Faculty member in the social sciences

In discussing their reasons for the changes they had made to their
courses, faculty described their specific reasons for those changes. In
addition, to get at general sources of change in teaching, we read faculty
a list of 17 possible sources of change, asking them to rate each source's
overall contribution to the changes they had made in their teaching
over the years. Both sets of responses—faculty members' descriptions of
their reasons for change and their ratings of our 17 sources of change—
were remarkably similar. Together, their responses suggest that change
emerges more from internal interactions between faculty members and
the students in the courses they are teaching than it does from external
influences, such as reading about best practices.

Reasons for Changes Made to Specific Courses

Altogether faculty members gave 234 reasons for the 211 changes that
they identified making in the 107 classes they described. Similar to
the categories of change that we noted in chapter 4, faculty members'
reasons for the changes overlapped and interacted; one reason for change

often suggested others that were not stated but that could be inferred from faculty comments. However, as before, we categorized only what the faculty members explicitly stated.

Faculty members gave two kinds of responses to the question of why they made the changes they had described. First, they said they made changes for specific reasons, such as "I wanted students to learn X" or "I wanted to spend more time focusing more deeply on Y." Second, when answering why they had made changes, faculty sometimes spoke of sources of information about needed change, such as "I noticed from their quizzes that they were not getting X" or "I went to a workshop and learned how to do Y." Obviously, the two kinds of responses often overlapped, but in our analysis of faculty responses, we preserved this difference.

In addition, the reasons for change that faculty gave separated themselves into "internal" reasons or sources of change—those that came from interaction between the students, faculty member, and subject inside the class—and "external" reasons or sources of change—those that came from sources outside the class.

Table 5.1 shows how the reasons for the changes faculty gave in their interviews were distributed. The table separates reasons from sources of change, as well as internal from external causes. As the table shows, internal reasons and sources of change—those that emerged from the interaction between faculty members and their classes—far outnumbered those that were external to the classroom. In fact, 85% of the 234 reasons and sources for change that faculty members described were the results of interaction between the faculty member and the particular students in the specific course he was teaching. Furthermore, as the table shows, close observation of a variety of course components, which revealed what students were learning, together with the faculty member's desire to advance her learning goals or increase student learning accounted for half of all the *reasons* that faculty gave for changing their teaching.[1] These two findings powerfully suggest that change in teaching is primarily the result of what happens between the faculty member, the students in her class, and the subject she is teaching.

Internal Reasons and Sources: Change Arising from Faculty/Class Interactions

As table 5.1 shows, 14 reasons and sources for change were rooted in faculty interactions with their students and courses. As noted in chapter

Table 5.1. Reasons for and sources of change

Reason and Sources N=234	# of times	% of reasons	% of changes made for that reason/source*
Internal Reasons for Change:			
Between the Instructor and the Class	139	59.4%	65.9%
To advance instructor's learning goals/increase student learning	66	28.2	31.3
To address the instructor's own values or teaching philosophy	16	6.8	7.6
To increase student engagement/motivation in class	15	6.4	7.1
To keep the class and its content current	13	5.5	6.2
To continuously improve the class	10	4.3	4.7
To slow the pace of the class	6	2.6	2.8
To get students to reflect on their own learning	3	1.3	1.4
To bring the faculty member's own expertise/experience into the class	3	1.3	1.4
To help the instructor assess students' learning	3	1.3	1.4
To give students particular information at the particular time they need it	2	0.9	1.0
Fairness—to make sure all students had access to all resources	1	0.4	0.5
To improve class climate	1	0.4	0.5
Internal Sources of Change/Awareness That Change Was Needed:			
Between the Instructor and the Class	60	25.6%	28.5%
Instructors observed—by paying attention to students' questions in class, performance on assignments or exams, and level of students' attentiveness in class—that changes were needed	51	21.8	24.2
Instructors talked to previous students or paid attention to what students wrote in course evaluations	9	3.8	4.3
External Reasons for Change:			
Outside the Interaction between Instructor and Class	7	3.0%	3.4%
Instructor was more confident about own teaching	3	1.3	1.4
Instructor based change on successful changes made in previous courses	2	0.9	1.0
To improve own lecture performance	1	0.4	0.5
To improve own course evaluations	1	0.4	0.5
External Sources of Change/Awareness That Change Was Needed:			
Outside the Interaction between Instructor and Class	28	12.0%	13.3%
Learned from others: instructors attended a conference where changes were being discussed, worked closely with other faculty/staff who helped them see the need for change, or observed other faculty teaching	13	5.5	6.2
Instructor took the needs of subsequent courses in the major into account	4	1.7	1.9
Changes in the student population	3	1.3	1.4
Instructor's department/college wanted the changes made	3	1.3	1.4
Size of the class was significantly increased	3	1.3	1.4
Unclear	2	0.9%	1.0%

*Adds to more than 100% because sometimes faculty gave more than one reason for change

2, these categories of reasons and sources emerged from an inductive analysis of faculty responses; they were not imposed on the open-ended responses. Here, we consider the most frequently mentioned internal reasons and sources of change and some of the changes they brought about.

To ADVANCE/INCREASE LEARNING. As table 5.1 shows, the most frequently given reason for change focused on the faculty member's desire to advance her learning goals or increase student learning, with more than 28% of the reasons that faculty gave for changes in their teaching falling into this category. This category also accounted for close to a third of all the changes that faculty described. Obviously, the kinds of learning that faculty members hoped to increase were varied. They included better understanding of content and concepts, a clearer sense of disciplinary processes, deeper grasp of the assigned reading, integration of hands-on and theoretical aspects of the course, as well as other kinds of learning.

Many faculty members described making changes in assignments as a way to advance students' learning or help them meet faculty learning goals. For example, several faculty members spoke about changes they had made to assignments as a way of getting students to complete reading assigned for their classes. The faculty member had assigned the reading as a way to advanced student learning, and assignments were designed to ensure that students engaged with it. In the faculty quotation that follows, the faculty member described wanting students to read more and think more about conceptual issues in the class:

> The reason for that was that it became pretty clear that students were enjoying the activities and the project, but the problem was that they weren't spending enough time reading and thinking about the concepts that would help them understand the longer-term issues at play. So the writing assignments got them to think more about those concepts that I was trying to get them to be better prepared for. (Faculty member in the social sciences, 400 level, 35 students)

Another example of faculty members making changes in their assignments to advance learning came from those who added assignments or a series of assignments into their courses. For example, the following quotation from a faculty member in art describes building scaffolding into assignments in order to help students learn the importance of making mistakes and consulting others in the process of making art. In her words:

> I build in more and more moments where they have to bring in their work in progress. I see it and they have to tell me about it. If you don't do that, they don't do anything until the last minute. It's at Stage One, and they haven't made all the mistakes they need to make to get to the thing they want. Knowing human nature is what made me make the change. The piece never replicates exactly what's in your head; there are always roadblocks, and you have to deal with them and shift your idea in relation to them. You need time to negotiate that new information. I have learned that the more often they bounce their ideas off someone else, like me or the other students, with enough time to get to the next step, the more successful their projects will be. So I've increased this kind of interaction over time. (Faculty member in the arts, 300 level, 20 students)

Similarly, a faculty member in biology added weekly learning summaries to the course requirements in order to help students learn how to connect concepts in a science course as they learned them:

> Often I see students come to class, and it's as if the faculty are giving them Lego pieces, and all they do is hoard all the pieces together, so that the night before the exam, they can try to put them together. The faculty member has this beautiful castle in mind that really explains everything, and when he looks at what the student puts together the night before the test, it's really bad. So I'm just trying to get them to start building that earlier. Again, this was based on my reading on concept maps—they need a framework and they need connections. (Faculty member in the sciences/math, 300 level, 100 students)

As these examples indicate, the learning that faculty members hoped to advance was quite particular to courses, as well as to the disciplines in which those courses resided. Another example along these lines came from a faculty member teaching a writing course that was linked with a course in international studies. He described changing an assignment in order to help students learn to make decisions about what was necessary for their arguments:

> One change I've made that I mentioned earlier is that I've mul-
> tiplied the first set of assignments—giving them many more
> options about what to write about. . . . when they see this as-
> signment initially, I want them to see that the challenge isn't
> filling up five pages but the challenge is figuring out what the
> most important things to put in those five pages are. So when
> there's a lot of current debate and discussion, they really have to
> make those decisions—what is necessary to my argument and
> in what way is that necessary? Also I want to put them into a
> situation where they have to look at a lot of documents—de-
> velopment indicators that are statistical or pieces out of the
> *New York Times* or a few articles from journals, more academic
> pieces—and figure out how they are going to use these. (Fac-
> ulty member in the humanities, 100 level, 20 students)

Faculty members also described a range of other changes designed to advance student learning, as these two examples—the first about changing the structure of a course and the second about adding technology to the class—illustrate:

> Another change I made was that I introduced the peer facilita-
> tors. Before there was a TA, and they met with the TA once a
> week for 50 minutes. I found that to be not enough. I wanted
> them to engage every day of the week with the topics we were
> addressing. I wanted them to have a social setting in which
> they could express themselves without hierarchy. So I intro-
> duced the peer facilitators, and that has worked really well.
> (Faculty member in the social sciences, 300 level, 100 students)

> I'm putting a video textbook on the web that they can access
> from home. They can hear Polish for more hours or minutes in
> a day. For foreign language instruction, the more you can get
> your students in contact with the language, the more they are
> going to learn. Learning a foreign language has elements of a
> content class, but it is also experiential and oriented to contact
> with other people. It's a unique thing. It is not like learning a

musical instrument or like taking a course in math. It is very different. So I don't think there's a question that the more input of the Polish language they have, the better. (Faculty member in the humanities, 400 level, 20 students)

As these examples show, the learning that faculty hoped to advance and the changes they made to advance that learning were specific to each course and context. However, the large number of changes made in order to advance learning suggests that faculty entered their classrooms with an awareness of what they hoped students would learn there, and, if they did not see evidence of that learning, faculty made changes to their courses until they did.

TO ADDRESS THE INSTRUCTOR'S VALUES OR TEACHING PHILOSOPHY. Another frequently given "internal" reason for change was that the faculty member needed to put his teaching philosophy or learning values into play in the classroom, a reason that accounted for close to 8% of the changes faculty noted. Like the changes we observed related to advancing students' learning, these changes were about the values that related to the particular courses the faculty members were teaching or to the disciplines in which those courses were situated. They were not rooted in generic values, such as valuing collaboration or leadership. The following extended example illustrates change emerging from values. The faculty member began her description of an installation class and the value that shaped the course, ending with what she hoped students would learn about her discipline from her class:

One of the things that really is important in this class is seeking out opportunities to open the parameters in which we make art—open the contexts, the places, open our work up to new audiences—rather than constantly making work for our fellow students, our professors, and the art world, which is a rather small piece of the human pie.

I had a student interested in architecture, and she had this interest in a building in Magnuson Park. She photographed it in a series of 4 x 5 shots, just the outer walls of it. She made those photographs the inside of a big white cube—and hung it from the ceiling, so to see the building you had to kind of crawl inside and stand in it. You could see the different sides of the walls of this building inside her white cube. So it was kind of inverting how you would usually see the walls of this building—the inside was the outside.

Another student made this room of string. At regular intervals, she made a matrix of string in the room and projected white noise on it with a video. The strings got very highly charged and floated. It was visually very beautiful. And she talked about it in a very articulate way—about networking and excess information—it ultimately predicted another installation for her thesis show. I think it was the first time she ever worked truly three dimensionally. This experience gave her the freedom to figure all that out.

Another student interacted with a man who was confined to a wheelchair and had very little use of his body in the Harborview Medical Center project. [Our contact at Harborview] was really impressed with his interaction. [The student] did a portrait of [the man]—but to do a portrait of someone like that man, who may be very self-conscious about his body, the student had to go in and get to know this guy again and again. And in the end the guy was thrilled with this portrait.

These installation situations asked students to step outside their comfort zones. You're going to fail a lot but you're going to find something amazing as well. The next time that student is doing an installation, he's going to think about how that idea translates into actual space. There's a big difference between your ideas as you imagine them and how those ideas actually look in that space. (Faculty member in the arts, 300 level, 20 students)

A faculty member in mathematics also spoke of how his beliefs about his discipline brought about change in what he was doing in the classroom. In his words:

I like to humanize the subject if I can, by introducing personalities, for instance. There's something they learn called L'Hospital's Rule. It's interesting to learn that the Marquis de l'Hospital thought math was neat, but he wasn't good enough to do a theorem himself, so he bought his rule from one of the Bernoullis. It's still called L'Hospital's theorem, but he didn't discover it. He bought it. I throw in a little math history like that along the way. I believe that math is a human creation and a lot of people view it as this tectonic structure out there. I think of it as a cathedral that somebody built. I try to bring in the human side of it—these people who built it, that it is not something that was handed down by Zeus. I try to let my students know that it's a very human creation, and it might even be flawed. (Faculty member in the sciences/math, 100 level, 160 students)

A third example shows a faculty member trying to put a belief about learning into play in the classroom and the less-than-perfect result:

I made this change because the philosophy of discovery-based learning was quite appealing to me, but the result wasn't quite what I expected. My original intent was to bring in as much of the constructivist idea as possible, but it was not entirely as successful as I thought it would be when we went through it. Students still appreciated looking through data, but it wasn't quite as discovery-based as I had hoped, with me helping them set up the problem in more detail than I had first intended. But what I did ended up being about half-way between what I wanted to do and what I was doing without these homework assignments. They did make nice changes. Students do learn more and they are more involved in their learning. (Faculty member in the social sciences, 200 level, 375 students)

Although changes made because of a faculty member's values or philosophy of learning were rarer than those made to advance students' learning, the overlap between the two is clear in these examples. For instance, the faculty member whose students created installations because she wanted to expand students' understanding of what it meant to show art were learning about the creative process—an area of learning that she clearly hoped to advance. The faculty member who felt it important to share his view with students that mathematics is something people have built was also teaching them about the discipline and about their roles as students in it. These examples fit into the "values and philosophy" category because that was the reason the faculty members foregrounded in their explanations of the change they had made; however, it is obvious that other reasons and sources of change may be at work in these changes, as well.

To increase student engagement/motivation in class. A third reason for the changes that faculty made to their courses was to increase student engagement in the class. This reason was given for about 7% of the changes that faculty described. For example, one faculty member described changing writing assignments in order to keep students engaged in the course:

> My change in assignments reflects my thinking about my change in expectations for the course. I really want students to be engaged, and if they're not, it's really depressing to me. There's really no point in teaching. They aren't easier assignments, but I want students to talk more, to be more interested, to be more engaged, so I worry less about them getting the coverage over a period of time, for example, or about understanding a novel the way I do. I want them to argue about what is going on in there rather than about an interpretation I think they should have. (Faculty member in the humanities, 300 level, 35 students)

Another faculty member spoke of using technology in the classroom as a way of keeping students engaged with class material:

> I think clickers help students stay interested, because they provide a break. I think the students like the clickers. It makes them engage more in the material in a way, because they have to respond. I think it affects attendance—more students show up for class. (Faculty member in the sciences/math, 400 level, 90 students)

Instructors observed that changes were needed. Observation that change was needed was one of the two most frequently given reasons for changes that faculty described making to their courses. As were other reasons for change, observation was linked with the desire to advance students' learning. As table 5.1 indicates, this category represented more than one out of five of the reasons faculty gave for change, and it was noted as a reason for one out of every four changes that faculty identified making. We included as "observation" any monitoring of in-class behavior and interaction, as well as faculty monitoring of the "products" of the course. Therefore, we counted the following as "observation":

> Students' in-class, nonverbal responses
> The kinds and frequency of questions asked or comments made in class
> The content and depth of class discussion
> The work students turned in—for example, homework, papers, projects, and performances
> Students' performance on exams

Many faculty members who made changes in their teaching did so because their students' poor performance on an assignment or an exam revealed that they were not learning what the faculty member hoped they were learning. For example, the following faculty member described providing scaffolding for a research assignment, based on her observations of her students' performance on an earlier assignment:

> I've changed this class by reducing the amount of reading and the amount of reading responses. I've also gotten much more specific with the assignments, laying out how to do fieldwork and the stages of doing the research, for example. I got more specific because I didn't get the results I wanted, so I thought about how I could get closer to what I'm hoping for. I think more specific instruction helps, more steps, doing things in smaller steps. We'll get a better product at the end if we do it in smaller steps. It just seemed like that would be better. Our job is to teach—to not give up on the student. (Faculty member in the humanities, 200 level, 35 students)

Similarly, a second example shows the thinking that led another faculty member to revise all the work he assigned in his history class, based on his observation of students' midterm exam performance:

> Students always did miserably on the midterm. But for the first five, six, seven years, I had no idea why students did miserably, because my whole testing method wasn't designed to reveal

that. [I came to understand] there were three possible reasons why. One, they didn't know the material. Second, they knew the material, but they didn't know how to put it together in an essay. Third, they may have known the material and how to write an essay but just freaked under the time pressure. So I realized I had to break the pieces up so I could figure out where the problem was. (Faculty member in the social sciences, 100 level, 350 students)

One faculty member described monitoring results of multiple-choice exams in order to see where change was needed:

We use the Scantrons, the machines that grade the exams. It gave me a breakdown of which questions students missed, and whether the people who missed this question correlated with the people who missed this other question. I spend a good deal of time looking at the results of the exam. (Faculty member in the sciences/math, 200 level, 80 students)

Another example of observation as a source of change resulted in integrating an assignment more fully into the class:

The first time I taught the class, I tried the portfolio. Then I stopped it, because of student perception that it was busy work. But when I did that, I felt that the quality of engagement with the theories was down, and I realized that the portfolio functioned as a pop quiz and that it made them have to try to engage with the texts before class. So I went back to it. The portfolio helped people stay on track, and it's easy to get off track when they are managing so much. I realized when I took the portfolio away that I had not adequately diagnosed why they felt it was busy work. The "why" question is so important! I had to show them that their work is part of my class and show them that it is integrated into my class. I had to bring the portfolios into the classroom. (Faculty member in the humanities, 300 level, 40 students)

In addition to observations that were based in student work, faculty members also described observation of students' behaviors that caused them to change their teaching. As this faculty member put it:

I think sometimes it wasn't so much the exams that showed me they weren't understanding, but it was the look on their faces. It was just too much, and as I started to back off and get it to the right level, I could tell if they were understanding by looking at their faces and listening to their questions. That would help me know, "Okay, I should do this." (Faculty member in the sciences/math, 200 level, 55 students)

Another faculty member described a similar kind of in-class observation:

One thing I've noticed that I've changed is that now I take a little break at some time during the class. This has developed over the years. I like the students. I look at them and talk to them, and if they ask questions, I walk up to them. I'm not up at the front of the class, but I am always somewhere in the middle. I pay attention to them, so I can tell if they are bored or daydreaming. I just look around. Eventually I started noticing that 25 minutes to a half hour into the class, most of them were daydreaming. So that's when I started teaching them [colorful] French words for 30 seconds or so. I usually say something, usually something just off the top of my head in that little break, or I'll think of something ahead of time. I'm pretty good at keeping it to a minute or so, and then they all wake up and we get back to the math. (Faculty member in the sciences/math, 100 level, 160 students)

Along with monitoring students' behavior and work, faculty members also described paying attention to the questions students asked in class or to their responses to questions the faculty member asked as indicators of learning. For example:

Question-asking helps me in keeping on track and paying attention to the students, because it's always the best students who ask the questions. It's good to know where they're confused, [because] most students are much more confused. (Faculty member in the sciences/math, 200 level, 80 students)

These examples, as well as the comments of other faculty members about this source of change make it clear that observation of students' behavior and performance was an important source of change for most faculty members. Furthermore, the examples show how closely linked faculty observations were with their desire to advance student learning. What faculty were looking for in their monitoring of students' behaviors and questions in class and their perusal of assignments was evidence that students were learning or were not learning what faculty members hoped they were teaching. When they observed that students were not learning, faculty members responded with changes to their teaching.

INSTRUCTORS TALKED TO STUDENTS OR NOTED WHAT STUDENTS WROTE IN COURSE EVALUATIONS. Faculty members also spoke of reactions from students who had completed or were just completing their courses as a source of information about change. Often those reactions came in the form of written comments on course evaluations. For example several faculty members described making changes to the texts they assigned, based on what students told them, as this observation illustrates:

> I made changes in the literature over the years I've taught this class because I found that I had initially used too much institutional material—what is the EU? what is the Parliament?—which for me as a political scientist is nice fodder. But I realized that my population in that class is too diverse for that. I have a variety of majors in there. So I diversified the literature. I read the [comment] sheets on my course evaluations quite carefully, and I would ask people how things went after the class was done. In Europe there is always that last class—a tabula rasa—where you ask them how it went for them. I did that the first year here, and people were absolutely silent. But after the class was done and the grades were in, they felt free to talk to me, and they always do. (Faculty member in the social sciences, 300 level, 100 students)

Faculty had more to say about the role course evaluations played in the changes they made to their teaching when we asked them to rate 17 sources of change, discussed later in this chapter.

External Reasons and Sources of Change

In addition to internal reasons and sources of change, faculty members talked about causes of change that were external to the particular courses they described. However, as table 5.1 shows, few faculty members noted external *reasons*. More frequently, faculty noted external *sources* of information that change was needed. This group of responses accounted for about 12% of the reasons and sources of change that faculty members gave and about 13% of the changes they described. Here we discuss two of those external sources.

LEARNED FROM OTHERS AT A CONFERENCE, BY WORKING CLOSELY WITH OTHER FACULTY/STAFF MEMBERS, OR BY OBSERVING OTHER FACULTY MEMBERS TEACHING. Close to one in four of the faculty members whom we interviewed spoke of learning about the changes they made from other faculty members—both colleagues at the UW and colleagues across the country. Learning from other faculty members constituted 5.5% of the reasons and sources faculty members gave for changes they made and more than 6% of the those changes. Several faculty members spoke of making a change in their teaching because they had observed others, including faculty who were in a mentoring role, faculty who had reputations for good teaching, and faculty whom they were observing as part of the peer-review process. One faculty member described this source of change:

> I didn't always do the learning enhancements, but I started them when I sat in on a colleague's class. I heard she was a good professor, and I wanted to observe her. I liked that she had these different games she played with them to get them excited about the material. I asked her if it was okay if I stole the learning enhancement piece. I had a lot of ideas about teaching— what I wanted them to learn, and in these large lectures a large part of it is performance and getting them excited so they want to stay awake. I thought the learning enhancements would do that. (Faculty member in the social sciences, 200 level, 275 students)

Other faculty members described learning from colleagues at workshops and conferences—sometimes with mixed results, as the following faculty member noted:

> I did a couple of innovative things. I really tried. I embraced the Faculty Fellows[2] mantra of active learning. I tried to do some active-learning things, and I did a partnering workshop,

where they role-played, taking turns in front of the class, and playing a role in a meeting. They take on being an engineer, the architect, or the contractor [in a scenario]. The first time I did it, it worked really well, and since then, it's not worked. (Faculty member in architecture/built environments, 400 level, 60 students)

Finally, faculty members also spoke of change in their teaching that came from close interaction with other faculty members over time. Some spoke of faculty members with whom they had team-taught; others spoke of close relationships established over time with peers. One faculty member described making sweeping changes to his class, because of his extended interaction with a faculty member teaching a writing course linked to his sociology course. In his words:

Having the writing links attached to the class was helpful. The writing link instructor was telling me that [the students] were just plowing through the readings. I saw that the students were getting the broad brush but not the deep understanding. So I realized I needed to be way more selective about the reading and ask them to do more in class. I knew that they would write a good essay at the end, but I was getting them to a point where they really got it, really understood what the field was about. So I tried to make sure that not every article was on the reading list that I thought might be relevant, but to put only the most critical on the list that we could structure the writing around. So I became much more purposeful in the planning. In those early conversations, [the writing link instructor] was just really up front about it, [saying], "Just because you assign that reading doesn't mean that students are going to learn it."

The second major [change] was to be really explicit about the goals. When you have to explain to another teacher what you are trying to accomplish, what that article you are assigning is trying to accomplish, that really caused me to reflect on what I was doing, to recognize things like—"I never liked that article; it's just horrid!" So being explicit about the learning goals to the other teacher, who had to figure out how the writing would support that or not, made me rethink things.

[The writing link instructor's] first assignment focused on teaching them to read an article. He told me that this is what he does, because I jumped into reading these three or four articles on expansion of education, and that's really tough for students. So [the writing link instructor] said he went through one article and asked students what they saw on the page, taking them through the acknowledgment section, for example, and asking them why they thought that's important. I never even thought of that—that the acknowledgment section tells you the street credentials of people—who are they and who they are connected to. It talks about a community of scholars. So [the writing link instructor] brought the sociological disciplinary perspective to that. To me it was totally implicit. (Faculty member in the social sciences, 300 level course, 35 students)

INSTRUCTOR TOOK THE NEEDS OF SUBSEQUENT COURSES IN THE MAJOR INTO ACCOUNT. Another external source of change was the faculty member's awareness of what was coming next in the major. Often this awareness allowed faculty members to eliminate parts of their course content that they knew would be explored later in the major, but sometimes it caused them to add content to their courses, as this faculty member described:

So one of the things that really has changed in my thinking is that I try to include a lot more theory than I did early on. Institutionally, I think it's important for English majors to engage in theory. They're going to get it in other classes and if they go on to grad school, they'll need to know something about theory. At the 400 level they'll need to understand the ways that theory is important. (Faculty member in the humanities, 300 level, 25 students)

Matching Reasons with Changes

As we noted at the beginning of this chapter, the desire to advance or increase students' learning and observing the need for change from a

Table 5.2. Reasons for specific kinds of change

Kind of Change	% of all changes	Reason #1 (% of kind of change*)	Reason #2 (% of change)	Reason #3 (% of change)
Changed assignments	27.0	Advance learning (66%)	Observed need (50.9%)	Address values; keep current; talked to students; engage students (8.7% each)
Reorganized/revised class	18.5	Advance learning (71.8%)	Observed need (30.8%)	Address values (23.1%)
Added active learning	13.7	Advance learning (69%)	Observed need (37.9%)	Learned from others (34.5%)
Changed technology	10.9	Advance learning (73.9%)	Observed need; engage students (26.1% each)	Keep current (17.4%)
Became more explicit	7.1	Observed need (73.9%)	Advance learning (46.7%)	Address values (26.7%)
Covered less to teach more	5.7	Observed need (83.3%)	Advance learning (41.7%)	---
Responded to changes in self	5.7	Observed need, keep current, constantly changing teaching, and respond to changes in students (25% each)		
Changed logistics	5.2	Observed need (81.8%)	Advance learning (63.6%)	Address values (36.4%)
Added real-life examples	3.8	Advance learning (50.0%)	Observed need (50.0%)	---
Misc.	2.4	Observed need (60.0%)	Address values (60.0%)	---

*Numbers do not add to 100% because faculty sometimes had more than one reason for a given change.

variety of sources were the two most frequently given reasons for the changes in the courses that faculty members discussed. Table 5.2 underscores that result, matching the changes we identified in faculty members' responses (the subject of chapter 4) with the most frequently given reasons for each type of change. As the table also shows, often one of the two reasons was more important than the other, such as changing assignments in order to advance learning and becoming more explicit about expectations because faculty members had observed the need to do so.

Furthermore, sometimes the third most frequently given reason for change provides the most information. For example, more than a third of the faculty who noted that they began using active learning strategies said that they made this change because they learned to do so from others. Most of the teaching training workshops and retreats at the UW emphasize active learning, so it is likely that many faculty members learned about active pedagogy by participating in those events, by hearing about them, or by observing others on campus who had. Similarly, keeping current was an important reason for faculty to make changes in the technology they were teaching or using in their courses.

End-of-interview Ratings of Sources of Change

As noted at the beginning of this chapter, the last question in our interviews with faculty participants in UW GIFTS asked them to rate the contributions of 17 possible sources of change to overall changes in their teaching. Faculty were given a 4-point rating scale, with 1 = "played no role in the changes I've made to my teaching over the years"; 2 = "played a minor role in changes I've made"; 3 = "played a moderately important role in changes I've made"; and 4 = "played a significant role in changes I've made to my teaching." We told faculty interviewees that their comments on each of the sources of change were welcome, as well as their numerical ratings.

Figure 5.1 shows the faculty ratings of the 17 sources of change. As the figure shows, on average the seven sources that faculty rated as the most significant in their thinking about change were:

> The students' behavior in class—their nonverbal communication, the questions they asked, their level of participation, and their attentiveness (a mean of 3.69 out of 4)
> Students' performance on assignments, such as papers, projects, and presentations (3.44)
> The faculty member's own maturity and growth (3.36)
> Technology (2.85)

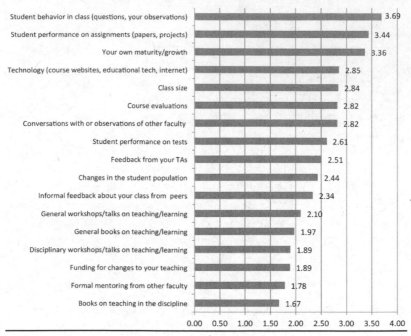

Figure 5.1. Faculty ratings of sources of change in their teaching

Class size (2.84)
Course evaluations (2.82)
Conversations with or observations of other faculty (2.82)

In addition, the four least significant roles in change in faculty teaching were played by:

Disciplinary workshops/talks about teaching/learning (1.89)
Funding for changes to teaching (1.89)
Formal mentoring from other faculty members (1.78)
Books on teaching/learning in one's discipline (1.67)

In this section, we provide details on the sources of change that faculty members ranked as their top seven and those they ranked as the bottom three. In addition, we provide information on two other results of this survey—the effects of general workshops and books on teaching and learning—and details about the "18th" source of change—those influences on change that faculty added to our list of 17.

The Effects of Students' Behaviors in Class

On average, faculty rated students' in-class behaviors[3] as the most significant of the 17 sources of information about change that we listed, giving that item a mean of 3.69 out of 4. This high rating for observation of students' behaviors in class is highly consistent with faculty members' descriptions of reasons for the changes they made to their courses, discussed earlier in this chapter. In addition, more than a third of the faculty members we interviewed commented on this item after they rated it. Most of the faculty comments concerned the value of monitoring students' in-class behavior both as a way of tracking students' engagement in the class and as a way of ascertaining if students were learning what the faculty member hoped they were learning, as the following two comments demonstrate:

> I change things on the fly in a lecture, based on how they are behaving. Sometimes it's Friday, and they've had a long week, so we'll do something more interactive. (Faculty member in engineering)

> This is probably the biggest thing, maybe because it's the easiest. It's the most tangible thing I can use to adjust during the quarter and then from quarter to quarter. (Faculty member in the social sciences)

In addition to the faculty members who spoke of monitoring students' behavior in class as a way of assessing teaching and engagement, faculty in some academic disciplines, such as foreign languages and dance, spoke of such monitoring as essential. In the words of one instructor:

> If you're teaching dance, you look at their bodies and see what they do. It tells you a lot instantly. You get instant feedback about whether or not they've got it, and you know whether you need to slow down or speed up. (Faculty member in the arts)

The Effects of Students' Performance on Assignments

Faculty members rated students' performance on assignments, such as their work on papers, projects, and presentations, as the second most important source of information contributing to change in their teaching, giving this item an average of 3.44. Like their rating of the importance of in-class observation, this rating is consistent with faculty members' open-ended descriptions of sources of change to their courses. The consistency between qualitative and quantitative findings points to the singular importance of observation of students' behavior and performance as a source of information about the need for change. In addition, they underscore our earlier finding about change being rooted in the interaction between faculty and students in class.

Faculty members who taught small classes spoke of monitoring their students' work directly. When we asked how faculty members teaching large courses monitored students' work that teaching assistants graded, faculty members often noted that they read or graded a sample of students' work. Many also said that they consulted with their TAs to understand how well students were doing and where they might need additional help.

Twenty-three faculty members—nearly half of our sample—added comments to their ratings of this item, with close to half of them noting that they used student performance on assignments to assess learning. Some faculty members said that students' performance on assignments allowed them to integrate changes into class time. For example:

> If the TAs tell me that the students' proposals show that they are having trouble, then I will make changes to lectures. (Faculty member in the social sciences)

Other faculty members noted that students' performance on assignments allowed them to assess the quality of the assignments they had given, so that they could improve or kill the assignment, such as these two faculty members described:

> I might look at papers and say, "These are crappy. How did I fail? How do I make it better so they get it next time?" (Faculty member in the humanities)

> I had them do group projects this year, and I won't next year because I don't think they learned enough doing it, so out it goes. (Faculty member in the sciences/math)

Faculty members also noted that when they used a draft/revision process or a sequence of similar assignments, students' performance on the first version of the assignment helped faculty shape lectures and class time to improve students' performance on the second version. For example:

> I use that feedback to refine assignments for the rest of the quarter, or I'll talk to the class about them: "Here's what really worked on the WebQs this time and here's what didn't." (Faculty member in the social sciences)

While observation of students' performance on assigned work and exams often stimulated change, it did not always do so. For example, one of the faculty members we interviewed indicated that students' performances on assignments raised questions about their abilities, rather than his teaching. He said:

> I like them to do a good performance on papers and projects, but I don't change the class because of that. I might change my opinion of them, but not the class. (Faculty member in the sciences/math)

The Effect of the Faculty Member's Own Maturity/Growth

The third most significant contribution to change in faculty teaching among the items on the list we gave faculty was their own maturity or growth, averaging 3.36. We prompted most faculty members to explain their rating of this particular item, and 49 (89.1%) of the 55 faculty members did so. One faculty member's response to this item seemed to sum up all faculty members' responses. In his words:

> You can't separate people from processes. My own process is everything. It expresses itself in how I look at the job, how I am growing, how I can help them to grow. It's huge. It's central, big, enormous, critical. (Faculty member in engineering)

Although faculty members identified maturity and growth as one of the three most important sources of change in the list of 17 sources we provided them, they rarely mentioned maturity or growth when they were talking about their reasons for the changes they had made to the classes they described. In fact, only three faculty members said that their own maturity and growth were important when they described the changes they had made to the specific courses they discussed. This inconsistency is puzzling but perhaps not surprising, in that we often have difficulty tracking the ways our own growth affects other aspects of our lives.

Regarding faculty comments about changes in themselves, we were able to identify some themes among their responses, including increased confidence and comfort in the classroom and changes in views of and interactions with students.

CHANGES IN CONFIDENCE AND COMFORT IN THE CLASSROOM. In discussing the ways their own personal growth and maturity had affected their teaching, nearly half (49%) of the faculty members who commented on this item said that they had become more confident in themselves as teachers and more comfortable in that role. Within this category of response, we could identify several subthemes, including the following:

Faculty members came to see that they could teach from who they were

Faculty members became less afraid of making mistakes in class

Faculty members realized that they knew what worked and what did not work in the classroom

Faculty members gained awareness of their own expertise in their fields

Faculty members had a new understanding about what it meant to teach.

These aspects of change will be discussed in detail in chapter 6.

CHANGES IN ONE'S VIEW OF AND INTERACTIONS WITH STUDENTS. In speaking about the role of their own growth and maturity in change in their teaching, several faculty members (about 20%) spoke of changes in their views of and interactions with students. Changes in this area came from multiple directions. Sometimes one's experience as a parent gave faculty members a new understanding of students that rippled out into other areas, as the following faculty member described:

One of the big things I've learned is that human brains work in a wondrous variety of ways. When I started off as a teacher, I used to think that if brains worked properly they would work the way mine did. And it was really raising an ADD child who had some learning disabilities that really brought home to me what a huge variety there was in the way people's brains worked.

Has this meant that I've reorganized my classes to try to better reach multiple intelligences? Well no, not really, not a lot. I tend to think that what universities do is what universities do, and they aren't suited very well to everybody. But I no longer mistake what universities do for an objective test of intelligence. It just happens to be how we do things, but there are many other quite different ways to think and act and be that are every bit as intelligent but may not lead to success in the university. I think I recognize the ADD kids in my class now in a way I didn't used to. I'm more open to allowing alternative assignments than I used to be.

I'm [also] clearer in my own mind in saying historical thinking is a very peculiar and particular way of thinking, but it's not the only way to think—it just happens to be what we are doing here in this class. (Faculty member in the social sciences)

Sometimes faculty members noted changes in their interactions with students that happened over time, as these two faculty members described.

Earlier on I think I tended to be more "Here's the rule; follow it." Now I'm more understanding of the students. (Faculty member in the social sciences)

Age has taught . . . an understanding of and appreciation for the complexities of people's lives. I kind of left thinking I was just teaching economics for thinking I'm teaching people, teaching students—so you are looking at a more complex picture of a student body than just people with empty brains, brains as raw grist that we can write on. (Faculty member in the social sciences)

Finally, some faculty members spoke of getting older as changing their relationships to their students, as this faculty member's comment illustrates:

> I feel more and more distant from the experiential world of the bulk of the students I teach. I just feel more distant from them. I don't know the same points of cultural reference. I much more have to draw them into my world than I used to have to do. Movies, music, technology—I'm not sure what's important to them. (Faculty member in the social sciences)

Technology

Classroom technology is both a source of change and a reason for change for the faculty members we interviewed. As noted earlier, only about 20% of the faculty we interviewed reported that they did not use or teach technology in the classroom, and about 11% of the changes that faculty mentioned they had made in their courses were changes in technology. Often the reason faculty members gave for making changes in technology in the courses they described was to ensure that the course "kept current" with both technological and other changes in the world.

In the list of 17 items, faculty rated technology as close to "moderately important" (a mean of 2.85) to change in their teaching and more than half (58%) of the faculty we interviewed commented about technology and change in their teaching. The majority of faculty members who commented on technology as a source of change spoke of their specific uses of technology. The following example illustrates this category of response:

> There's a lot of stuff I can now do in small groups—having the right room is about technology. The new room we've just created is good. And we're now wired—wifi so they can do their searches at their desks any time they want. "Is this a good reference?"—they can ask that question right there in class. (Faculty member in the sciences/math)

In addition, faculty often commented that technology did not serve as a reason for change in their teaching but rather as a resource they could use, as these faculty members said:

> I didn't change things because of technology, but when it became available it was an extra incentive to use it. (Faculty member in the social sciences)

> I do like all the technology we have access to and I want to teach in rooms that are well-teched up, because I use it. I use all the technology. It is that variety, which is probably something I learned from some workshop. You need to change constantly what's going on and technology helps me do it. (Faculty member in the arts)

Finally, just as students do, faculty become frustrated with technology when it does not work as it is supposed to work, as this faculty member's comment illustrates:

> I got thrown into this classroom where there wasn't a way to make the classroom dark, and I had this cart that I had to haul up to the third floor every time I taught. And every time I taught there was some other technological snafu to it. And I would get so mad. I'd go down and say, "This didn't work, and it's not just me. None of the students could figure this out." Now it's 40 minutes into my class and things still don't work. And I get to have that room again this quarter. [Technology has] affected my teaching but in a negative way. (Faculty member in the arts)

It is clear from our data on classes (chapter 2) and on changes (chapter 3) that technology plays an important role in teaching for most faculty members, even though many faculty members point to the challenges that the use of classroom technology brings with it.

Class Size

Of the 17 sources of change we gave them, faculty members ranked class size as fifth in importance, with an average rating of 2.83 out of 4—close to "moderately important to change in my teaching." About

60% of our faculty interviewees commented on class size, and nearly all of them noted that smaller classes allowed them to do things that larger classes did not. Many faculty members spoke of larger classes requiring more formality from the faculty member, including greater "control" over the class and less flexibility in interactions with students.

About 75% of the faculty members who commented on this item pointed out teaching opportunities in smaller classes that were not available in large classrooms. For example, many faculty members noted that they could facilitate discussion more easily in smaller classes, often because students were known to them. In the words of one faculty member:

> Large classes are impersonal. You can hide in there. I liked that best as an undergrad too. (Faculty member in the sciences/math)

In addition, several faculty members said that in smaller classes, it was easier to track students' learning, as these two quotations illustrate:

> Monitoring students is a personal relationship. (Faculty member in architecture/built environments)

> I want to have first-hand knowledge who the students are. I call on them in class, of course, not to be mean, but to tell them we are going to examine them—that is part of the class. They have to prepare so much each time, and they should be willing to do that. (Faculty member in the social sciences)

Faculty members occasionally spoke about getting the perspective of the students in their large classes, as these two faculty members reported:

> When I gave my 700-student lecture class, I went up one day to the balcony to see what my students saw, and I realized that in the back of the balcony, the students couldn't even see me talking. So now I try very heavily to make a personal connection with my students and to use technology to augment skills or creativity, but not to do the bulk of the teaching. (Faculty member in the humanities)

> What you can do in a class of 440 is totally different from what you can do in a class of 40. It's different, and I'm different.

The teacher I am in a big class has got to be different from the teacher I can be in a small class. One of my problems is that I'm this big [makes an inch with her fingers] in front of the classroom, and when I smiled they couldn't see it. (Faculty member in the social sciences)

One faculty member's comment seemed to sum up most of what faculty noted as the effects of class size on change in teaching:

It's incredible, the difference. I can interact with students, directly challenge them at the same time I'm comforting them in a smaller class. I can let them know there's a huge handrail; they aren't going to fall. I can get them to speak up more readily, so they can make these ideas their own. I can address what each student needs better and get a better sense of that. Anything to heighten the amount of feedback between the student and me is all good. Class size is the thing that has the most direct effect on these things. (Faculty member in the social sciences)

Course Evaluations

Faculty members rated course evaluations as a 2.82, on average; course evaluations, therefore, play a moderately important role in changes that faculty make to their teaching. Forty-six (83.6%) of the 55 faculty members we interviewed commented on their use of and regard for course evaluations. Many faculty members told us that they evaluate courses even when they are not required to do so, as these two faculty members noted:

Even though I only have to do one a year, I did three this year, because I'm interested in knowing what's working, particularly if I've changed the format. (Faculty member in the social sciences)

At the end of this quarter, I was exhausted. I had a friend ask me, "Why did you do course evaluations at all? You've got tenure. You don't have to do them." "I want to know," I told her. (Faculty member in the social sciences)

At the UW, course evaluations[1] include two parts. The first is quantitative. Students rate the course and the faculty member on a number of items by filling in bubble sheets. Students' completed forms are collected and sent to the Office of Educational Assessment (OEA) for scanning and scoring, and statistical results are sent to the faculty member and the department chair at the beginning of the next quarter. Four general items on this part of the student evaluations are common across all types of evaluations and are used in tenure and promotion decisions. The remaining items are more specific in nature.

The second part of the course evaluations are comment sheets that pose the following four open-ended questions for students:

> Was this class intellectually stimulating? Did it stretch your thinking? Why or why not?
> What aspects of this class contributed most to your learning?
> What aspects of this class detracted from your learning?
> What suggestions do you have for improving the class?

Comment sheets are collected with the bubble sheets and sent to the OEA. OEA does not process the comment sheets but returns them untouched to the faculty member, along with the statistical summary of bubble-sheet results, after grades have been turned in and the new quarter begins.

Many faculty members commented on the contribution of course evaluations to change in their teaching, specifically noting that they paid attention to trends that evaluations reveal. One faculty member noted:

> I look at the items that are the highest and the lowest—the ones that stand out the most to say what's working and what's not working. When I see that something like "clarity of grading and assignments" is lower, that one stands out and I realize it's an area that is still a challenge for me. (Faculty member in the social sciences)

In addition, several faculty members said that the statistics on their teaching did not change much from course to course, and a few faculty members noted that course evaluations were the most useful when they were teaching a class for the first time or had implemented a change in the course from a previous version of it.

Although in tenure and promotion decisions, the institution focuses on the four common items that students rate on the bubble sheets, more than half of the faculty members commenting on course evaluations said that the comment sheets, which only they see, are the more useful sources of information about their teaching than are the statistical summaries. In the words of two of the faculty members:

> It was nice to get the statistical part of the evaluation, because it gave me encouragement. But for the things I used to improve my teaching, I found the [comment] sheets more helpful. (Faculty member in the humanities)

> I look less at the numbers than at the [comment] sheets. They really give you specific hints about what worked and what didn't. They give you specific suggestions. (Faculty member in the social sciences)

Although faculty members pointed to problems with consistency in students' open-ended comments, in general they described specific information they had received from comments that led to changes in their teaching.

However, faculty also identified problems with course evaluations. Several noted, for example, that course evaluations were not as helpful as they might be, because they did not assess what students learned in the course. As one faculty member put it:

> I get good ratings, but course evaluations don't really talk about learning. In some ways they are more like a little bit of a popularity thing. I know my persona comes across well in the classroom, and that seems to have a good influence on the students, but that's not really a measure of learning. (Faculty member in the sciences/math)

Another problem that faculty members noted was that course evaluations were sometimes difficult to interpret, as this faculty member pointed out:

> I need a class on course evaluations! (Faculty member in the sciences/math)

But by far the most challenging problem in course evaluations that faculty described addressing was that student comments sometimes crossed the line between constructively critical and mean-spirited or unkind. Many faculty members—several of whom had been honored for excellence in teaching—described this problem. As one faculty member said:

> It makes you lose your enthusiasm for teaching. It can be nit-picky critical. There's always kind of a zinger in there, one person who didn't like anything. It sets up a negative dynamic when the course is done that hopefully doesn't carry on into the next course. Students use the evaluations to get things off their chest, their frustrations that they feel about succeeding or what they're doing. Sometimes there are useful things in there; if they liked one part of the course more than another, that becomes evident. But you have to be pretty thick-skinned with some of the evaluations. (Faculty member in the arts)

The problem of intentionally unkind student comments on course evaluations was so pervasive that more than one in four (28%) of the faculty members in this group described methods they had developed for reading evaluations that minimized the damage. One commonly used method was postponing reading course evaluations for weeks or even a full quarter, as these two faculty members described:

> I have to put them away for awhile though. I am sensitive, and sometimes they make me angry. A lot of them are very thoughtful and come up with constructive things, but there are a fair number of them that say these phenomenally clueless and irritating things. Of course it's a minority, but it's the minority I remember. (Faculty member in the sciences/math)

> The [comment] sheets I will read later. They're hard sometimes. People will make comments about how you dress, your physical appearance—things that are not appropriate. I try not to read them for awhile, and then I try not to give them too much weight even though it's hard. I get more from having conversations with students vs. the anonymous evaluation at the end. (Faculty member in the social sciences)

Others tried to keep their focus away from the unkind comments, as this faculty member said:

> One thing I've found is that the really bad ones tend to stick in your mind and that isn't always a good thing, so I've been trying to be better about not paying attention to what one student says but to look for trends. (Faculty member in the humanities)

One faculty member described a creative method she had developed for handling unkind student comments on evaluations. She said that she gave the comment sheets from her large class (440 students) to a colleague in her department, asking him to read them before she did and to remove any that were "mean" before he gave them back to her. In her words:

> I always have someone else read them from the big class first—a colleague in the department. And that colleague takes out the mean ones and doesn't tell me whether he took any out or didn't. He always says he didn't take any out, and I don't know one way or the other whether he is telling the truth or not. I've had some really mean ones, and that spoils the other feedback. I don't hear what anyone else is saying after reading mean comments like some of them have been. And the other comments have helped a lot—the ones that are very constructive about my teaching. I use them to think about changes. I've had that colleague pulling out the mean ones for four or five years. (Faculty member in the social sciences)

Another faculty member said that when he received an unkind comment, he physically destroyed it.

In spite of problems that faculty members had with course evaluations, they appeared to make use of them as they considered change in their teaching. Furthermore, many found course evaluations to be a source of encouragement, as this faculty member noted:

> Course evaluations have provided me with great encouragement over the years, because they were positive. Students will say, for example, that they appreciated your enthusiasm and that makes you realize that you project enthusiasm when you were just being who you are. Course evaluations helped me

forge an image of myself as an instructor that I didn't have. (Faculty member in the humanities)

Conversations with or Observations of Other Faculty

Faculty gave conversations with other faculty about teaching and observations of other faculty the same average rating that they did course evaluations—a 2.82, close to "moderately important" to change in teaching. In addition, 30 faculty members provided additional comments about this item. Four of them said that they did not have many conversations with fellow faculty members about teaching.

Most of the other comments centered on two kinds of interactions with peers. The first were informal conversations about teaching. Close to half of the faculty commenting on this item said that informal conversations with peers had been helpful to their teaching. For example, one faculty member spoke of speaking with peers in a variety of settings:

It's those collegial conversations you have with people that has shaped what I do from then on. Some of these happen at the programs, workshops, and so on, which is great. Some of it is just lunchtime chit chat or the mailroom. (Faculty member in the social sciences)

Another faculty member mentioned speaking with other faculty members in his discipline across the country:

We are always trading stories about what worked and what didn't, what students did. It usually happens in our specialty, so I'm talking to other seismologists, comparing across universities about how the classes go. (Faculty member in the sciences/math)

Finally, one faculty member described conversations about teaching that happened in the past in his department:

One of the great things about [my] department when I first came here was that there were a bunch of people who ate lunch together in a seminar room. It was just a brown bag lunch we would have together, and it was very striking how often those conversations turned to teaching. I got a lot out of those. It was just something the older members of the department did, and it is totally gone now. (Faculty member in the social sciences)

In addition to speaking of the effects of informal conversations with peers on teaching, faculty members also talked about the value of observing others teaching. Sometimes faculty members described conducting those observations on their own, as this example illustrates:

There are a couple classes I sat in on—one in oceanography. I'd heard she was a good teacher, and what I found amazing was how the jargon in that discipline was giving me a hard time, and that was a 100-level class. All of a sudden that made me appreciate how my jargon that I'm used to could be getting in the way of students understanding the concepts. Supposedly I was an intelligent novice in that class, but I wasn't feeling so intelligent. (Faculty member in the sciences/mathematics)

Also, several faculty members spoke of learning about their own teaching by observing other faculty as part of the peer-review process at our institution. For example:

We do peer evaluations of one another, and I've been asked to do that for a lot of my colleagues. Also when we are doing three-year reviews or ten-year reviews we look over teaching material. I look over those, and I read their statements where they talk about teaching philosophy. I admire my colleagues a lot. (Faculty member in the social sciences)

Finally, a few faculty members spoke of continuously observing others in order to learn more about teaching, as this faculty member described:

I'm very aware of what I learn when I go and observe other people teach and what I learn at public lectures by watching people speak. I notice even small details—how they start, how they introduce themselves, how they end, how much they walk around, how fast or slow they speak, how much information or how little information they put on a PowerPoint. You get to know what works. (Faculty member in the social sciences)

Items Receiving the Lowest Ratings

Faculty members' comments on the four items rated the lowest of the 17 sources of change suggested that the reason these sources of change were in last place was because they were all hard to find. For the most part, the faculty members who did find these resources reported that they had helped faculty think about their teaching.

For example, faculty members rated the effects on their teaching of workshops/talks on teaching and learning in their disciplines and funding for changes to their teaching at 1.89 on average, close to "played a minor role" in changes in teaching. Of the 19 faculty members who commented on teaching training workshops in their disciplines, close to half said that there were few such workshops. Most of those who reported attending workshops on teaching in their disciplines, however, found them to be useful, as this faculty member said:

> There aren't too many, although I love to go to these. I think they are super important because they provide you with new ideas, so actually I'm leading some of these workshops myself. I would love to go and get some ideas here and there. There is a worldwide conference biennially. The next one is in England, and it's money and time and happens in September during the TA orientation, and that's the one I would like to go to. (Faculty member in the humanities)

The same was true of funding for change to teaching. Many faculty members noted that there was little funding available for work on teaching. However, those who had received such funding—about half of the 28 faculty members who commented on this item—said that the money they had received to improve their teaching was beneficial to their work. For example, one faculty member spoke about receiving funding to participate in a week-long teaching training session:

> They pay us to go out to Forks, so that counts I think. It did make me feel that the university really values this enough that they would spend this much money on it—the people teaching the classes and those of us going. To me it was really a statement about the importance of good teaching. (Faculty member in the social sciences)

A second faculty member gave a similar response in describing receiving funding from the College of Arts and Sciences for improving her large lecture class:

> I received funding from the College of Arts and Sciences to improve [my 200-level class]. I was paid for my time, and it was a great incentive. I felt I needed to show I'd used those funds productively. (Faculty member in the social sciences)

Among the four lowest-rated items, formal mentoring from other faculty members received a mean rating of 1.78. Similar to faculty speaking about disciplinary workshops or funding for improving teaching, more than half of the 26 faculty members commenting on faculty mentors said they had never had mentors. Furthermore, all but two of the remaining comments were faculty members talking about help they had received from peers who had observed their classes on single occasions.

Just as faculty members reported that the previous three items were not very helpful to them because of their scarcity, books on teaching and learning in one's discipline received the lowest mean score of all 17 items in this set—1.67—for the same reason. Eight of the 18 faculty members who commented on reading books or journal articles in their disciplines said they had done so and most of the remaining comments focused on such books being unavailable.

Therefore, the four lowest-ranked items in the list of 17 were not necessarily the least effective sources of change in faculty teaching; they were the scarcest. Faculty members who were able to take advantage of these four items usually found them to be helpful.

General Workshops and Books

As figure 5.1 shows, faculty members appeared to get little benefit from general workshops (2.10 mean rating) or general books (1.97) on teaching and learning. Yet, we asked 53 of the 55 faculty members we interviewed if they had received any formal training in teaching since they had been graduate students, and close to 74% of them said they had, with most of them identifying UW workshops, retreats, and talks as the training they had received. Although three-quarters of our sample had attended at least one teaching training event, they designated such experiences as playing a "minor role" in change in their teaching. Eighteen faculty members commented on that item, as well, but their comments ranged from very positive to very negative, and we could identify no strong trends in them. The same was true for faculty comments on general books on teaching and learning.

Results on the effects of general books and workshops on change in faculty teaching support what we saw earlier in interview descriptions of reasons for change. The interactions between the faculty member and her students in the particular context of the class are more important motivators for change than external sources or reasons.

Other: Faculty Additions

Finally, we asked interviewees if there were other things that influenced change in their teaching that we had not asked them about. More than half of the faculty members we interviewed (53%) added an item. Five influences on change were mentioned by more than one faculty member, as follows:

> Chairs, deans, other administrators, and university/departmental culture, mentioned by eight faculty members: "I don't think the process of change I've undergone would have happened to me if I'd been in a different department. I've learned to value teaching and to think carefully about what I'm doing. The department culture definitely is very powerful. I have powerful role models around me in the Jackson School."
>
> Time the class meets, mentioned by two faculty members: "The time of the big lecture has some effect. I had an 8:30 lecture once that was podcast, and that combined with putting my PowerPoint slides on line took attendance down to 30%. It was not good."
>
> Having a teaching spouse, mentioned by two faculty members: "My husband is a teacher . . . and he taught junior high for 13 years. He sort of widened my scope of thinking about what teaching means."
>
> Getting tenure, mentioned by two faculty members: "I think

getting tenure has had an effect. It helps with that confidence thing."

Working with graduate students, mentioned by two faculty members: "I think my teaching is more creative and pedagogically more rigorous when I work with a TA. It can be a lot of administrative work—a weekly teaching meeting, other things—but I really do enjoy it. This is a change factor."

The rest of the sources of change that faculty mentioned were unique to the interviewee and were as follows:

Chairing a cross-college committee on writing
General technology
Connections between the course and the world
Literature outside that of the discipline
Having guest lecturers
Winning a teaching award
Competing demands on time
Running the math study center
A book on undergraduates
A life-coaching experience
Faculty member's research interests
World events
Loving the students

Summary: Reasons and Sources for Change

Using the analysis of the reasons that faculty gave for the changes they made, as well as their ratings of the 17 sources we gave them, we can say that the following causes played the most significant roles in the nine categories of change that faculty made to their teaching:

1. The desire to advance one's learning goals or increase student learning
2. Observations of students' behavior in class
3. Observations of students' performance on assignments
4. Changes in the faculty member's own growth and maturity

5. The desire to address the faculty member's values, particularly discipline-related values or teaching philosophy
6. The desire to increase student engagement or motivation in class
7. Availability of or changes in technology
8. The need to keep the content of the class current
9. Face-to-face interaction with peers—mostly at conferences and through informal conversations with peers
10. Conversations with previous students or comments on student evaluations

These reasons led to the following changes, described in chapter 4:

1. Changed assignments
2. Restructured class
3. Added active learning strategies
4. Changed technology
5. Became more explicit
6. Covered less to teach more
7. Responded to changes in self
8. Changed logistics
9. Added real-life examples

Reasons and causes overlapped and interacted in ways that seemed obvious and, because they were sometimes obvious, in ways we assumed that we could not disaggregate. For example, one reason for change implied others. One change might bring in evidence that became a reason for a new change, to give another example. Because of the interaction between faculty members' reasons for change and the changes they made, it is difficult to tell a linear story about change, even though the path that we were seeing seemed to tell a fairly consistent story. That story is displayed in figure 5.2.

As figure 5.2 suggests, faculty members began their courses with a sense of what they wanted students to learn—the knowledge and perspectives of their subject areas and the skills that they wanted students to develop. Their goals for students' learning may have been explicit or implied, crisply stated or vague, but it is wrong to assume that if faculty members did not articulate those goals in measurable terms, they did not have them. Indeed, without some sense of what they hoped students

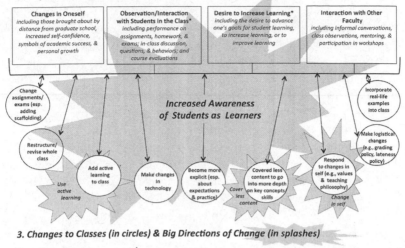

1. Starting Point ~ What the Faculty Member Hopes to Teach: Content, Perspectives, Skills

2. Major Causes of Change

Changes in Oneself	Observation/Interaction	Desire to Increase Learning*	Interaction with Other Faculty
including those brought about by distance from graduate school, increased self-confidence, symbols of academic success, & personal growth	with Students in the Class* including performance on assignments, homework, & exams; in-class discussion, questions, & behaviors; and course evaluations	including the desire to advance one's goals for student learning, to increase learning, or to improve learning	including informal conversations, class observations, mentoring, & participation in workshops

Change assignments/exams (esp. adding scaffolding)

Incorporate real-life examples into class

Restructure/revise whole class

Make logistical changes (e.g., grading policy, lateness policy)

Increased Awareness of Students as Learners

Use active learning

Add active learning to class

Make changes in technology

Become more explicit (esp. about expectations & practice)

Cover less content

Covered less content to go into more depth on key concepts

Cover less skills

Respond to changes in self (e.g., values & teaching philosophy)

Change in self

3. Changes to Classes (in circles) & Big Directions of Change (in splashes)

Figure 5.2. Interactive paths in change in faculty teaching

would learn in their courses, faculty members could not even select the readings.

At some point in their teaching—perhaps when they had reached a certain level of confidence in the classroom—something called on faculty members to rethink what they were doing in the class. Perhaps their own values about teaching in their disciplines changed. Perhaps they observed students' in-class behavior and performance in relation to their goals. They may have watched for signs, asked for signs, or were given signs—perhaps a row of confused faces, perhaps a series of questions—that indicated how much students were learning. They may have noticed that students' papers, projects, homework, or exams revealed a lack of understanding. They may have thought about how they might challenge students further, advance their learning goals, deepen or complicate students' understanding. Maybe course evaluations suggested a change in direction. In addition, faculty may have observed peers' classrooms or had interactions with colleagues at conferences that helped them think about what they might do in their own courses.

One or more of these causes led faculty to make specific changes in their teaching, as figure 5.2 shows. They may have integrated more active learning strategies into their courses or sequenced assignments in a way that helped students gain skills in the second week of class that they would need to use in the fourth week. They may have spelled out their expectations for assignments and the kinds of responses their disciplines wanted more explicitly, or they may have changed their grading policies to bring them more in line with their new understanding of what they believed about teaching. These changes could have, in turn, further shaped how faculty members observed students or their thinking about what they needed to do to advance student learning. The causal arrows in figure 5.2 are shown moving in both directions to show the interactive nature of the causes and their changes.

These interactions eventually led to big directions of change. The big direction of change given by 53% of the faculty we interviewed had to do with a growing awareness of the student as a learner and what that meant faculty needed to do in their classes. This awareness of students as learners made it clear to faculty that students were moving along a path from not-knowing to knowing—a path that the faculty member was building, with the classroom as his building site. Furthermore, it was a path to knowing something specific—what students needed to know how to do in order to write a strong philosophy paper, for example, or how to identify types of soil by touch. In addition, faculty members' success and comfort with other changes—integrating active learning strategies into the classroom, tossing out chunks of content, or responding to changes in themselves, to give three examples—made some of these practices big directions of change in their teaching. As figure 5.2 suggests, these big directions of change spilled into many areas, touching both reasons for change and other kinds of change. Over time we imagine that these big directions of change became an almost unnoticed or automatic part of a faculty member's course planning.

One clear implication of these results is that growth in teaching is a dynamic, iterative, complex, and challenging process. It is not linear, self-evident, or easy. As faculty members have told us, it is difficult to yield authority in the classroom, not necessarily because of ego issues but because faculty members feel responsible for the class. It is hard to know how much time to spend on getting students engaged in the subject, how much content to delete from one class that leads to another in a sequence, how to design a series of assignments that teach. It is challenging to be open to students' suggestions for change when some of their comments are intended to hurt and others may be silly. For example:

I wish the faculty would come dressed appropriately and wear a bathing suit when she's talking about the tropics. (Faculty member in the sciences/math)

In the grip of observing student behavior in class, faculty members might be at a loss to know what to do next, and a single change might require several iterations in order for the faculty member to feel as though he were answering the questions that his own observation of students' work raised. The process of change is, therefore, challenging and bumpy, and the faculty member is creating it as she moves forward. Faculty members are not moving along a superhighway as they evaluate and make changes to their teaching; they are tracking through a dense forest that they have no maps for. The lucky few may have a compass, a view of the night sky, or a companion with stories about her own classes.

A second implication in the findings we have discussed in this chapter concerns faculty monitoring student learning. Tracking what students are "getting" in a variety of ways and making changes in response to those observations is something that students see and note. Such monitoring communicates to students that faculty members care about their learning (Beyer et al., 2007). As one student said:

In class, it registers with them more easily if the student is not catching on to the concepts. They have a tendency to say, "I feel that everyone is not completely getting this, so let's go ahead and break this down a little further." They are monitoring in some way. (p. 346)

Therefore, change in teaching may increase student learning in two ways. First, the changes, themselves—the improved assignments or the increased interaction between the faculty member and the class may lead to improvements in student learning. Second, such monitoring sends the message to students that their learning matters to their instructors, a message that is also likely to improve learning.

6

WHAT ALLOWED FACULTY
TO TEACH FROM THE SELF?

I think a lot of it is just that I'm more relaxed and confident. I'm older than
when I started. I don't project as much about being a young woman. It's
a shift for me . . . where I'm more comfortable with my own authority. I
feel competent and not afraid of making mistakes. I make them routinely,
which I don't feel compromises my authority as a teacher. Being relaxed
has been the key for me. I try to go in "willing"—willing to be in the classroom for the two hours, to just park things before I go in there. It's kind
of delightful. It's one of the few spaces and times in my life where the goal
is to not get distracted by things to do with me. It's two hours where my
research doesn't matter, my personal life doesn't matter, grocery shopping
or cat litter doesn't matter. It's a time where a group of other people are
thinking and talking and hopefully enjoying struggling with ideas.
—Faculty member in the humanities

In *The Courage to Teach* (1998), a remarkable book about teaching and
the human spirit, Parker Palmer refers to a comment from a student
about what characterizes good teachers and bad teachers. The student
said that she could not describe her good teachers because they differed a
great deal from each other. In contrast, she was able to describe her bad
teachers because they were all alike in that they distanced themselves
from the subject they were teaching and from their students. In Parker
Palmer's words, "Good teachers join self and subject and students in
the fabric of life" (p. 11). One faculty member in the UW GIFTS spoke
about this connecting of subject, students, and self in almost the same
terms that Parker Palmer used, saying:

[I heard] a speaker at the first part of the Collegium [a teaching training retreat for faculty teaching large lecture classes]. He said there are three parts of teaching: the content, the students, and yourself. He said when he first started teaching, he just thought about the content. Then he thought about the students. And it wasn't until recently that he thought about himself in the classroom and who he wanted to be there, with the content and those students. That's a really freeing concept. (Faculty member in the social sciences)

Palmer goes on to say that this connecting of subject, students, and self is not centered in the methods faculty members use:

The methods used by these weavers vary widely: lectures, Socratic dialogues, laboratory experiments, collaborative problem solving, creative chaos. The connections made by good teachers are held not in their methods but in their hearts—meaning "heart" in its ancient sense, as the place where intellect and emotion and spirit and will converge in the human self. (p. 11)

Ken Bain, in his equally remarkable book, *What the Best College Teachers Do* (2004), echoes that idea, saying that one big obstacle to being a good teacher "is the simplistic notion that good teaching is just a matter of technique . . . a few easy tricks that [faculty can] apply in their own classrooms" (p. 174).

Thus far in this book, we have focused primarily on those "tricks"—the methods and techniques that faculty members sought and used to better join their subjects with their students. These were the changes that faculty members explicitly described. For example, they described moving to more active learning strategies in the classroom as a way both to engage students more fully and to advance their learning of the content, perspectives, and approaches of their subject matters and disciplines. Furthermore, in focusing on these kinds of changes in technique, faculty members tended to describe the immediate causes of change. They reported that they had noticed that students were not learning how to read historical accounts critically, for example, or that students were not doing the assigned reading. Only a few faculty members mentioned changes in themselves as causes for the changes they made in their classrooms.

The Importance of Changes in the Self

However, when asked to identify "big directions of change" in their teaching, one in five of our interviewees mentioned responding to changes in themselves as a direction of change. In addition, when given a list of 17 items at the end of their interviews and asked to rate how much each one of the 17 contributed to change in their teaching, faculty members rated "my own maturity and growth" as the third most important cause of change. In explaining their responses to that item, faculty members often spoke about a growing sense of confidence and comfort in the classroom. This change, in turn, allowed them to bring themselves into the classroom, to teach from who they were rather than from a set of ideas about what a professor "ought to be." One faculty member spoke about this shift in these words:

> There's one [change] that happened just in the last couple of years that I don't fully understand yet, but I know it is a huge part of how my teaching is changing. It's something I'm calling "teaching from the heart." And part of it is who I am in the classroom. I think in the past I've felt I needed to prove my competency, just like I needed to prove the seriousness of the field when I first began teaching. And I don't need that anymore. Now I just really want to engage with the material and the students and have them engage with the material with me and with each other. I feel more comfortable now to work within whatever emerges. (Faculty member in the social sciences)

Another faculty member spoke about it in this way:

> . . . I'm not a warm and fuzzy natural teacher. I've taught with [Professor X] who expressed more overt enthusiasm in her little toe than I had in my whole body. But over time, I became comfortable with who I am, with teaching from who I am. I became comfortable with what I do, and I brought that to the classroom with a little more confidence. (Faculty member in the sciences/math)

According to Palmer, this move to teaching from the self closes the distances between instructor, subject, and students.

We did not set out to track this shift because we did not anticipate it. Nor did faculty members foreground it in their conversations. However, we saw its footprints across the interview questions with faculty. For example, one faculty member spoke about learning to have faith in her own ability to teach in these words:

> I'm getting a little bit more confident that in the end—whatever happens along the way—to have more faith in what I'm doing and if I'm faltering, to go back to the things that work. To do my own thing. Every day I have to get up and say, "You were meant to do this and you were meant to do this in your way, so don't be insecure that people are doing it a different way." Be yourself, I guess I'm trying to have the maturity to do that. (Faculty member in the social sciences)

Another faculty member linked his growing comfort in the classroom to a general acceptance of himself:

> As I've become more comfortable in my own skin as a person, I've become more comfortable in my own skin as a teacher. I think that frees me up to do things in ways I think are best, rather than worrying about whether everyone else is doing it in the same way or whether the students like me any more than they have to in order not to tune out. It's nice if I have some connections with the way others are doing their classes but now I know how I need to do things in my own way. (Faculty member in the social sciences)

A third faculty member spoke of the importance of revealing oneself and one's own perspectives to students:

> I sometimes have encounters with students who come in, notice the Bible on my desk, and we'll have a discussion. I think the diversity is important—and helps connect us as people. We as instructors can and, I believe, ought to share the ethnic or gender perspectives we may have to contribute—and also other things like our faith. I think it's important that the students see all of us as people—whether we happen to be gay or not, Christian, Jewish, Muslim, or atheist. (Faculty member in engineering)

Our interviews suggest that faculty often experience some specific kinds of new awareness in order to be free to teach from their authentic selves. A very general description of this highly individualized process would begin with what we have come to think of as moving beyond (or "recovering from") the graduate school experience. This step leads faculty members to trust their own authority over time, give themselves permission to make mistakes, and discover that they know how to teach. As a result, they pare down course content, which is the first moment when many of them free themselves from what they believe they "should" do as college teachers. Then they embark on the path of teaching from themselves. Once they have started down this path, it can take them in teaching directions they may not have anticipated, sometimes calling on them to abandon what they have been doing and to pursue new passions.

Moving Beyond the Graduate Student Experience

The freedom to be oneself in the classroom, to "teach from the heart" as one of our faculty members put it, begins by stepping away from content. This was not an aspect of teaching that the graduate students with whom we spoke mentioned. The graduate students in the small focus groups we conducted were remarkably experienced instructors. As a group, they had a great deal more teaching experience than many graduate students do. Furthermore, as we note in chapter 9, some of them indicated a growing sense of comfort in the classroom. However, none of them was even close to the kind of freedom that our faculty interviewees described. That seemed to be a gift that only time and experience could bring. The following interaction with three of the graduate students, all from different disciplines, in one of the focus groups illustrates this difference:

> Student A: "I've created a lot of 'do not do lists' from watching other people teach. I've been somewhat humbled recently, though, because I've been doing my own classes and it's hard to do your own classes. You have to have organization, charisma, a good plan, good lectures. I'm working on it. I was a good TA, but organization is hard for me, and not being comfortable with the content knowledge makes it hard for me to know what to do in class. That level of confidence."

Student B: [Nodding]: "Knowing what you need to have and coming up with it and organizing it. I'm not sure I'm capable of that now."

Student C: ". . . the grading part of it was really difficult for a lot of reasons, one of which was I wanted to be liked."

Student A: "I feel I'm getting to be a better teacher, but I'm actually less confident because I'm experimenting so much. I don't know where my center of gravity is or who I am as a teacher anymore. I knew who I was and what I was good at as a TA."

As the focus group discussion suggests, even after several years of teaching experience and experience observing and working with faculty members whom they considered to be both good and bad teachers, the graduate students were uncertain about their own abilities to teach effectively. Selecting and organizing course content, having "charisma" or presence in the classroom, being able to create good lectures, and difficulties with grading were worries even for these students. Student A's first moments in the classroom left him not knowing "who I am as a teacher."

Biggs (1999) noted more than a decade ago that beginning teachers often believe that their primary responsibility is to know content thoroughly and be able to speak about it clearly. This concern with content may be a by-product of students' graduate school experience. Both faculty and graduate students with whom we spoke often described the graduate student years as a time when they felt they were frequently called on to display "content knowledge" and to defend their expertise in their fields. Not only did the graduate process and their advisers call on them to demonstrate expertise, but often graduate students were in highly competitive environments with other graduate students and felt compelled to demonstrate their right to be there. A study by Baiocco and DeWaters (1998) shows that, in contrast with a group of faculty members who had been recognized for distinguished teaching, graduate student teaching assistants were focused on "the content they were responsible for conveying" and with staying just ahead of the classes they were teaching (p. 236). Confirming this finding, UW GIFTS participants spoke explicitly about the challenges in making the switch from graduate student to professor in terms of content knowledge. As two young faculty members said:

Going from being a graduate student one day to being a professor the next means that all of a sudden you have to have answers. It is weird being considered to be an expert in a field I'm still so new in. (Faculty member in the social sciences)

My impulse as a graduate student was to go in and teach—to go in and just model, do, be smart, provide some information, and then give them discussion questions that they could do for themselves. (Faculty member in the humanities)

This idea that professors should "have answers" and "provide some information"—an almost automatic focus on content as faculty begin teaching—came up frequently in our interviews with faculty. As one faculty member put it:

I suppose earlier in my career I spent more time trying to teach facts than I do now. I'm still interested in factoids, but I probably emphasized them more at first because I was more scared of teaching, of whether I knew enough to teach. What was I supposed to communicate if not facts? (Faculty member in the sciences/ math)

Faculty members sometimes spoke of this automatic focus as amplified by the sense of urgency they felt at having to create a course that they would offer for hundreds of students, often within the next few weeks. In the words of one faculty member:

Someone drops a teaching assignment on you, and you are just trying to figure out what is the content, what am I teaching? (Faculty member in the social sciences)

Another faculty member's description of beginning teaching also serves as an example:

Certainly in the beginning, I really didn't think about it. I kind of frantically put together courses without thinking about what it was that I wanted the students to learn and how best to do that with undergraduates. (Faculty member in the social sciences)

It is important to note that the need to display one's expertise and focus on content was not about individuals' egos. In fact, it is driven by just the opposite—by wanting to do the right thing for one's students and having had little instruction in how to do that. New faculty members are not likely to have learned much about teaching and learning as graduate students. As Bain (2004) points out, the best teaching is usually the result of a "struggle with the meaning of learning within our disciplines and how best to cultivate and recognize it" (pp. 174–175). This process is hidden from most graduate students. Thus, when they arrive to teach in their own classrooms, new faculty have had little time or help engaging in that struggle; rarely have they been told by advisors or mentors to come by their classes and observe the ways experienced faculty are wrestling with "the meaning of learning in their disciplines." Therefore, when suddenly responsible for the learning going on behind 300 pairs of eyes—or even only 20—every week, a conscientious instructor is likely to focus on the "what"—what "should be" taught—rather than on how people learn or who he might be as a faculty member in the classroom. As one faculty member said:

> When you are a beginning teacher in Latin, you think that nobody will get the right answer unless you ratify it and authenticate it for them. (Faculty member in the humanities)

Given these realities for new faculty—graduate experiences in which they were expected to display expertise, no training in teaching, the need as new professors to create courses quickly, and the desire to do a good job in their classes—it should be no surprise, then, that faculty members in the UW GIFTS talked about their early years of teaching as challenging. As one faculty member said:

> You can name anything that somebody does wrong when they first start teaching, and I was doing it. As my chair said it, "The great thing about your teaching is that your evaluations just go up." But that was because they started so low! (Faculty member in the social sciences)

So many faculty members mentioned an early need to display expertise—as well as their growth away from that need—that we finally asked one faculty member directly whether experienced faculty members had warned her about focusing too much on content. Was there a shortcut for new faculty, advice that might allow them to skip that step, we asked. She responded:

> Oh yeah! But even if people tell you that, and even if you understand what they are saying, you still go in there feeling that you have to demonstrate that you know what you are doing. For me, there is no getting around the fact that teaching is a kind of performance. And there are risks to that performance. Especially when you are just starting out, the fear of failure is very high, and so even if someone tells you, "Look, you know more than anyone else in there," it doesn't matter if you know more than they do if you don't know the answer to one of their questions. For you there is just this overwhelming fear of public failure. I'm sure that there are people who don't have that fear coming in, but I think that would be rare. Also, gender may play a role, and I think I look very young. Coming into a big course looking the same age as the students somehow raises the stakes again. I have to do something to demonstrate my authority, and I am going to demonstrate my authority with what I know.

She went on to discuss how that need changes with time into having enough authority to "open free space for the unpredictable *and* enforce an educative order," in the words of Parker Palmer and Arthur Zajonc (2010, p. 39). As she put it:

> Showing that you are in control of this discussion, that you can engage with them, take what they say, and lead the discussion forward in a purposeful way—that's how you show that you have control and authority over the situation. It's not by lecturing to them and showing them how many facts and figures you know. I couldn't have learned that until I did it—until I just got in there. I didn't know how to do that in my first year. That's a skill you develop over time—how to develop questions and build them to a good discussion. If that is the best way of showing your authority it's something you have to learn by mucking around in it for awhile. (Faculty member in the social sciences)

Therefore, we can surmise that one crucial step, perhaps the first one, in teaching from the heart—or in weaving the strands of students, subject, and self together in the classroom—appeared to be getting over the need to demonstrate one's expertise and stepping away from content as the primary focus in the classroom. In the words of one faculty member:

> One of the things you learn over time is that you know this material and you don't have to prove it to them by showing them how much you know. (Faculty member in the humanities)

Learning to Trust Their Own Authority over Time

It takes time to learn what else to do. Like all learning, learning to teach effectively is a process that takes place over time. As one faculty member noted:

> . . . getting to a place where I really focus on teaching the material for what it has to offer to students and what the experience has to offer me, that's taken place over time. (Faculty member in the social sciences)

Time and practice give faculty members a sense of comfort and increased confidence in the classroom. UW GIFTS interviewees often linked these changes to getting older and trusting their own authority, as the following quotation shows:

> I think there's a certain extent to which the older you get, you are often more confident in who you are and the less you need to project some kind of authority. I think that the older I get, the less I might need to project inapproachability as a way of projecting authority. I don't have to perform it anymore. (Faculty member in the arts)

Another faculty member spoke about knowing that she could trust her own judgment, as follows:

> I try to be responsive to students, but I don't doubt myself as much as I used to. They have to buck up and do it. They can

roll their eyes around, but if there are 18 people in the class who are lost and two who aren't, those two are just going to have to suck it up and be bored. I think if it's for the greater good of the class and 98% will benefit, I'm going to go with that. I think this change is because I've done this a lot. I know what works, and I think before I didn't know what works. But now I've done all these things in all these different directions, so I really know what works. So if a student comes to me and suggests that we translate all day, I just say no, because I know now that doesn't work. And I won't second guess myself about it anymore. (Faculty member in the humanities)

A number of experiences may help faculty accept their own authority over time, but faculty specifically mentioned publishing, tenure, and successful classes as helpful in their development. As one faculty member said:

Having a little more authority—that perspective of having a successful art career helps. My experience in the field certainly comes into play, my perspective on it. (Faculty member in the arts)

Echoing that idea, another faculty member said:

Time has given me that confidence, and publishing has too. I have a record of research. I can stand on my own. That's helped boost my confidence a lot. (Faculty member in the social sciences)

Permission to Make Mistakes

Faculty often reported that no longer being afraid of making mistakes in front of students also freed them to be more comfortable teaching from themselves. Many faculty members described coming to a point of accepting that perfection was impossible and that they would be able to handle mistakes they made in class. In the words of two faculty members:

I'm just more confident. I guess one thing that I will say is that every now and then you're up in a class and you explain something incorrectly—or more often in a way that you realize is correct but not very helpful. I guess originally that would really affect me. I'd think, "Oh my gosh, why did I say that? How am I going to dig myself out of this hole?" And now, I realize that that's kind of okay. I am a little more comfortable with dealing with that when it happens. (Faculty member in the sciences/math)

When things do go badly—and we all have those days—learning that it's not the end of the world, knowing you can have off days, days when you fail, and it doesn't ruin the course. When you're young, it's hard for you to realize that. (Faculty member in the humanities)

Similarly, another faculty member noted learning that giving a bad lecture did not destroy the class:

I've gotten more confident about it and that makes me more comfortable speaking in front of a group of students. I learned that the world didn't end after a bad lecture. (Faculty member in engineering)

Knowing That They Know How to Teach

Faculty members also said that their confidence in themselves had increased because they understood that they now knew what worked in the classroom. In the words of one faculty member:

I'm more confident. I also have a better understanding of what teaching is. And the question that I ask the TAs—"Is what you are thinking about doing going to help them learn?"— that question—I don't know if I knew that before. I may have been living by it. I just never said it like that before. (Faculty member in the arts)

This knowledge of their own teaching expertise gave them confidence to do things in class that may have been difficult for them to do earlier in their careers. For example, one faculty member spoke of knowing how to handle challenges to her authority in the classroom, as well as being looser with examples. In her words:

> I think I'm more confident in the classroom of my abilities and knowledge of the material. Early on, those first couple of years—women of color are often challenged by some students. They challenge your understanding of the material, for instance. As an authority figure, I'm just more confident now, and I don't get that as much in class. I feel more confident in saying to a student, "Take off your hoodie," because I know they are going to do it. I feel more confident in playing with examples, too. I don't have to have everything so planned and perfect. (Faculty member in the social sciences)

Paring Down, Opening Up, and Weaving In

Often beginning to pare down the material "covered" in class was the beginning of freedom to teach from the self. Many faculty members described change in their teaching as an awareness that they had to eliminate content in order to do something else. As two faculty members put it:

> What has changed is my thinking about how much material I can effectively cover in the 50-minute, three-days-a-week time that I teach—especially with someone like Kant, recognizing just how difficult that material is for someone who has never taken any philosophy, let alone someone who has never read something written in the 18th century. (Faculty member in the humanities)

> I've come to the point where I want to do less and do it deeply than to try to do everything in one class. (Faculty member in the social sciences)

Connected to loosening their grip on content, faculty also talked about yielding some control of the direction of the course to the students. As one faculty member said:

I'm not so set on a direction—as I used to be. I used to bring in examples of things every quarter, but now I ask them for examples and if they have none, that's okay and I can play with it. If they offer an example of a theoretical perspective that doesn't work, it can crash and burn, but at least they see me trying to make it relevant and we play around with the ideas. (Faculty member in the social sciences)

Sharing the direction of the class with students often led to the use of new teaching methods and classroom techniques, such as active learning and scaffolding assignments.

These shifts began or advanced the process that Parker Palmer described in which the faculty member weaves the students, the subject, and the self together. One of our interviewees spoke of this awareness that some of the content needed to go as coming from "an interaction" between herself and her students. In her words:

I think the direction for me has been more clarity and more streamlining. I have had to streamline. . . . I haven't made this change as much by my own design as it is an interaction between my students and me. The first year I had a whole set of stuff I wanted to do. It went okay but I got some criticism that there was too much to do. The next year I would ask myself what it was important to focus on, what is the biggest bang for the time I have. So I have gone by the way of productivity of learning. That has meant teaching less material but teaching some of it more in-depth. (Faculty member in the social sciences)

Another one of our faculty members described Palmer's weaving of students, subject, and self as a learning process in this example:

First, I should say that I had zero teaching experience when I first came here. [That 200-level class] was my first class ever. I got four weeks' worth of lectures ready, and I thought I was way ahead, but I was behind so fast I couldn't believe it. My first mistake was not being prepared enough. My other mistake was—never having taught—I think I basically was insecure about it and just trying to throw too much at them. I figured that out over the years. Since my first time teaching, to this day, I still eliminate a few things almost every time.

Just showing respect for them is really important. I think I was too busy those first few years to realize that. I think I became aware over time that when you are having a discussion with them and trying to get them to see something—rather than just telling them—they are so much more receptive; they are so much more open. I would say that was one of the things that was a key turning point for me back there along the way.

I think that when they feel like you care whether they learn, they learn better. So that's another thing. They see my enthusiasm, and they see that I care that they learn and 90% respond to that. The vast majority respond to that.

It's simply a matter of me having to learn to teach, and it just took me awhile to do it. I think I became more secure and more comfortable in the role of teaching. After my first year of terror, it became a challenge. I wanted to do this right, and I wanted to figure out how to do it right. It became an intriguing challenge. I think I got more comfortable with making mistakes, with just letting things happen, seeing how things worked. I just got more comfortable with the idea, more interested in the challenge and that made it easier for me to experiment. When I figured out something worked, I stuck with it. But until I get to that point I keep tweaking it. So I guess that's why I was saying that maturity mattered. My own learning over time made a difference; I have learned. (Faculty member in the sciences/math)

This faculty member also gave us an interesting metaphor for learning to teach by describing one of the things she helps her students learn—identifying some of the properties of soil by touch. In her words:

The purpose of the lab is to teach them to texture with their hands. You use your hands to feel the soil and learn how much sand and clay are in it. To be really good at identifying soil with your hands, you have to do it a lot more, but they learn that you can do that and that you can get good at it. They practice it.

Faculty who, in Parker Palmer's (1998) words, "join self" with their subjects and students in the classroom know when they are teaching from the heart by "touch." Practice has taught them.

Listening to Changes in the Self

Finally, faculty members sometimes talked about the ways that major changes in their intellectual passions brought about major changes in what they taught as well as in how they taught it. That faculty members' intellectual interests might change over time is not surprising. Many faculty members spend 40 years or longer in academia—a long time to pursue only one research interest. However, it seems likely that only faculty members who have already felt free to teach from themselves will feel free to incorporate new passions into their teaching, and this was certainly true for the faculty members who described such profound changes to us. For example, one of those faculty members began his academic career as an Americanist, teaching survey courses and other classes in American literature. He described the change he experienced in himself and how he carried that into the classroom in this extended example:

> I went to the Holocaust Museum in Washington, D.C., and what was powerful to me was the fact that not only were these people killed but also that what was taken from them was their everyday lives. Everything there in the museum was about the details of their lives. And it made me think about what it was that had been taken away from them. I started doing research on the everyday, coming to the question of what everyday life is and what are the stories about it. And there really are a lot of stories about it.
>
> So I began to put together a whole set of ways to get students to think about the everyday life. I grew tired of having to overcome the inertia in a classroom of convincing students that a subject was worth studying. Now I use their lives. Even though we are also talking about fictional lives, I engage them in their lives—what their favorite object is and why, what they have for breakfast and when do they eat it. And they all have

answers. Everybody has answers—they always have responses. They all have something to talk about.

What I do is I have them read literary texts, for example, Nicholson Baker, a novelist, who writes about these really compressed periods of time, like what he thinks about when he's giving his baby a bottle of milk or what he's thinking about when he takes an escalator from the bottom floor to the mezzanine where he works. So I'm also using these texts to get students to think of what is work to them, what is life.

But the real reason I do this is I can get them to read really hard theory to help them understand what it is that they're engaged with in their lives—Marx, Freud, French theorists. It makes sense to them because it's about their lives. So I might have them think of space—about a neighborhood and how it's structured—and read Lefebvre and Foucault. Once they read the theory, they get the connection between that and how it is important for them to theorize about their lives. They understand that the importance of having these outside theoretical perspectives is that it helps them think about their own lives— why that thing they just bought, for example, is a commodity. They get it. They understand that their lives aren't just their lives but are connected to all these other things, globally, nationally, and otherwise.

I tell them that this class will change their lives, and it does. I teach this class as often as I can. I love the course. I love their writing for the course.

In terms of writing, I give them models, the first thing they have to do is engage one of the theorists and put that theorist in conversation with a text, for example, Marx on commodities and a novel I've assigned. Then I want them to "close read" an object. I give them examples for how to do it—essays on objects. This is an object of their choice, and I've had everything—ballpoint pens, coffee mugs, toys, dolls, everything you can think of, I've received. Students have written about vases they've broken and pieced together that they somehow made their own by repairing. Mr. Potato Head. I had an uproarious discussion in class about Mr. Potato Head. I never get bored by reading these essays, because the objects are never the same.

Another assignment is an experiential assignment that has to do with space. I get them to use Foucault or someone else writing about space, and they have to go out in the world and be attentive to a space they select.

The whole course is about that—being attentive to their own lives. (Faculty member in the humanities)

Obviously, this faculty member's growing interest in the everyday led him to create a new course for undergraduates and a new research focus for himself. It also changed how he taught, affecting how he graded students ("I don't care if everyone gets a 4.0 or a 2.0; I grade much differently now than I once did. If they do what I ask them to do and do it well, I don't care if they get high grades."), his assignments, and how he conducted class time.

A second example of a shift in one's intellectual interests reshaping the classroom came from a faculty member in the social sciences. As he described:

I was originally hired to teach [a course on] Constitutional Thought, which is very focused on American history, and that plus the American Political Thought class were connected. I thought of the American Political Thought class as a course in non-legal thought and politics, which was parallel to the Constitutional Thought class. But I gave that class up a few years later, as well. . . . at the time I was undergoing a change in my own identity—focusing more and more on law and society studies, which became the Law, Societies, and Justice Program a few years later. That didn't take off until after I dropped the American Political Thought class. I think dropping that class may have left me thinking, "What am I going to do now?" But I was already thinking about law a little bit. So since the mid-1990s, I've had a change in identity. How much of that was the pull of the new direction and how much the push of the old? I don't know. (Faculty member in the social sciences)

This shift in the faculty member's intellectual "identity" ended up not only in changes in teaching and research, but it created an entire academic program at the university.

As these two examples show, faculty members sometimes experience profound changes in their own intellectual passions, and, when faculty members are teaching from themselves, these changes end up changing their teaching, as well as the learning of undergraduates.

Summary: Teaching from the Self

We can summarize the theme of freedom to teach from the self as a change that often begins with faculty loosening their grip on *what* they believe they must teach, which allows them to focus on the other two aspects of their classes—the students and who they, themselves, are in the classroom. This shift is, itself, a learning process that parallels the learning processes of students and that is as complex, dynamic, and iterative as all learning processes are. Faculty began without much sense of where to look to improve their teaching work, but at some point—usually early in their teaching careers—they began to question what they were teaching and why. They began to ask what mattered and, in response to the answers to that question, to pare down the course content. When faculty members began teaching from their authentic selves their connections to both their students and their subjects deepened and changed. With that shift, it became easier, as this faculty member noted:

> I'm really comfortable in front of this group of 450 students and especially when I come in feeling really myself. (Faculty member in the social sciences)

It is important to remember, however, that this is a risky process for the individuals engaging in it. As their comments in this chapter show, teaching requires them to be willing to fail and to take risks. They have to have some idea at the beginning where they hope to end today, next week, and at the end of the quarter and some plan for getting there. But they also have to be willing to change directions on the spot if they observe a need to do so. And they take these risks and make these judgments very publicly—in classrooms of 20 and in classrooms of 700 students. In his book *The Courage to Teach* (1998), Parker Palmer points out that "unlike many professions, teaching is done at the dangerous intersection of personal and public life" (p. 17). He contrasts teaching with counseling, which is done in the private sphere, and with law, which is conducted primarily in the public sphere, noting:

> But a good teacher must stand where personal and public meet, dealing with the thundering flow of traffic at an intersection where "weaving a web of connectedness" feels more like crossing a freeway on foot. As we try to connect ourselves and our subjects with our students, we make ourselves, as well as our subjects, vulnerable to indifference, judgment, ridicule. (p. 17)

This path away from the comfort of content and into teaching from the self, then, is a challenging one. When faculty members start their journeys along it, they have no guidelines and no one pressuring them to move forward. They move along that path because of their own desire, often propelled by their own personal growth.

7

WHAT DID FACULTY
SAY ABOUT STUDENTS?

I think back on it and wonder why it took me so long to think about the
sequence of the assignments I was giving, that I needed to help them build
a set of skills sequentially. I think that was partly the way I was taught—
you either could do it or not, and grading separated the people who could
from those who could not. . . . It slowly began to dawn on me that there
really is a sequencing of skills that needed to be built and that I couldn't
presume that students were bringing those skills with them. So it was my
job to try to teach them.

        —Faculty member in the social sciences

Barr and Tagg (1995) changed the focus of assessment from teaching to learning more than 15 years ago, but in her book on student-centered teaching, Maryellen Weimer (2002) notes that faculty
members often move from a focus on content to more student-centered
approaches only as they mature. In chapter 6, we discussed changes
faculty made to their teaching that made space for themselves in the
classroom. Interviews with faculty members in UW GIFTS also support Weimer's contention—changes were often related to the growing
perception among UW GIFTS participants that students are learners
and that faculty have to use the classroom as a place to help them learn.

  We have already briefly discussed this shift to a deeper focus on the
students and their needs as learners in the section in chapter 4 that reported faculty responses to the question about "big directions of change"
in their teaching. However, the shift from thinking about students as
people who "either could do it or not" to the understanding that students
are engaged in a learning process that takes place over time was a theme
that crossed faculty responses to a number of questions. Furthermore,

faculty members' sense of students as learners often seemed present even when unspoken, touching many areas of change. Therefore, we thought this theme deserved further consideration.

Students as Learners

When students enter college from high school experiences, they often confuse knowing with learning, believing that learning is an "either you know it or you don't" proposition, rather than understanding that learning is a process (Beyer et al., 2007). Even faculty members can confuse knowing and learning in the early days of their teaching, as the quotation that starts this chapter indicates. Therefore, learning what learning is and requires is a learning process in itself, and it is a process that both faculty and students sometimes experience together.

When asked what the "big directions" of change in their teaching were (described in chapter 4), more than half of the faculty members we interviewed spoke about changes that related to the awareness that students are learners. For example, one faculty member in the sciences spoke about realizing that students "have to learn how to learn" as well as learning other skills. In his words:

> I guess the one thing I would say as far as change [goes] is that I've felt increasingly comfortable with the notion that it's not only the content of the class, but it's also the process of learning in the class that's important. Students have to learn how to learn, how to write a wiki, how to write short analytical essays, how to facilitate a discussion, how to do a research paper . . . it's simple to memorize but more difficult to think. I've constantly tried to grow with that. (Faculty member in the sciences/math)

Another faculty member talked about "correcting" the "preach and teach" style he had adopted as a younger professor:

> You know it is so easy to teach in the "preach and teach" style. You roll in and say, "Here's the stuff," and roll out. Give them a test, assign a grade, and start over next quarter. I think the biggest mistake I made in my initial stages of teaching was to take for granted that the material I was presenting was sinking in. I think I corrected this by invoking impedance matching

techniques. With this approach one has to take time to be really prepared [and] have good examples so you can draw out what is happening in the learning process. (Faculty member in the sciences/math)

There were many sources for this shift in focus. Sometimes it came about because of faculty members' interactions with other faculty members or because of their reading, as this faculty member said, speaking of Eric Mazur's ground-breaking book, *Peer Instruction: A User's Manual* (1997):

In thinking about this change—I think there has just been this emphasis—and I couldn't tell you when it started—with the type of model Eric Mazur uses—the learner-centered instruction. It all heads us away from a pure lecture teaching method, which has been shown is not a great way to teach students. (Faculty member in the sciences/math)

Mostly, however, faculty described moving into an understanding of students as learners by being careful observers of their own classes and of students' behaviors and performances in those classes, as noted previously (chapter 5). In the words of one faculty member:

I needed to come to the understanding that these are not students who have been studying ethics intensely for the last five years and they have to understand every detail of these arguments. I learned to step back and teach it slowly enough so they were getting the big picture and the important arguments and not the details that they can investigate on their own later. (Faculty member in the humanities)

In addition to the big directions of change that faculty noted, many of the specific changes that faculty described making in the two courses they discussed—such as adding scaffolding to assignments, moving to active learning strategies in the classroom, becoming more explicit about expectations and disciplinary practice, and even changes in technology—were related to their observations that students were not learning what they hoped they were. Therefore, many of these changes, themselves, suggest a growing understanding that students were engaged in a process that faculty members were helping them move through. For example, this faculty member spoke of thinking about exams as part of a learning process, rather than as just a place for students to demonstrate what they knew:

> I make sure they have those kinds of questions in the exam and the TAs have the exams early so they can prepare students for them—to tell them, for instance, that they will need to apply concepts as well as know what they are. My hope is that students are learning something in the process of preparing for the exam, not just for this material but for other classes. (Faculty member in the social sciences)

Other faculty members spoke about making changes to their courses in order to extend students' learning into their futures beyond the university, as this faculty member's comment illustrates:

> That first time I was insecure, but after I taught it for a few years, I kept working on understanding not what was important for me to teach but what was important for them to understand if they were going to work with soils in the future. (Faculty member in the sciences/math)

Just as bringing one's whole self into teaching required faculty members to begin asking whether content should be the only driver of a course, the shift to an awareness of students as learners called on faculty to ask new questions. In some cases, faculty spoke of having to challenge their own undergraduate experiences where the question of whether they were learning a subject was not separated from the assertion that faculty were "covering" it, as this faculty member suggests:

> There has been a change in approach to student learning. For example when I was an undergrad, the notion was that there is a good library, figure out how to use it and incorporate the literature into your learning. Learning how to use a library was completely on your own. When I was an undergrad it was essentially sink or swim. Some [faculty] were old school. For example, "I'm only teaching upper-level courses and if you have basic questions, get out of my face." Now, I think we do a

much better job at educating students. We expend much more effort to make sure students understand the material and think about it. (Faculty member in the sciences/math)

Another question that faculty began asking themselves as they became aware of new ways they might help students learn was how to help students help each other along the learning path, as this faculty member described:

> The last thing in the world I want is for the class to be about me—that somehow this is about my ability to motivate them, like a coach, "Let's go out there! Let's do this!" And that's not an abstraction. I'm looking at how they review each other's work in the writing groups, and it's the extent to which you can get the students to trust and respect one another so they work productively in groups [that matters]. They don't need you there monitoring them. They don't need you there disseminating information. You produce a context and a classroom in which that sort of collaborative work is valued and does take place. (Faculty member in the humanities)

Similarly, faculty members often tried new ways to motivate students to learn. One faculty member spoke of discovering encouragement as a motivator of student learning:

> In the beginning I had no idea what I was doing. I came from a very traditional background, where you were right or you were wrong—the whole idea of encouragement rather than punishment was bizarre. You start to see immediately the results of reassurance and encouragement. I was amazed that within two weeks I could walk into a classroom, speak in full sentences in Italian, and the students would understand and respond. And would be the ones talking most of the time, and talking Italian! That was a major discovery about encouragement and affirmation. It's astounding. (Faculty member in the humanities)

Faculty members spoke of other ways to engage students, as well, such as this faculty member speaking about giving students permission to be creative:

. . . most people, when they are allowed to realize their own creativity and when they are allowed to bring that to learning can get to "Wooo-hoooo! why wasn't learning like this before?" Being right on that edge is what makes it terrible and wonderful. (Faculty member in the social sciences)

Finally faculty members also spoke of reminding themselves that students are novices in fields in which they, themselves, are experts. Research has shown that expert learners differ from novice learners in many ways but that faculty sometimes have difficulty remembering what it was like *not* to know what they know (Bransford et al., 2000; Nathan & Petrosino, 2002). One faculty member in the UW GIFTS, for example, spoke about the difference between teaching experts and teaching novices:

But I also think that experts are different from novices, and you teach experts differently than you teach novices. There are going to be people who are very good at teaching experts who are not good at teaching novices and vice versa. (Faculty member in the sciences/math)

Furthermore, two faculty members said that their own experience as novices helped them understand students as learners:

In grad school, I started taking ballet for the first time, and bizarrely that had a huge effect on my teaching. Being the dumbest person in a class in a leotard and tights where other people can really see how you make mistakes really helped me see what students feel like when they are that exposed. Taking a class where I knew absolutely nothing and usually I was the worst in the class—that was very helpful. (Faculty member in the humanities)

I took Italian here, which was wonderful, not just for seeing my wonderful Italian teachers in action, but seeing how the students handled the class, what they found helpful, what they didn't find helpful. It totally made me committed to putting everything on the syllabus on the first day of a term. Up until then—usually, I'm very detailed in the syllabus—but in the beginning language classes, sometimes I'd do a weekly syllabus. Then we were doing that in Italian, and I was like, "You expect me to keep track of this? I need one piece of paper; I can't be writing down something every day." (Faculty member in the humanities)

Throughout their interviews, when faculty spoke of the changes they had made to their courses, their comments often implied a shift in awareness of their students as learners and in a deepening understanding what that meant for teaching. As chapters 4 and 5 suggest, this shift motivated change and identified the change that was needed. Like the opening that allowed faculty to teach from themselves, the awareness of students as learners required faculty to give up some content in order to open time for students to take the steps necessary for learning. Once they made that change, they often found they valued it, as this faculty member's comment illustrates:

And this is my favorite sound at the university—young people actively saying, "Yeah, but what about this?" "Have you thought of this?" (Faculty member in the social sciences)

Students Today . . .

Before faculty members can shift their focus to ways to help students along the path to learning, they have to believe that students want to learn—that they are at least as interested in learning as they are in getting a good grade or completing a degree. Indeed, Ken Bain (2004) noted that: "Highly effective teachers tend to reflect a strong trust in students. They usually believe that students want to learn and they assume, until proven otherwise, that they can" (p. 18). Studies of students' attitudes toward college show that students not only want to learn, they want to be challenged in that learning. In the University of Washington's longitudinal study on undergraduate learning (Beyer et al., 2007), for example, students throughout their four years at the UW spoke positively about courses that had challenged them to stretch their thinking and skills and negatively about courses that had not, even when they had received high grades in the latter.

Even so, believing that students want to learn can be challenging. Often faculty hear only from students whose focus is on getting the grade they need to move to the next step on their intended career paths, rather than on acquiring the skills and knowledge they need to be good in those fields. Furthermore, most faculty members have heard the arguments that "students today" are different from students in previous generations. For example, faculty have heard that today's students are driven by a consumer mentality about college (Delucchi & Korgen, 2002), a mentality that allows both students and their parents to put pressure on faculty to give them the classroom experience or the grades they believe they "purchased" with their tuition. Faculty have also heard that "today's students" are driven by the need for instant gratification brought on by the digital age (Lowery, 2004).

Although faculty members were aware of these ideas about change in today's students, participants in the UW GIFTS did not seem to think that changes were great enough to have a strong effect on their teaching. When asked to rate the effects of changes in students on changes they had made to their courses, faculty rated that source of change a 2.44 on average out of a possible 4—a little more than a minor source of change. Interestingly, all 55 of the UW GIFTS interviewees added a comment about changes in students. Some faculty members told humorous stories about differences between their own generation and that of the undergraduates they were teaching. For example:

> So then he [asked], "Like if you wanted to know something before the Internet 10 years ago, how did you find out? I'll bet there are a lot of students who don't have a clue about this." I said, "Well, we went to the library," and he asked, "What did you do there?" I said, "You'd go to the card catalog, look up your book, and it would tell you where to find it in the library." And he said, "Yeah, I saw that once." (Faculty member in the social sciences)

About a third of the faculty members we interviewed said that they saw no major changes in their students over time. Some of those faculty members noted changes in the landscape around students, but said that such changes did not essentially alter the student population. For example:

> By and large they come in with enthusiasms; they are willing to work hard; and they have their ideals. And they have a harder deal than I ever had. Tuition, finding somewhere to live

in Seattle these days—everything is more difficult for them these days. And then we turn around and say they don't have the ideals we had in the 60s. That's ridiculous. They have an influence on my teaching because I love their idealism, their hope. They work very, very hard. (Faculty member in architecture/built environments)

Their access to technology and the impact of that on their contribution to their own knowledge and stuff like that have changed. But I've had people talk to me about Gen X-ers vs. this, that, and the other, and I don't see things like that in students. We went through another big thing about that topic last week at a meeting, but I think, you know, they're just people. I just don't see that. I don't think students have changed that much. (Faculty member in business)

. . . we now have those "millennial" students right now, so that's different. Although, I like to think that we're all people and they're just young. They're like us, but just younger. Even though they are from a different generation, they aren't from a different planet after all, and they were raised by us. (Faculty member in business)

As all three quotations show faculty members were aware of the pressures on students, as well as of the literature about how current students differ from those from previous generations. Along these lines, about 20% of the faculty commented about the effects of technology on students. Many of them noted that students were more technologically savvy than they had ever been. Some noted in this set of comments and elsewhere in their interviews that they were working to understand the effects of students' technological understanding on their teaching, as this faculty member said:

One of them has been me trying to figure out how my students interface with technology. I like technology too, so I can make websites and all that, but how to make them so they aren't just a syllabus put online. Students are really technologically savvy, and they get a lot of their knowledge from technology these days. So I think about how to use technology, like in the key word mapping assignment, and how to get them interacting with each other outside the classroom using technology. A lot of the model I got taught to as an undergraduate is that I got lectured to and I took a lot of notes. But these students are different. I have tried to figure out how I can get them to absorb the information when they tell me that they only write it down if it's on the PowerPoint slide. When I was in school, there was relatively little visual material introduced in class. So I bring that into class a lot. But how to use slides, how to get them to be interactive and not just sort of being passive—this is my dilemma. (Faculty member in the social sciences)

Sometimes faculty expressed concerns about the effects that increased access to technology might be having on students. In addition, some faculty members expressed concern over the potential for distraction posed by the use of laptop computers in class. For example:

The use of text messaging and computers in class. That keeps them from focusing their attention on the class. It focuses their attention on everything else. I swear I have students on YouTube and Facebook and stuff because I've had two students looking at a computer and laughing in class, and I know my lectures aren't that funny. (Faculty member in the sciences/math)

I guess the other change in students that's affected the way I teach is just their access to technology, and their presumption that the technology is just an extension of themselves. So texting in class and surfing the web in class, answering their phones in class—that stuff completely took me by surprise. So trying to engage them in their learning while they are in their space has made me change the way I think about who I am in the classroom and how I get them to check in. (Faculty member in the social sciences)

Faculty members also expressed concern that technology has caused students to need quick answers. For example:

They are so used to being able to find things on the web, with a few mouse clicks find the program or the answer, that many of them aren't encouraged to seek a deeper understanding. There is more of an instant-gratification approach—a bit like when slide rules left and calculators came in—only now they do it on websites, where a key word can give them the answer. (Faculty member in engineering)

. . . they go in sound bites instead of studying for hours to figure something out. That idea of sitting down and figuring it out for hours seems to have gone by the wayside. In the early 1990s, I used to go ask them to figure things out, and about half the class really loved that. Now about 5% like that. Most of them now want it to be more directive. Pouring into the material and digging in is simply out. (Faculty member in the social sciences)

Technology was not the only concern that faculty members had for today's students. In their comments about how changes in students had affected changes in their teaching, several faculty members noted that students were working more and busier now than they used to be. Faculty members often pointed to students' need to work in order to pay for rising college costs. As one faculty member said:

Twenty-six years ago maybe a quarter were working, and now they all are. (Faculty member in the humanities)

Faculty also expressed concern that students were less well prepared to handle college—particularly college math—than previous students had been, as these faculty members noted:

The students are really the same as they were before in terms of smarts. In terms of the power of their intellect, I think they're as good now as they were before. However, their preparation is lacking. Their preparation especially in mathematical terms now is weaker than it used to be before. (Faculty member in the social sciences)

I feel that students aren't learning basic math in high school anymore. They rely too much on calculators. This whole idea of having to do your times tables a million times before you can do algebra—they don't do that anymore. I feel that people teach them the concepts but don't make them do a whole lot of algebraic computations. I think they get to our classes at the UW, and the things that used to be more familiar to them are now more difficult, because they haven't had the practice. (Faculty member in the sciences/math)

Faculty sometimes attributed students' level of preparation to poor conditions in public high schools, such as large class sizes and underfunding. However, faculty members also spoke of students needing better preparation from the university to "do" college, as this faculty member described:

Fall quarter I ended up doing a "freshman check-in." I dismissed lecture 15 minutes early and anyone who wanted to attend could, but I emphasized that the freshmen could stay. We had a discussion about basic questions and fears they had and how they could be successful in the class. It felt like some of them are underprepared for college learning, so next year I will be much more explicit and I'll definitely do the freshman check-ins for fall quarter. (Faculty member in the social sciences)

Praise for Students Today

Although faculty members identified concerns they had about their undergraduates, they were primarily positive about their students and what they could accomplish—both in their responses to the question concerning the effects on changes in students on their teaching and throughout the interviews. Many faculty members spoke of students as having always been good, as these two examples illustrate:

They have always been great kids. I haven't noticed any changes. (Faculty member in the humanities)

People always talk about students as not knowing things, but I can't tell that they don't, I really can't. They know as much as they did when I first started. (Faculty member in the humanities)

Faculty members also spoke of today's students as better in some ways than previous students had been, as these two examples show:

> Actually our students in classics have only gotten better and better, which is an amazing thing and I would not have expected it. (Faculty member in the humanities)

> One of the more exciting things in my field is that students are becoming more engaged. Students have always been interested in the environment, but they are becoming more agitated, more indignant about these issues. (Faculty member in the sciences/math)

According to some faculty members, current students' approaches to learning were better than were those of students before them. For example, one faculty member spoke of students' willingness to challenge knowledge:

> They are much more apt to challenge knowledge which I think is really good. (Faculty member in the sciences/math)

Another faculty member praised students' willingness to experiment:

> There was a period of time when students were much less interested in experimentation and wanted the formulas given to them, and I'm finding that to be less so now, which I like so much more. (Faculty member in the arts)

In addition, some faculty members pointed out that today's students are being asked to learn more than their predecessors were, as this faculty member said:

> The one difference I'll say is I think we are asking students to learn more and more information. Certainly, compared to when I took intro psych, the amount of information has expanded just because of the advancements in the field, so they are having to study biopsychology and intro to psychology to a degree that we didn't need to do earlier. That's hard stuff for a lot of students, so to the extent that their performance is staying the

same overall, when being asked to learn more, is something [of note]. (Faculty member in the social sciences)

Finally, a few faculty members noted that students seemed more self-confident now than they seemed in the past. For example, one faculty member said:

> In the 1980s, you felt that students had developed blinders because they thought that life was precarious. They hoped they could do as well as their parents did but they were looking at the prospect of downward mobility. Japan was coming up, and the U.S. was going down. They were very directed to get something secure and go out there and do it. This is a horrible generalization, but that's my impression. But in the late '90s, they said they were going to start some new company or go to Africa and stop poverty. All the possibilities opened to them and sometimes dysfunctionally. Now they are getting back to that. You talk to them—and they remind me more of the students at Harvard back in the '70s. They tell you, "I want to go work for *National Geographic* and become a wildlife photographer" and you think—"Wait a minute! How can you just do that?" They are self-confident and I think we empower them in this university. I think we empower them in the major. (Faculty member in the social sciences)

Summary: Students and Other Learners

Overall, faculty members had concerns about students, particularly in the area of technology, but they saw their students as capable learners. Many faculty members explicitly noted their respect for their students and their thinking, as this example demonstrates:

> I have always been committed to an underlying respect for my students. I want them to know they are important contributors to the learning in the class, that I take seriously what they have to say, that I'm not going to ask them to do things that are a waste of their time. I understand they have busy lives outside of class, so what I'm asking them to do is important to

their learning. Those ideas have been consistent and what has changed is my execution of those principles, especially the first one. How do we ensure that students are active participants? How do we foster an environment in which they can be active participants? (Faculty member in the humanities)

In addition, many faculty members did not believe that students had changed much and most of them believed that changes in students had minor effects on their own teaching. In contrast, faculty members' responses to questions throughout the interviews suggested that instructors' growing awareness of students as learners had profound effects on change in their teaching.

In his book on excellence in college teaching, Ken Bain (2004) says that the best college teachers are "engineering an environment" in which students learn (p. 49). The UW GIFTS did not set out to demonstrate that faculty had created such environments, but our interviews with faculty clearly show them learning to create them. Indeed, we saw evidence of a deepening awareness that students are learners engaged in a process that takes place over time. With this awareness came its partner—that, therefore, faculty have to guide students along that path. These shifts in perspective are, themselves, steps in faculty members' own learning processes—processes that they are moving along in the act of teaching.

8

WHAT "RESEARCH" METHODS
DID FACULTY USE?

I try to watch what other people are doing. Once I went to this lecture by [Professor X] in Anthropology. It was to high school teachers, and she used a film clip, and I thought, "This is great." I had never thought about using films like this. I had thought about it in terms of having narratives, but she was using it in an entirely different way. While I was doing a peer review for [Professor Y], I watched him put slides up in his class, and I adopted that. I had never done that before.

          —Faculty member in the social sciences

Students in some fields report that the line between research in their majors and living is blurry, at best (Beyer et al., 2007; Peterson et al., 2009). Architecture students, for example, have described being unable to walk down a street without critically analyzing every structure they encountered—with some of them lamenting the loss of the gift of inattention. Art majors have described constantly gathering images, no matter what else they were also engaged in, for potential use in their next creations. Engineering majors have reported being engaged in online conversations about interesting problems with people far away, deep into the night. Sometimes these walks, images, and conversations were directly related to students' assigned work, but often students described them as habits of being—the accidental consequences of *being* architects, artists, or engineers. They described a curiosity about their work that was neither bound by location nor time, and they spoke of sources of information as infinite. For lack of a better term, we called the continuous gathering of information that these students were describing "research" (Peterson et al., 2009).

Similarly, after listening to faculty discuss the changes they had made to their teaching, the sources of those changes, and the reasons for change, it seemed to us that over time many faculty become consummate researchers in this same way. The many ways faculty gathered information about teaching and learning were revealed in their responses to many of our questions; thus, research on teaching was a theme that recurred throughout the interviews.

Our sense of faculty as researchers on learning lies outside the "Scholarship of Teaching and Learning" movement begun by Boyer (1990) in his book *Scholarship Reconsidered* and refined by others, particularly Pat Hutchings and Lee Shulman in their work with the Carnegie Foundation and with faculty from many colleges and universities. According to Hutchings and Shulman (1999), the Scholarship of Teaching and Learning differs from faculty members seeking ways to improve their teaching primarily because such scholarship is public and, therefore, open to the scrutiny and critique of others. Hutchings and Shulman explain that the Scholarship of Teaching and Learning is not the same as excellent teaching; instead: "It is the mechanism through which the profession of teaching itself advances, through which teaching can be something other than a seat-of-the-pants operation, with each of us out there making it up as we go" (p. 14).

Since Boyer, Hutchings, and Shulman defined the Scholarship of Teaching and Learning, others have added to that definition, such as the ideas recently put forward by Cranton (2011). However, the research that we are talking about in this chapter lies outside those recent changes, as well.

Occasionally, there was a public aspect in the course-based research of the UW GIFTS' faculty members. Several faculty participants in the UW GIFTS were familiar with the language of the Scholarship of Teaching and Learning movement, and a few of our interviewees published results of their research on learning or presented workshops on teaching and learning for other faculty. However, for the most part, faculty were not generating ideas about what would improve capital "T"-teaching. They were working to discern what might improve the learning of the students in their individual classrooms with no intention of making their work public. Even so, that making-it-up-as-they-went process, intimate and nonpublic though it was, called on faculty to gather information from every possible direction in the same way undergraduate architecture, art, and engineering students described.

Obviously there are problems with labeling what faculty described they were doing as "research." Like that of the students in art, architecture, and engineering, the work of gathering information that faculty members described was often neither formalized nor systematic. Frequently, it was a big net continually cast out into the classroom, rather than a carefully planned and targeted search for results with all variables under control. Furthermore, the researchers, themselves, were not disinterested. They hoped to find that what they were doing in the classroom was working, and we did not set up any measures to determine if their senses of their own success or failure were accurate. Also, faculty members' tracking of the effects of the changes they made presented challenges that they, themselves, recognized. With these caveats in mind, however, we could still see the evidence of a research-like stance toward teaching in the ways that faculty members described going about making changes to their classes, as well as in their reasons for change.

Sources of Information on Teaching and Learning

We described sources and reasons for change in chapter 5, and as that chapter makes clear, faculty gathered information on teaching and learning from multiple sources. As noted in that chapter, what happened inside the class—between faculty, students, and subjects—accounted for the majority of the sources of information for change. Looking across the interviews, we saw approaches for gathering that information that resembled many kinds of research methodologies.

Observation

Observation as a research method involves watching events, objects, or organisms in their actual environments. Although observation—or fieldwork, as it is sometimes called—is often considered to be a method most often used in the social sciences, both astronomy and biology, as well as other sciences, make use of observation as a research method. Jane Goodall's observations of chimpanzees, for instance, permanently altered the field of animal behavior and its research methods, raising interesting ethical and scientific questions about results from experimental research on animal behavior.

In using observation as a research method, the researcher can either become involved with those she is observing (participant observation) or maintain a distance from them (direct observation). The position of the faculty member as observer in the classroom does not fall comfortably into one of these models. However, like researchers engaging in observation methodologies, faculty members who reported gathering information from their observations worked hard to be objective about what they were seeing. They frequently described careful observation of their students' behaviors, as well as observing the teaching behavior of colleagues in order to learn more about effective teaching. The following two quotations illustrate the use of this method:

> One more thing I've changed is that when I first started teaching, I think I was overprepared in the sense that I came to class with really dense lectures and I felt I needed to cover a lot of material. I wasn't taking cues from them to see how they were receiving the information, how they were comprehending it. (Faculty member in the humanities)

> I'm very aware of what I learn when I go and observe other people teach—what I learn from them and what I learn at public lectures by watching people speak. I notice even small details—how they start, how they introduce themselves, how they end, how much they walk around, how fast or slow they speak, how much information or how little information they put on a PowerPoint. You get to know what works. (Faculty member in the social sciences)

In their book on qualitative research methods, Lindlof and Taylor (2010) speak of the challenges in observational research or fieldwork, and these challenges are consistent with what many faculty members reported. Citing other scholars, Lindlof and Taylor note:

> . . . actual fieldwork presents challenges that test researchers' ability to cope with ambiguity, adapt to change, improvise plans, and adequately reflect on their role in co-creating social worlds. Somewhat disconcertingly, fieldwork requires

researchers to deliberately abandon their certainty and expertise . . . to adopt a stance of curiosity and openness to the un-
expected, a kind of epistemological vulnerability that can be
frustrating and humbling. (p. 134)

"Textual" Analysis

According to Alan McKee (2003), textual analysis is the interpretation
of documents or objects (such as books, movies, clothing) in order to
gather information about how others are making sense of the world
around them or their experience in it. "Observing" the texts student
produced for a class was one of the major causes of change that faculty
noted. Often, faculty talked of reviewing incoming written assignments
or a sample of them if they were working in a large class in order to
determine if students understood concepts and were improving their
writing and thinking skills in the discipline. However, "texts" are not
necessarily written pieces of work, and faculty in the arts also described
engaging in textual analysis when they regularly reviewed and analyzed
students' performances. Faculty members reported that analysis of both
written and other kinds of texts informed their teaching. Two examples
of textual analysis:

> I'm better at making topics more focused, very clear, and hav-
> ing them tackle that. I think I learned I needed to do that by
> not having success in the overall performance of the students
> on the first papers. It became clear that the questions were too
> hard; the students weren't at a level yet to understand what was
> motivating the question so they couldn't answer the sub-ques-
> tions that were implicit in the main question. (Faculty member
> in the humanities)

> A benefit to having two related classes in back-to-back quarters
> is that you can see any changes that you implement in that
> cohort of students. The student presentations in my 302 course
> significantly improved with respect to my 301 class. Students
> were more prepared, poised, and overall had significantly im-
> proved presentations. (Faculty member in the sciences/math)

Quantitative Analysis

A simple comparison of numerical results is the most basic kind of quantitative research. Sometimes faculty members gathered or studied numerical data on student performance in order to determine what they might do to improve learning, as the following two comments illustrate:

> It was interesting for me to see that there was a significant improvement on their test scores—comparing students in a quarter without any activities to students in a quarter with them. (Faculty member in the social sciences)

> But I'd get a big variance on their exams—and my personal thing is that I want them all to get at least 60%. But I got huge distributions, very spread out—some were way up there and some could figure out how to put their names on the exam and that's it. It became apparent from that distribution that some people would just go straight to the solutions. So I had to figure out a way of giving them practice work. (Faculty member in business)

Consulting Experts

Consultation with colleagues and other experts, either one-to-one or at academic conventions and meetings, is a time-honored research practice (Lindlof & Taylor, 2010). The faculty members we interviewed described seeking out experienced faculty in their departments or others for help. In addition, they engaged in formal training and informal conversations about teaching and learning with other colleagues both locally and internationally at conferences, workshops, and retreats—those public places where the Scholarship of Teaching and Learning might be presented. The five examples that follow illustrate this method of gathering information and show that faculty consult a range of "experts":

> The key, the breakthrough, event for me was—and certainly because of [my colleague's] prod—was going to this week-long workshop on active learning, because I was not familiar with the literature, not familiar with even with basic approaches to

active learning. It was sponsored by a group called the FIRST, an acronym for Faculty Institutes for Reform of Science Teaching. It was an NSF sponsored thing. Subsequent to that, I started reading papers and reading literature on teaching and started going to other workshops. (Faculty member in the sciences/math)

I talked with the librarian after the library lab, and she said that students often don't have adequate background knowledge for their papers, based on the questions they asked her. So even though the TA had told them that the topic was okay, they didn't really understand how this event they were writing about was an anomaly. So she told me that in the library labs, sometimes they have them do a one-minute talk about their topic. So I thought—"Aha, I'll have them do that!" (Faculty member in the humanities)

When I first got here, I talked to a lot of my colleagues and asked for copies of their syllabi and essay questions. I just talked informally with people. I collected a lot of material. That was really very helpful. (Faculty member in the humanities)

I think maybe my attendance at one of the UW retreats, where I learned about some faculty doing this. I think [Professor X] spoke about one-minute essays, so I adapted that. I figured I could have some time for them to sit down and draw a graph and explain it, for instance, usually on what I'd just discussed, to see whether they got it or not. (Faculty member in the social sciences)

Some of the stuff I pick up by reading or by going to teaching workshops. If I come across a good idea, I steal it. The idea for the class notes exercises came out of reading John Bransford's book, *How People Learn*. (Faculty member in the sciences/math)

Experimentation

Conducting experiments is a common research method in the sciences and social sciences. Researchers develop a hypothesis and test its validity using clearly defined, repeatable methods and logical analysis. Furthermore, researchers can control potentially confounding variables by conducting experiments in carefully arranged laboratories and by using regression models to analyze results. One of the faculty members in the UW GIFTS has done well-regarded experiments on teaching and learning in his classroom and has published his results. In his words:

> Since about 2005, I've gotten interested in trying to innovate the way the course is done. I've been trying new course designs and collecting data on student achievement to try to see what's working and what's not working. (Faculty member in the sciences/math)

For most faculty in the UW GIFTS, though, conducting experiments often meant something less formal. They hypothesized that X would be more effective as a method or strategy than Y; they tried X; and they analyzed its effects, often speaking of this experimental approach as "trial and error" or "trying things." If X did not seem effective, they tried Z. For example, one faculty member described this experience of "tinkering" with aspects of class, based on her "educated guess":

> Usually, it seems to me that something has registered for me or for them as ineffective, and then I'll tend to tinker with it, and usually something else appears that I have to tinker with later. My abstract concepts about my teaching, my theory of what is or isn't happening, is just an educated guess. I just try to be in the practice of it a lot. I might be curious about what it would be like not to do it that way, so I'll do it this way. Usually I know if something didn't work—and I'll try something else. (Faculty member in the humanities)

Another faculty member spoke about trying to get students to understand their own learning, as the following quotation, used also in chapter 3, illustrates:

> The other thing I do is the Bloom's [Taxonomy] with them. What I'm finding is that too many times students would come to me after the first test and say, "I studied so hard," but they haven't studied smart, because they don't know how. When

they look at the test, they can't figure out why they got some answers and why they didn't get others. I've started introducing Bloom's Taxonomy the first day of class, and explaining that we are moving more and more into more sophisticated and higher levels of Bloom's. So in class, when I ask questions, I will tell them what level of Bloom's it is—"This is a knowledge question." "This is an application question." And I ask them, too, which is easier for them. I tell them the best way to get good at those upper-level questions is in study groups. And when they get their exams back, they not only get their scores, they get their Bloom's scores, too. The answer key gives them not only the answer, but the general model the question represents and what level of Bloom's the question is. Also [two of my colleagues] and I came up with a Bloom's study chart for students. "If you scored badly in this, what can you do by yourself and what can you do in a group to improve this score?" I tell them that if they got 70% or less in any area of the Bloom's, they have to go to this chart and figure out how to change the way they are studying. (Faculty member in the sciences/math)

"Member Checks": Listening to Students

Member checking in qualitative research is a method of verifying a researcher's analysis of data with those who supplied the data. It is a way of finding out if the researcher's interpretation of her research subjects' experiences matches what the subjects think they reported about those experiences. Although faculty rarely initiate the kinds of organized member checks found in research studies, they often listen to students as a way of verifying or clarifying their own understanding of students' experience in class. For example, as reported in chapter 5, they pay attention to course evaluations to see if students' perspectives jibe with their own perceptions of the work they have done. Sometimes when faculty members make a change to their courses, they also send out short surveys or follow-up questions to verify their own ideas about the effectiveness of those changes. In addition, faculty members often get information from students in other ways and places, such as during office hours, from email messages students send them, or from students' comments in class. The following three examples illustrate these approaches:

I think I've made evolutionary improvements, incremental improvements, based on student feedback, both formal and informal. By formal I mean class feedback I do at week three and week six. [I do this kind of class feedback] so I can just get a real sense, some objective sense, of what students are thinking, so I can echo that back to students and say that I'll try to respond to things if there are things to respond to. That helps me clue into what is going on. And then there's the evaluation that happens at the end of the quarter. (Faculty member in the social sciences)

A quarter after doing this, I emailed my students and asked them what they thought about Bloom's. I got one student who said, "I can remember thinking why is she teaching us Bloom's, which has nothing to do with physiology. She could be teaching us about the heart. But then I realized she's helping me figure out where my learning problems are so I can spend more time at that level than at a different level. I kind of do that in all my classes now—look at what level the teacher is teaching to and adjust my learning to match that level." Some students see the benefit and some don't—and because responses are anonymous, I can't tell if there is a correlation between that and their grades. (Faculty member in the sciences/math)

Another reason I made this change was that students would come in and talk to me during office hours. That's really helpful to me because I can see one-on-one by asking them questions how much they are comprehending. I saw that students would come in confused, and then I'd know I needed to go back and cover that piece again so they would be able to understand the next stage of the argument. (Faculty member in the humanities)

Other Sources of Information

As the faculty member whose quotation began this chapter suggests, gathering information on teaching is often the result of a kind of openness to information about teaching and learning even when it comes from unusual directions. For example, in addition to the methods described in this chapter, faculty members spoke of learning about teaching and learning from their spouses, as the following two examples illustrate:

> I was cooking dinner and listening to [my wife] teach the [piano] lesson in an adjacent room, and she came in after her student left. She was done for the day and she said, "My job is to teach my students how to practice." And it was just like this Zen gong went off in my head and said, "My job is to teach my students how to study." That's really guided my teaching and everything we are doing with these students. (Faculty member in the sciences/math)

> My husband is a teacher. . . . he sort of widened my scope of thinking about what teaching means. He appreciates the experience students bring into class. I didn't used to do that. In the beginning, when they came in, whatever they had brought from home, that was immaterial to me. But in his teaching, he always considered that. So I have had over the years to consider that myself. And also he's given me specific tips for improving my teaching. (Faculty member in the social sciences)

Faculty also described parenting or interactions with and because of their children as helping them think about improving their teaching. For example:

> And the other thing that I've done in the last few years is that my children are in elementary school and not that often but once in a while, I go and am just that extra pair of hands in the classroom. I'm just watching how explicit their teachers are— their elementary school teachers. I think they are all gifted teachers. I think, "Oh yeah, I can do that. I could be explicit in that way. I could phrase a question in that way." It really gave me permission to do that. (Faculty member in the humanities)

In addition, faculty members described their own experience as learners as giving them insights, as this faculty member noted:

> Another little thing that I've done for the past couple of quarters, I've been in the UW Women's Choir, because a friend of mine is conducting it, and it's an amazing group. It really

impressed me how, about half of the people in it can't sing very well, but it sounds fantastic at the end. Thursday nights at 7 o'clock, I've been really impressed with those people who really aren't that good at what we are doing, but they have amazing focus. Just the amount of focus that a UW student can bring to a task—sometimes you forget that when you are standing at the front of a big hall, giving a lecture. But basically, I treat all my students like they are the girls in this choir. We had a concert the other night, and there was more than one [student] up in the balcony, waiting for it to be our turn, writing a paper. And that to me was the perfect UW student, because anybody else who had to write a paper might have skipped or they might be out in the hall. But [these] students—they want to get the full experience. But they still need to write the paper. And the concert was only going to be an hour. They could have not written the paper, there, but they were, "Oh a few extra minutes on the paper would help." So [I've learned to] appreciate that focus. (Faculty member in the humanities)

Finally, faculty members spoke of the gathering of experience as helping them to understand when they are teaching effectively and when they are not, as these two faculty members indicated:

I don't know how I learned to trust myself. You come out of a good class knowing you did well. You get a kind of a high from it. You come out of a bad one, and you know it, too. (Faculty member in the social sciences)

. . . changes in the diagnostic eye, being able to see what they are doing. I've always been able to tailor notes [on a performance] to a certain person, but those notes are better now. It's life experience that has made it better. (Faculty member in the arts)

Tracking the Effects of Change

In our interviews with faculty members, we asked them to tell us what the effects of the changes they described were and how they knew those were the effects. Faculty responses to this question were quite honest.

The most frequently given response was that it is hard to tell what the full effects of the change were, as this faculty comment illustrates:

> This is always the hardest point—measuring learning changes. Sometimes I might look at grades—are fewer students failing or is the average higher? But this gets pretty tricky because sometimes what I'm finding is that I'm giving harder questions, so the average is staying the same. Also there are many reasons why students fail. There could be other things going on outside in their lives. And the one study I did do, where I looked at their answers and compared the general model to the number of points they got on the question. That gave me some information, but were those just the smarter students? (Faculty member in the sciences/math)

In noting that they were unsure how to test the effects of change in students, faculty sometimes pointed to their own observations of the class as indicators that change was effective, as these two faculty members indicate:

> I don't know. I don't know how to test that. I know, for example, that students were doing the reading because they were doing the quiz, so for the first time I have documented evidence that they are doing the reading. I didn't have that before. Now I know that they are doing the reading. That makes me feel fantastic. I know that they got better at the readings, so I have a sense that they know how to read better. It's a crude measure but I think they know how to read an academic article better than they did before my class. (Faculty member in the social sciences)

> This is the best question. I don't think I have a way of measuring this or proving this in the sense that I can offer empirical evidence of improvement. All I can say is that I do cover more now in first-year Polish than I used to cover. I sense that I can go faster with the material, but I can't quantify that. (Faculty member in the humanities)

Furthermore, faculty members often distinguished between changes they could track and changes they could not, as this faculty member described:

[In this class] the grades have gone up, and the quality of the answers on the final has distinctly improved. I don't think it's an artifact of the expectation for high grades around here. I can tell by the quality of their work, by the student teaching evaluations that come in, from the things students say to me as they're walking out after the final exam, and from the students who stay in touch with you afterwards. [But in this second class] I haven't seen changes in students' learning so clearly. There was one time when I tried to put all the political stuff together, all the religious stuff—and that was a disaster. The course evaluations were kind, but it was clear from what came in that this approach to the class left them totally confused. I don't think the reorganization in that class has had a significant effect on their learning. (Faculty member in the social sciences)

For some faculty members, the idea of turning the classroom into a study of what worked and what did not seemed challenging, as this faculty member's comment suggests:

You know the thing that is a genuine deficit in my approach to things is I've never been able to figure out how to test that and how to control that. I don't think it's easy. I mean you can't divide the class in half and half of them do one thing and half do another thing. (Faculty member in the sciences/math)

But a few faculty members found ways to conduct such tests, comparing results of specific exam questions in the altered class with those of students in an earlier course or comparing fail and drop rates before and after changes.

Faculty members used other external indicators to measure the success of their changes, as well, such as improvements in their course evaluation scores or using mid-quarter evaluations to check in with students' perceptions of their learning. Several faculty members pointed to positive email or face-to-face conversations with students about changes to the class and their learning. One faculty member tracked his work from day to day. In his words:

I wrote things down—which exercises were more productive and which less. (Faculty member in the humanities)

For the most part, however, when faculty felt that they could tell whether the changes they made had been effective, they frequently pointed to improved student performance on papers, exams, and other assignments as evidence that the changes they had made had been effective, or they said that they had noticed a higher or more thoughtful level of in-class questions and discussions. As two examples from faculty explain:

> When I started doing this—making them work the practice problems outside of class, turn in their work, and go over it in class—the level of thinking was far beyond anything I'd ever seen before. It was jaw-dropping. I wasn't anticipating this at all, but it was a huge jump in the thinking. And students were more confident about saying things, because maybe they'd thought about it with their friends, maybe by themselves—I don't care how they do that—but they had thought about it. They were in a different place, which I could see by how they talked about it in class. (Faculty member in business)

> I could see a quality improvement in my students' work when I instituted the stepped-approach to the larger project. (Faculty member in the arts)

In other words, faculty members used the same research approaches to assess the effects of change that they used to determine that they needed to make change in their classes in the first place.

Those who believe that faculty members' observations and judgments about students' learning are not evidence of learning will be unmoved by our account of their efforts to hold themselves accountable to their own learning goals for students. For example, most assessment experts and practitioners believe that grades are not valid measures of the quality of students' learning because they are too subjective (Shenoy, 2011), raising questions about all faculty judgments of student learning. We suggest, however, in the face of the continuous work that faculty apparently do to know if their work is effective, this assumption must be revisited. The multiple methods that faculty members use to understand their students' learning have been praised by assessment experts (Bain, 2004; Angelo & Cross, 1993), and they bring those same methods to bear on evaluating the changes they bring to their classrooms. Our findings on the research approaches faculty members use raise questions about general assumptions regarding who can and should judge the quality of students' learning.

Summary: Researching One's Own Teaching Effectiveness

In his book on excellence in college teaching, Ken Bain (2004) said:

> . . . we must struggle with the meaning of learning within our disciplines and how best to cultivate and recognize it. For that task, we don't need routine experts who know all the right procedures but adaptive ones who can apply fundamental principles to all the situations and students they are likely to encounter, recognizing when invention is both possible and necessary and that there is no single "best way" to teach. (pp. 174–175)

Struggling with the meaning of learning within one's discipline and being able to recognize when invention is both possible and necessary requires a willingness to experience what Lindlof and Taylor (2010) described earlier as "a kind of epistemological vulnerability that can be frustrating and humbling" (p. 134). Faculty members described such moments as a normal part of their teaching experience, such as this faculty member described:

> I spent a lot of time and effort on [the class I was teaching]. I learned a lot of the students' names. I really enjoy teaching. I was using what I call a modified Socratic style. I stop all the time, and I am asking students' questions. I try not to talk more than a couple minutes before I'm asking the students to respond. And the students really like this teaching style, so the course got very high evaluations. But about 20% of the students failed, including drops. We have a very low drop rate, because it's very difficult to get into the class—we always have a waiting list, so drops are only about 3%. So we had 16–17% of students who were getting Ds or Fs, [which meant] they

were not able to go on in biology, and these are sophomores. So here my [department] chair was saying, "Oh wow, look at these evaluations. You are doing a great job." And I was looking at the failure rate and thinking, "I stink. This is disaster." I didn't sleep for a week. I just thought that my job was to help students learn and they are not getting it. (Faculty member in the sciences/math)

Perhaps not sleeping for a week was an extreme reaction to the evidence that one's teaching needed to change in order to advance students' learning. However, again and again, faculty reported creating ways to know if their students were learning and, as a result, ways to adjust their teaching. They struggled, in Ken Bain's words, with how best to cultivate the meaning of learning in their disciplines.

Some scholars of higher education, such as Derek Bok (2006), believe that leaving "appropriate teaching methods . . . to the discretion of individual professors" (p. 315) leads to faculty caring a great deal about keeping their course content current but not about improving their teaching methods. As Bok sees it, "Professors seldom receive clear evidence of how much students are learning," and faculty members who try different teaching strategies in order to improve learning are "a minority" (pp. 315–316).

Our findings in the UW GIFTS suggest that Bok is at least half wrong about that. It is true that faculty have difficulty gathering evidence of the effects of change in their classes—as the faculty, themselves, noted. However, we found that faculty used wide-ranging research skills to seek to know what might best cultivate learning. For example, after the faculty member speaking in the previous quotation had that conversation with his department chair, he entered into a series of experiments on teaching and learning in his large introductory classes that would dramatically improve the learning and the success rate in the class. Other faculty members made changes to individual assignments, pared away "content" to allow for greater student participation in the classroom, added field trips and labs, and experimented with technology, as we saw in earlier chapters. Furthermore, they tracked the effectiveness of these changes, as well, consulting experts for help, analyzing student-produced texts, conducting member checks, or observing student behavior in class. Faculty members used similar research approaches to assess the changes they had made and sometimes reported making changes to their changes until they were satisfied that students were learning what faculty had intended them to learn. This research "stance" was not an anomaly found in the work of one or two dedicated faculty members. It was widespread, crossing faculty ranks, disciplines, and genders. All of them were out there seeking and using a number of sources in order to know about their students' learning.

What motivated faculty to take on these research tasks? Conducting extensive and continual research on one's own performance is not a normal expectation in the world of work in general. Although they constantly criticize educators for their work, legislators rarely conduct "member checks" with constituents to see if their own perceptions of their successes are accurate; they rarely look for evidence that they have improved society in order to determine how they might better govern. Doctors do not mail evaluations to their patients to get feedback on their approaches to medicine, and lawyers do not scrutinize taped consultations with clients to see if their explanations of the law were clear to those in trouble with it. After the 2008 financial crash, we have no illusions about financial institutions checking to see if their practices are beneficial to the public they served.

In addition, as mentioned previously, college faculty have not been taught to conduct research on learning as part of their graduate training, and they rarely hear faculty or mentors discuss their teaching goals and practices. Furthermore, faculty have no expectation of external rewards for improving their teaching. Great teachers do not get raises or promotions; they do not get stock options, company cars, or holiday bonuses; they rarely get praise from administrators for their teaching work.

The faculty with whom we spoke may have been motivated to engage in research on their own practices for many complex and even personal reasons, but the only common motivator we could discern across the interviews was that they wanted to do a good job. Their work as teachers was creative and complex, and they cared about it. Therefore, as many who study motivation and behavior (Ariely et al., 2009; Kohn, 1999) would predict, faculty members were willing to work hard—including seeking and being open to information about what they were not doing well—because they cared about their work as teachers.

9

WERE THERE DIFFERENCES ACROSS GROUPS?

The class is positive. It gives them a very positive experience at the UW. That's important because it is hard to learn a language. As a young adult you are put back in the position of someone who is illiterate, and that is frustrating for students. So if you can keep a positive atmosphere in class, they learn how to trust you, and they thrive.

—Faculty member in the humanities

Thus far, we have identified some common changes that faculty make to their classes and some shared reasons for those changes. In addition, we have identified three themes that crossed our interviews and interview questions, discussed in chapters 6, 7, and 8. This chapter seeks to explore differences across groups of UW GIFTS participants. To do so, we group the interviews in three different ways: differences based on faculty characteristics, differences we noted in interviews with faculty of color and with white faculty, and differences in the interviews of faculty members in three disciplinary areas. In addition, we also compare faculty responses to questions about change in their teaching with those of graduate student participants in the two focus groups we conducted. Although the focus of this chapter is on differences, it is important to remember that the similarities across groups were stronger than the differences.

Differences Based on Faculty Characteristics

The strength of similarities across groups was brought into focus by the statistical comparisons we conducted of the changes and reasons for change reported by faculty subgroups. For this analysis, we used R (R Development Core Team, 2011), a computer language and software environment for statistical computing and graphics, and compared faculty responses in the following subgroups, also described in chapter 2:

> *Selection method.* We compared the responses of faculty who were referred to us by department chairs, were randomly selected, or were selected by researchers.
>
> *Gender.* Faculty members were identified by the UW as male or female, and we compared the two groups' responses to changes and reasons for changes they had made to their courses.
>
> *Ethnicity.* Because we had so few faculty members of color, we divided our sample into two groups—white (87.3%) and faculty of color (12.7%)—and compared their responses.
>
> *Academic rank.* We compared the responses of faculty in the UW GIFTS who were professors, associate professors, assistant professors, senior lecturers, and lecturers.
>
> *Years at the UW.* As a way of determining the impact of the UW environment on changes faculty members made to their teaching and their reasons for change, we compared faculty interviewees who had been at the UW for a short time (1–6 years), those who had been here an "average" amount of time (7–13 years), and those who had been working at the UW for a long time (14–40 years).
>
> *Disciplinary area.* We grouped faculty participants into four major disciplinary categories: 1) arts and humanities; 2) social sciences; 3) science (including faculty in forestry and oceanography), math, and engineering; and 4) "other" (business, architecture/built environments, and informatics faculty) in order to compare their responses to interview questions.

In addition to these faculty characteristics, we compared changes faculty made in teaching and their reasons for change by the size of their classes. For this analysis, we grouped classes into three categories: large (61 students or more), medium (30–60 students), and small (4–29 students).

Our analysis revealed no significant differences in faculty descriptions of the changes they had made to their classes. In other words, all groups were making similar kinds of changes in their courses, regardless of how they were selected for participation in the UW GIFTS, what disciplinary areas they were working in, whether they were males or females, and so on.

In addition, our analysis revealed only three statistically significant differences for faculty members' reasons for change, as follows (see also appendix C for relevant statistics):

> Changes in the courses taught by lecturers were more likely to be made in order to advance student learning than were changes made in the courses of faculty from other ranks (professors, associate professors, assistant professors, and senior lecturers). Although this difference was statistically significant, it was not necessarily meaningful, since advancing student learning was one of the major causes of change for all faculty members.
>
> Similarly, changes faculty made for large classes were more likely to be made in order to advance student learning than changes made to medium-sized classes, and changes to small-sized classes were more likely to be made in order to advance student learning than changes in medium-sized classes.
>
> The changes made by faculty members of color were somewhat more likely to be rooted in faculty members' values or teaching philosophies than were the changes white faculty members made to their classes.

The lack of significant differences among the various subgroups of faculty participants is an important finding. The lack of differences among faculty of differing ranks challenges those who argue that once faculty members get tenure, they no longer care about their teaching. In fact, several teachers spoke about tenure as the step that allowed them to experiment with their teaching, as this example shows:

> I take risks—and that's why I am glad I have tenure. I can fail. I can try things. (Faculty member in the social sciences)

In addition, this result challenges the ideas that women care about teaching more than men do; that faculty in the humanities are more concerned about teaching than are their colleagues in the sciences; that teaching improvement is something only new faculty do; and that faculty teaching large lecture-style classes do not concern themselves with the quality of learning in their classes as much as faculty members teaching small classes do. In addition, this finding challenges the notion that those faculty members who are *recognized* as "thoughtful about their teaching" are the only ones who think carefully about their teaching. In fact, we found no differences between faculty members identified by their chairs as good teachers and those we randomly selected for the study or those we selected because we were interested in talking with them. Indeed, the lack of significant differences between faculty groups suggests that faculty members—regardless of their differences—reported making similar changes to their courses for similar reasons. This does not mean that there were no differences across individual faculty, but in their thinking about change, faculty members were quite similar.

Faculty of Color

We were curious to learn whether the teaching experiences of faculty of color differed in any ways from those of majority faculty on our campus, particularly after our statistical analysis revealed that faculty members of color made changes to their teaching based on their values and teaching philosophies more frequently than did other faculty members. Therefore, after analyzing the interviews of all faculty members, we re-examined the seven interviews we conducted with faculty of color to see if we could identify any experiences that were shared across them that differed from those of Caucasian faculty.

Change Emerging from Values and Teaching Philosophy

As noted, our statistical comparison of changes and reasons for change across faculty groups showed a greater tendency among faculty of color than among white faculty members to make changes in their teaching because of values or teaching philosophies. We reviewed the interviews of the faculty members of color to see if there were any common threads linking the values they described. Aside from a commitment to social justice—a value common to many faculty members teaching in the social sciences and humanities—we found few similarities. The values and philosophies described by the faculty of color participating in the UW GIFTS were different from each other. For example, one faculty member spoke of a shift in her understanding of students that linked with changes in teaching philosophy, which, in turn, led to changes in the classroom. As she described it:

> When I started teaching undergraduates, I went in there think-ing that they would all find everything as fascinating as I did. Then I realized I had to convince them that this was important. I think I saw all these students who looked bored out of their gourds. Hearing them respond to my tests and my questions. Hearing what they said about their professors, like "All I had to do to get through that course is to just figure out what she wants from me." Then I realized how much fun it is to take people who haven't thought about this area and to convince them that it's interesting. It's a very different teaching philoso-phy. (Faculty member in the sciences/math)

Another faculty member spoke about the learning value in moving away from teaching the most famous poets in his culture to teaching those less well known. In his words:

> Those established poets, there is a lot of material on them al-ready, but the minor poets don't get as much attention, and they deserve some of that. The highest poets are more ornamen-tal—not ornamental, really, but more complex, dense, richer. But poetry is part of everyday life in south Asia, so people don't go to the master poets all the time. There is an everyday level. That came up with some of my students. They started compos-ing poems themselves. And if they are comparing their work only to the highest poets, they will feel discouraged. They need to be comparing them to others writing in the everyday. Poets who are simpler make poetry more accessible and closer to our everyday experience. (Faculty member in the humanities)

Finally, in a third example, a faculty member spoke about weaving her teaching philosophy into her classes, even though the content of those courses differed:

Even though you might think from reading my syllabi that I'm content-driven—there are only one or two things I am ever teaching. The first is opening critical perception and perspective, and the second is that in [my discipline], there's a lot about helping people work across differences, to find their place in contributing to social justice and social change. In every class I am working on those two things, but I teach really diverse classes. (Faculty member in the social sciences)

Because of the differences in the values and teaching philosophies that informed the changes these seven faculty members made, as well as the small sample size we were dealing with, we could not generalize about why faculty of color were more likely to make changes because of those values than were other faculty members. Perhaps faculty of color operate more from a set of beliefs than do white faculty members in general; perhaps faculty of color are more comfortable talking about their beliefs and values than are white faculty. We were unable to check back with our interviewees about this interesting finding.

Microaggression

Although the changes that faculty of color made in their classes and their reasons for change were more similar than different from those of white faculty members, we noted a few experiences that crossed some of the interviews of the faculty of color that we did not find in the interviews of Caucasian faculty. The first of these were a few incidents that we would define as microaggression. Solórzano et al. (2000) define racial microaggression as subtle visual, verbal, or nonverbal insults, which are sometimes unconscious or unintentional, directed toward people of color. The recipient of the microaggressive act or behavior is often uncertain whether that behavior was racially motivated or just generally thoughtless or rude behavior. Hearing about experiences with microaggression dismayed us but did not surprise us. The literature on racial microaggression (Sue et al., 2008; Solórzano et al., 2000; Pierce et al., 1977) shows that people of color in American society deal with racial microaggression daily. A staff member in an earlier study we conducted at the UW provided an example:

The other day, I tried to stop [my bus driver as I was running for the bus] and he pulled out a few bus lengths and made me walk to the door, and then says to me, "You were late." Then he waits there and three attractive women get on the bus. He waits for them. How do I read that? Is he a racist? I don't know. And that experience frames my morning. (Pitre et al., 2006, p. 26)

Microaggression is pervasive—found in every space people occupy, including virtual space (Beyer, 2012). All people of color—regardless of their gender, appearance, social status, education, age, or position— have experienced it, which means that all of them spend some part of each day weighing such experiences. Navigating them is a normal part of the life of students of color on predominantly white college campuses,[1] and, as Hurtado et al. (1999) point out, whatever students of color experience on campuses, faculty and staff of color also experience.

Microaggression is not just racial. People react in microaggressive ways to all manner of difference, making subtle comments to people with disabilities and behaving aggressively to those of the opposite sex, for example. Indeed, many faculty and graduate students report that students' treatment of female faculty differs from their treatment male faculty, although we did not gather information on those differences in our interviews.[2] In the words of one of the faculty members of color in the UW GIFTS: "Race, gender, and age matter in teaching on this campus." The common denominator in all microaggressive behavior is that it follows power relationships, with those in positions of power in society behaving and speaking in subtly aggressive ways to those who are perceived to have less power.

Although not mentioned with great frequency, some of the faculty members of color in the UW GIFTS described behaviors from students that fit the definition of racial microaggression. The faculty members describing such behavior identified other aspects of the courses they were teaching that might have contributed to it. For example, they spoke about the contribution to students' discomfort that the content of their courses might produce. All of them dealt with issues of social equality or justice in courses that included issues of race, class, gender, and/or sexual orientation—topics that the faculty members of color felt might be difficult for students who may not have discussed such issues before. One faculty member said:

I deal with a lot of intense topics around race, class, and gender that are new to a lot of people, and having those topics be taught by a faculty member of color may be a new experience for a lot of people, and they may not be sure how to respond to it.

Another faculty member spoke of the same challenge:

I have had a couple other difficult times in classes, I think related to racial dynamics and privilege, but I would have to say that my mistake is in taking on the teaching of classes that center the lives of non-white peoples in a resistance/empowerment modality and not being prepared for the resistance, in turn, from white students not used to having to navigate the periphery for a change. I have a lot to learn in that area, and I intend to do that learning in my lifetime.

In addition to pointing to the role that course topics might play in students' behaviors, two of the faculty members spoke about the effects that "safety in numbers" might produce—the anonymity that students often imagine they have in a large class. As one of them put it:

These were wonderful [students] when I got them one-on-one. They . . . were very respectful. But there was something about being in the group setting together and making it into a space that was not a classroom.

Although having to confront challenging topics and the safety that students might find in numbers both may have contributed to students' behaviors, it seemed obvious that racial microaggression was also at play in the teaching experiences that a few members described. For example, one faculty member noted:

I am not casual in class. I don't wear jeans or do things that [other] colleagues can do. I feel that's not so possible for me. I think you do get challenged quite a bit—I don't know if that's because [of my race or my gender]—but some young white guys are just not quite engaging with you. I've learned to kind of joke and play when a couple of those guys are in my class, and eventually they love what's going on because I just kind of work with them. But it draws my attention to a specific part of the class.

Another faculty member described a similar kind of experience:

One woman in a small class loudly told another student that this other faculty member was "a real professor" in contrast to me, for example. I feel that there is a sort of disrespect in that. My age, [race, gender]—they aren't used to seeing someone like me in front of them. I had a good number of students of color in [a large lecture class], and some students said on the comment sheets of the course evaluation that I talked too much to the [students of color]. One said that I was racist. But I knew those students' names because many of them were in [the class I taught the quarter before]. I think these things are normal for [people] of color.

Cultivating Respect for the Classroom

Another aspect of teaching that some of the faculty of color shared was a focus on actively cultivating respect in their classes. Other faculty members also spoke about respect, but their focus was on communicating to students that they respected students' ideas and presence, as discussed in chapter 7. Similarly, the faculty members of color who talked about respect in the classroom spoke about it in those terms. For example, all three designed classes that included students' participation and contributions, as this faculty member described:

Over the years I do more and more film and video clips . . . and I ask them to send me things that they find that they think may be relevant to class. They often do and then I'll show it in class and we'll talk about it. They like multi-media things. They're quick and flashy. And then I try to make them see those clips from this or that theoretical perspective. When I show something in class that a student sent me, I tell them that so-and-so emailed me this and it's related to what we were talking about yesterday. That also gets them excited because they start to pay attention to the media around them and there is always something relevant going on out there.

However, a few of the faculty of color also spoke of cultivating another kind of respect. They described setting rules to ensure that their classroom spaces, as well as the people in them, were treated respectfully. In their words:

I do pay attention to being respected, so I have a hypersensitivity about that, tuning into whether someone is disrespecting my classroom. I don't want them putting their feet up on the furniture or reading the paper. I tell them at the beginning of my class that I am really old-fashioned. I tell them, "I'm putting in a lot on my work here, so will you please put these things, like reading the paper or sleeping, in another place if you have to do them? Just take a day off if you need to do those things."

I make students take their hoodies off in class and keep their heads up. I tell them to do that. I don't want to further stigmatize [anyone], but I want respect in the classroom. The first day of class—one student came in late and said, "Yo, homie!" to another student while I was lecturing. I told him that was unacceptable and told him to sit down. Now, I have my 10 rules that I give them the first day of class—no reading, no texting—that kind of thing.

Commitment to Community

Another aspect of teaching that several of the faculty members of color shared was a sense of commitment to community. This sense of commitment caused faculty members to encourage students of color at the university in a number of ways; to bring information about race, gender, and ethnicity into the academic life of the campus and the greater community; and to help other faculty of color navigate the university successfully.

In speaking about commitment to students of color, and particularly to young male students of color—a population at risk in higher education—one of the three faculty members said:

For a lot of faculty of color, it is just different. There's a different sense of what my responsibility is to them and what I want it to be. It's not a burden, but I understand very intimately all of the challenges that these young men have on this campus, and I want them to succeed. That's not to say that some white faculty don't take that on as well. But for many of us who are where we are because of the support of our communities, we need to understand that we need to pay it forward as well. That's why I have such a hard time saying no to some things, because I know it's important to mentor students of color. And I enjoy doing that; I enjoy that part of my job. There was a piece in the job description about the ability to mentor students of color being a plus.

Another faculty member's interview echoed that sense of commitment, saying:

I feel responsible because these are my brothers, my husband, my children. Because I was an undergraduate here, I know how hard it is to be a person of color on campus. People like [Professor X] and others did the same for me when I was an undergraduate here. That's, of course, an additional responsibility. It creates less time. Again, I try to make sure I'm really fair. The extra things I do are going to events. I want students of color to see my face out there, to know that there are faculty of color on campus. It is so important to let these students know that we're here and we're supportive.

Often faculty members described commitments to their students of color as calling on them to track students they knew were having difficulty, to assist with programs that included large numbers of underrepresented minority students, to give talks that informed the public about race and society, and sometimes to provide emergency help to students who did not feel comfortable sharing their stories with other faculty members or staff. One faculty member described such an experience with a student athlete:

She came to see me and told me she was so unhappy and needed support. I drove her down to the Athletic Office and waited for her to tell the counselor what she told me. [When she didn't appear to be getting enough help], I tracked down the sports psychiatrist in the [student union building] and said, "You need to go talk to this student right now." I felt she just hurt so bad, and she was this big kid with tears in her eyes. And she was all alone. Her family was far away. I also found out in the car that she remembered me from a breakfast that I always go to.

The responsibility that faculty of color felt toward students of color was fueled by the responses from those students, who sought out their classes and their mentorship. As one faculty member put it:

The one change I've noticed has been that since students know about me, I have more students of color.

This phenomenon of students of color gravitating toward faculty of color is well reported (Hurtado et al., 1999), and faculty of color described both undergraduate and graduate students of color coming to speak with them, on one occasion before the faculty member was fully unpacked at the university.

Related to their commitment to students of color, some of the faculty members of color also spoke about their commitment to broadening access to ideas about diversity in their fields. For example, some moved from teaching small-sized classes to large classes, as this faculty member said:

I started off teaching this class the way it had been taught previously, which was as a 40-person class. I realized that [this] is a huge major and more students needed to go through this media literacy class, so I made it bigger. I'd never taught a large lecture before.

Another aspect of a strong sense of commitment to community that some of the faculty members of color in the UW GIFTS described concerned helping other underrepresented faculty members succeed in academia. In the words of one of those faculty members:

There have been some eye-opening things about being here, and that was one of them—I saw I was really kind of on my own. I didn't have the support I had as a PhD student in ethnic studies with all women of color mentors—people who were just looking out for me. So I tried to create a group of my peers.

Another faculty member said this about this group:

Three women formed [the group], because they felt that there needed to be a safe environment where we could share research interests and experiences as junior people of color in the tenure track. We meet once a month, in someone's house, and now there are 26 or 27 members. We do what we need to do to protect and support each other.

Differences: Faculty of Color

Although faculty members of color and white faculty members reported similar changes to their courses and reasons for those changes, there were some differences between the experiences of the two groups. Faculty members of color reported making changes to their teaching based on their own values and teaching philosophies more often than did white faculty members—a difference we could not explain.

In addition, a review of the interviews of the seven faculty members of color showed that some of the faculty members described what could be identified as racial microaggression from students. Faculty members attributed these behaviors as related, in part, to the challenging nature of their course material and to the "cover" provided by large classes.

Also, several faculty members of color expressed a powerful commitment to helping students of color believe in their own academic abilities and be successful at the university. Their desire to advance all students' learning put them in the position of expanding smaller courses into large lecture classes, even though this shift was not always immediately comfortable. As one of the faculty members said:

This large lecture class was not how I usually teach. My teaching is based on a pretty intimate relationship with the students; it's based on who they are. So it was pretty odd having a back row of students who put their hoods over their heads and went to sleep and to manage TAs for the first time.

Finally, some faculty members of color spoke of their commitment to strengthening their communities on campus—so much so that some of them created a group that continues to offer support and assistance to others like themselves. These differences may offer some explanation for why faculty members of color were more likely to make changes based on their values and teaching philosophy than white faculty members were, although we did not trace clear causal paths between them.

Three Disciplines

Another area of difference we investigated concerned the effects of disciplines on change in teaching. UW GIFTS participants included four or five faculty members from three disciplines—foreign languages, biology, and communication. We reviewed the interviews of each discipline separately to see if we could identify pedagogical differences that might be linked to those disciplines. Our findings showed some practices and values that might be said to be markers for classes in each field.

Foreign Languages

We interviewed five faculty members who were teaching foreign languages. Several themes emerged from their interviews, which might be identified as uniquely related to foreign language pedagogy. These themes included the importance of:

> Creating a safe classroom for students to practice new language
> skills
> Using daily assignments
> Providing students with early evidence of progress
> Giving students frequent opportunities to hear and practice the
> language; opening access to the language

CREATING A SAFE SPACE FOR TRYING. The strongest theme that emerged from the interviews with foreign language instructors was the need to make the language classroom feel like a safe place for students. Faculty members said that learning a language requires the learner's willingness to make mistakes publicly. Therefore, all five faculty members spoke of creating classrooms where correctness was secondary to trying and correction took a back seat to encouragement. As one faculty member described it:

> The atmosphere is hugely important in language classes. It has to challenge them, but you have to also create a place where it's safe for them to say something no matter how stupid they think it sounds. If you are trying to learn a language, you are vulnerable. You know you will sound ridiculous. Students are always comparing themselves to each other. So you try to make the place feel safe for them, that it's okay to try to share ideas, and others will respond.

Faculty members in this group spoke of creating activities that allowed students to make mistakes safely, such as this quotation illustrates:

> I do a lot of stuff where [we practice] whatever construction we are [learning] at the moment—today the genitive case. I gave them these cards, and let's say a card has a picture of a yellow skirt on it. They show the card to a student and have a conversation about that skirt. So that conversation is private between the two, and then they exchange cards and go on to converse with someone else about their new cards. By the end of this exercise, they have practiced with 20 people on 20 nouns, and it's a semi-private environment for them to have those conversations in. Anything you can do to make this kind of practice less threatening is good.

Furthermore, the need for safety and comfort in taking risks over correct use of grammar and vocabulary was something one of the faculty members we interviewed was trying to teach TAs in her department who were teaching first-year language courses. As she described:

> I really want them to understand how difficult it is for someone to be immersed in a language they do not understand. I don't want them to ever feel impatient, to not want to answer a question. I want them to totally respect the learner and understand where they are coming from. So we ask them to go sit in a class of a language they don't understand and see what it feels like.

I do want them to also give confidence to the students. I want them to communicate to the students that anyone can learn, and I do want them also to understand the way we teach the language, so that the students can actually communicate. Many people spend years in the language classroom and get out after three or four years of French or Spanish, and they can't even speak a correct sentence. So obviously there has to be a better way. Correctness and accuracy come over time—they will fall in place over time. The main thing is to make yourself understood with your own tools.

So the teacher has to understand that it's okay to make mistakes. I think beginning teachers make the mistake of thinking that because they explain all the rules to students, the students will say things correctly. So we do need to understand what happens in the brain, to be aware that students will do it correctly eventually. That takes patience from the instructor. Comprehension occurs before production. Even in my own native language I can understand everything someone says who is much more educated than I am, but I couldn't reproduce it.

In addition, a few of the faculty members in this group spoke of this emphasis on creating a safe space for students as a new idea, describing language instruction that they had received in other countries as focused on correctness and as somewhat punitive. In addition, one faculty member said that the idea of creating a safe space was not new but the ways she was implementing that idea had changed over time. In her words:

What I think is important hasn't changed, but the way I bring it about has changed. I've always thought that students need to feel comfortable and in an environment where they can participate. But the way I've tried to bring that about has changed, depending on where I was, what the students were like, and my level of motivation or confidence in any particular quarter.

WORK THAT IS DUE EVERY DAY. The second theme we could identify from the five foreign language faculty members' interviews was the importance of giving students daily assignments. Four of the five faculty members explicitly described requiring students to complete or turn in short pieces of writing, homework on grammar or vocabulary, quizzes, or other activities both online and on paper every day of class. The reason such daily assignments were necessary was because language learning, like mathematics, is cumulative and because foreign language faculty often spoke of wanting to devote class time to "communication" or learning to speak and interact in the language of study, rather than on rote learning activities. For example:

> Students have to do online work in the workbook every night—practicing vocabulary and the old-fashioned drilling type stuff. I also have them study the same stuff in their language book that they are practicing online. And then they have conversations and do activities in groups in class. They bring what they've done online and what they've studied in their books to class. We do work in groups or have a debate or whatever.

> I give them all kinds of assignments. They may not like me sometimes! They have an assignment every day. In the first three weeks, when they are learning the script, they have to produce three pages of writing. After that, once we go into formal grammar, they do written grammar three times a week, and one day a week, they have a quiz. Sometimes I ask them after every week or two to send me a recording—some conversation they have learned modeling the tenses we have done.

The fifth faculty member in this group did not mention daily work. However, this faculty member taught only 400-level language courses, so it is likely that daily assignments were less important for students familiar with a language than for those new to it.

PROVIDING EVIDENCE EARLY THAT STUDENTS ARE PROGRESSING. A third theme that emerged from the interviews with foreign language faculty was the importance for language learners to see (or "hear" in this case) their own progress quickly, identified in three of the five faculty members' interview responses. In the words of one of the faculty members: "Students see that within a few weeks they went from knowing nothing to functioning at a basic level, and they are amazed by how much they've learned."

OPENING ACCESS TO THE LANGUAGE. The importance of finding a wide range of opportunities for students to hear and practice the language they were learning was a theme mentioned by this group of faculty in response to a number of different questions. For example, when asked about big directions of change in their teaching, three of the five faculty members spoke of making changes that gave students more opportunities to use the language they were teaching—helping students to be "learning all the time" in the words of one faculty member.

Providing students with multiple opportunities to hear the language they were learning and to see images from the places where people spoke those languages was a reason three of the five faculty noted for using technology. They specifically spoke of the gifts that the internet and YouTube have brought to language instruction. According to these faculty members, use of foreign language videos and images found online have allowed students to hear more of the languages they were learning, which has been particularly important for less-commonly taught languages. In the words of two of the faculty members:

> The thing that has made the biggest impact on the class is that I can tell them to watch a YouTube video or show it to them in class. I'm putting a video textbook on the web that they can access from home. The availability especially for a less commonly taught language like this—and my colleagues who teach other less commonly taught languages say the same thing—gives students so much more input now than they used to have. They can hear Polish for more hours or minutes in a day. That was the really big breakthrough in that class—the availability of Polish language that they can listen to.

> Right now through the internet I can create real clips, songs, or movies, or whatever. You can get a lot of information, and sometimes I need to infuse the class with real-life examples—so they believe that the language I'm teaching in class is actually used in other places—so they feel happy with that. Even in the first year, if they are not able to pick up all the material, they can pick up a few sentences and can make sense of some of the things that are going on. When they are poking around on the internet on their own—they hear Urdu and they wonder, "Are these Urdu sounds?"—and that recognition gives them a sense of satisfaction.

In addition, faculty members found ways beyond the internet to amplify students' exposure to the languages they were teaching. For example, one faculty member organized a table at the student union building and cricket matches where his beginning students could come together with more advanced students to have fun and speak the language. Another faculty member spoke of getting students involved in community events. As she put it:

> I have them involved in the Polish community, so they participate in events and they can try to use their language at those events. I do that even in the first year. The more Polish people you know, the more practice you can get. The Polish community in Seattle is not big, but it is very active. There are two competing film festivals and many other events.

Biology

We interviewed five faculty members from the Biology Department and were able to identify three teaching themes that appeared to cross their interviews. These themes were:

> Teaching students how to think scientifically rather than teaching them to collect scientific facts
> "Making" students learn
> Understanding that biology students are novice learners

It is important to keep in mind, however, that this group of faculty was unique even in their own department. Three of the five had received UW distinguished teaching awards—one after our interview was completed. Furthermore, three of the biology interviewees frequently interact over teaching. Therefore, it is not clear whether we have picked up pedagogical values and practices that are disciplinary or whether these practices relate only to this unique group inside the larger group of biology faculty. Nevertheless, the similarities we noted were interesting.

A FOCUS ON CRITICAL THINKING. Faculty members we interviewed in every department valued critical thinking, so its importance in biology was not unique. Even so, it was notable that all five of the biology faculty members we interviewed spoke about needing to help students move from a science learning model that focused on "academic memorization and puke-back answers on tests" to courses that "infuse a lot more critical thinking skills" into the class. One faculty member described addressing this challenge in the first biology course students take in the introductory series:

> We have this very difficult transition in biology, because we are getting these star students. They have been successful all their lives, [getting all As] in high school. . . . Then they come to biology, and we make them think. The most common written response that I get on the [comment] sheets that go with [course] evaluation forms is, "This is the first time I had to think." It's new to them.

Seymour and Hewitt's (1997) book about why students leave science, mathematics, and engineering (SME) majors provides evidence that supports this view. In carefully itemizing the difficulties that students—particularly women and minority students—have with SME majors, Seymour and Hewitt note that students often leave the SME fields in college because they have had "no introduction to theoretical material or to analytical modes of thought" (p. 79) in their high school science classes. In addition, our own assessment work at the UW with students majoring in biology suggests that there is a gap between high school and college biology. Students often characterize high school science classes as emphasizing memorization and college courses emphasizing deep conceptual understanding and the ability to use scientific reasoning to question or create information (Peterson et al., 2009).

For the biology faculty members we interviewed, the level of critical thinking they wanted their students to achieve could be more precisely defined as "thinking like a scientist," or in the words of one of the faculty members, quoted earlier in this book:

> I think I'm teaching them rigorous standards of scientific thinking and reasoning. I think the reason why paradigms don't shift very well in science is that we overlook things we don't expect to see. You have to examine alternative hypotheses—that's a critical thinking skill. And if they don't pay attention to their data, they won't see the things they don't expect. So I want

them to learn to write scientific papers but mostly I'm trying to teach them to think.

And in the words of another:

> But that's what we are trying to do in the whole biology se-ries—moving them from sticking in a number to actually syn-thesizing and applying concepts.

Faculty interviewees in biology reported that asking students to use scientific reasoning began in the first course students took in the form of written exams that required students to explain their thinking:

> We give these written exams. These are an enormous invest-ment on the part of the course coordinators, the lab TAs, and faculty. And we are devoted. For us it's all about, "We don't want you to understand this stuff well enough to pick a pre-cisely correct answer out of a list; you need to explain it to me."

Faculty members also described asking students to apply skills to unfa-miliar problems, as this interviewee noted:

> In the lecture, as a way to help them move from just taking the material, memorizing it, and giving it right back, I give students different situations, sometimes unique situations that they will actually see on tests. In these situations, they have to take a set of skills that were discussed and apply them to different organisms that perhaps don't exist—that were sent from Mars or another planet, for instance, and they have to figure out, "Okay what do you do?" These are real-life scientific problems, where we try to get them to take information and apply it.

Another of the biology faculty members described a similar kind of thinking activity:

> I tell them I will give them some novel situations and they will have to be able to transfer their knowledge to that new thing. I tell them that I realize that they haven't had a lot of practice,

so they aren't very good at it yet, but that I have to start giving them that practice so they can get good at it.

Although all five faculty members required students to learn factual information, the purpose of that kind of memorization was so that students could apply it, connect it, or use it as a way into scientific inquiry. For the biology faculty, facts allowed students to think scientifically, and they saw their teaching work as helping students do that—actually, as "making" them do it, as the next section describes.

"MAKING" STUDENTS LEARN. Related to the previous quotation about giving students practice, three of the five faculty members in biology spoke explicitly about the importance of practice in learning science— or of "making them learn," in the words of one of the faculty members. To make students learn, faculty usually required many small assignments—often daily activities—in the introductory biology courses they taught. One of the faculty members called the use of such activities "adding structure to the course."

This idea of giving students daily activities that required them to learn or to study course material was similar to the use of daily assignments that foreign language faculty described. However, in foreign languages, the focus of daily work was to help students accumulate vocabulary and usage skills early so that they could see their own early progress in the language. It was motivational as well as educational. In biology, the use of daily or near-daily activities inside and outside class was really more about forcing students into a regular study practice— hence, "making them learn."

Faculty members in biology required a variety of activities to foster learning. One faculty member teaching the first in the three-course introductory series in biology described assigning daily work:

> . . . we have to help them get better at [thinking], and we get better through practice with feedback. So the whole thrust in my changes in my teaching is just to help my students learn to be better students through practice. That's why they have to do reading quizzes and practice exams. That's why there are daily clicker questions. I am going to make them write down the three most important concepts, the three most important ideas every day in class. And I tell them that's where my exam questions come from. And then every day they have to declare

what they don't understand and take that to the tutor at the Instructional Center,[3] CLUE,[4] or our biology tutors here, and have them check it. To get them to use the help, you have to make them. I have to get my students to be better students. I have to make them.

Another faculty member talked about using clickers as a way to get students to learn. In her words:

They have these clicker questions and earlier questions in class. These questions make them study and keep up-to-date. They learn more when you force them to do the work even though they don't want to. . .

Activities were not necessarily daily. Another faculty member described the use of weekly summary sheets in her 300-level biology classroom:

I realize that students in the sciences have so much information coming to them so fast, they don't make connections. They keep all the pieces separate. My gut feeling is that the smartest kids in the class do make the connections. So I tried to think of a way to force them all to do that. So I make them turn in the summary sheet each week. It's one page and it's about what we've done that week. They are allowed to build from week to week. In this sheet, I strongly encourage them to use pictures, because I think it's easier to remember pictures and words. It's almost an annotated picture—a picture of the GI tract and then on the side expand it. Also I encourage them to include graphs—patch the pictures to the graphs and to flow diagrams. The first week they kind of struggle with it, but then after that week I show them some examples of what I think are good ones, and the second week, they catch on to the ideas much faster. I do score them, and they are kind of a pain, but I think they have really helped the students make connections— forced them to make connections. Again, this was based on my reading on concept maps—they need a framework and they need connections. I realized that I do summary sheets myself, and I thought: if I did them, why not have them do them? And then the feedback from the students reinforced that it's worth it. And I know it's important to make their thinking visible, and this really does that. I can use it diagnostically then too.

STUDENTS AS NOVICE LEARNERS. Biology faculty members spoke of students as being beginners in a learning process and of themselves as needing to track students along that path. Like the other characteristics that appeared to define instruction in the discipline, the sense of students as learners was a prominent theme across the UW GIFTS faculty interviews. However, it seemed especially strong among the biology faculty with whom we spoke, and especially the awareness that students were new learners in the field and, therefore, that faculty would need to help them advance from that point. For example, one biology faculty member spoke of what beginning learners need:

> . . . they are novices—they don't know that they don't understand. They underline everything in the text. They memorize everything in their notes. That's not because they are stupid or lazy. It's because they are novices. They can't do this. We need to help them get better . . . novices need [structure].

Two other faculty members in the department noted:

> I've finally gotten learning in the right place—not centered on me but on the students. And that's how teaching should be.

> I became more realistic in how students develop over time, what they're ready to incorporate and how many times you have to give them examples for them to understand something complex—teaching them in different perspectives so they can get it different ways.

In addition, one of the biology faculty members pointed out the personal benefit of viewing students as learners:

> [I changed] from teaching as something you do to your students to helping the learner to learn. Now I'm a diagnostician. Students always bring a different angle to things each quarter and that keeps me on my toes. And to engage with their minds is so much more interesting than to have them be a stenographer for my discourse on the biological systems.

Communication

Four faculty members we interviewed in the UW GIFTS taught in the Communication Department. We reviewed their interviews as a group to see if any teaching themes crossed them, and although several themes emerged from different pairs of faculty in this group, only one theme arose in all four interviews—asking students to apply course-based learning to their everyday lives. Although faculty members across the disciplines hoped that students would connect aspects of their courses to the world outside the university and to their own lives, the faculty we interviewed in the Communication Department appeared to require students to do that as part of their learning process. One motivation behind this approach was to ensure that students applied communication theory to the world around them. For example, one faculty member said:

> I want them to have these theoretical frameworks and concepts, and I want them to be able to apply them or relate them to everyday circumstances and experiences.

Another said something similar:

> Students like that class because theory becomes real to them; it's not just confined to the classroom. Incorporating speakers, plays, etc. helped my students think about the academic theories we learned outside the classroom.

One of the faculty members described mixing the "outside" with the "inside" in her use of class time. In her words:

> We might have a discussion at the first part of class, and then I'll send them out with a small group. I mix those groups so they aren't just going out with their friends. Sometimes I have them work in class and figure out what they want to look at first, and sometimes I have them just go out and take field notes. These are just class activities, and they aren't graded. That's the great thing about teaching this class. It's all around them, and I really want them just to start looking at things differently, so they are learning something that they didn't know about but that they live in their daily lives.

Also, one faculty member described this shift as one of the big directions of change she experienced in her teaching and noted that she felt some conflict in doing so. As she put it:

> I think the biggest change I've made over time is getting students to apply the concepts to their own experiences. And this is a shift I go back and forth on. I often have them write research papers or analyze a research article—so the class is very transparently research based. That's the "serious academic area" side to the class. And the whole thing about applying it to one's life—that sounds softer, but I've grown much more comfortable about doing that. I know they are getting a lot of depth about the material in class, but I also want them to have that depth for their own thinking and knowledge. So they get a lot of research still, but they also get a lot of trying out research conclusions. I've made that change, because I know that's what they are going to remember.

Differences: Foreign Language, Biology, Communication

There are some obvious differences across the three disciplinary areas—foreign language, biology, and communication. One difference is what we might call areas of primary value. For the foreign language faculty, creating a safe place for students to take risks was necessary if students were to learn a language, so that value was primary to faculty in those disciplines. For the biology faculty members, learning to think like scientists appeared to be the primary value. Furthermore, because students may come to introductory biology classes thinking that the study and practice of science was more centered on memorization—a view that may have negative effects on their performance in college-level classes—faculty felt they had to begin teaching students to think like scientists in their first biology courses. For the communication faculty, awareness that the theories and concepts in the discipline could be found walking around in the students' everyday worlds was of primary value.

Those central values played key roles in the changes the faculty made to their teaching. In order to help students feel safe enough to try speaking unfamiliar languages, the foreign language faculty, for example, reported creating in-class work that allowed students to risk speaking without immediate correction. As one language instructor said: "I learned that when they are talking in small groups, they are not watched by me or the whole class, so they aren't as hesitant or as worried about making mistakes. So I did more group activities after that."

Similarly, biology faculty reporting giving certain kinds of exams—even in very large classes—because they needed to require that students think, rather than just memorize. Communication faculty required students to apply theories—sometimes in class, sometimes during class but outside its four walls, and sometimes after class—because the living nature of those theories was of value. Thus, in each of the three disciplinary cases we examined, the primary learning value determined to a large extent the teaching practices the faculty members put into play.

Does this mean that faculty members have to be embedded deeply enough in their disciplines to know those primary values before they can begin to make meaningful changes to their teaching? Certainly their experience as graduate students embeds faculty members in their disciplines, giving them a deep understanding of the values, practices, and conventions that shape their fields. However, we suspect that being deeply embedded in the discipline and being deeply immersed in the *teaching* of the discipline may differ. It is possible that faculty must be deeply embedded in the *teaching* of their disciplines before they can begin making meaningful changes to their teaching. Ken Bain's (2004) words seem relevant to this point. Bain asserted that for good college teaching to occur, "we must struggle with the meaning of learning within our disciplines and how best to cultivate and recognize it" (p. 174).

In our three cases, we found evidence of faculty who had struggled with the meaning of learning in their disciplines and perhaps in that struggle, learned, themselves, how best to cultivate it.

Graduate Students and Faculty Members

Our work lives in higher education have brought us in frequent and close contact with graduate students, and their contributions to the learning of undergraduates is difficult to overestimate. Working as TAs who lead discussion sections for large lecture courses, graduate students are a critical element in the learning of early undergraduates. In their roles as TAs and in nearly all academic disciplines, graduate students translate, clarify, and expand students' content learning. Often, they also translate, clarify, and extend new students' understanding of how the university operates. In addition, most graduate students work one-on-one with undergraduates, helping them learn the skills necessary for success in the disciplines—for example, how to read in the discipline, how to writing effectively, how to think critically in the field, and how to conduct research appropriately. Graduate students often encourage undergraduates to keep going after they have received a hard grade and help them navigate the major. In addition, as we note later in this section, they are often good colleagues to each other, working hard to help each other become good teachers, sharing class notes and assignments, briefing each other on what has worked and not worked in particular courses, and sometimes leading teaching training sessions for new graduate students—some of whom have never *had* a TA before, let alone *been* one.

As we noted in chapters 2 and 6, the eight graduate students who participated in our two focus groups on teaching were in some ways exceptional. Many had taught their own courses, as well as led discussion sections as TAs for faculty members. They had reputations in their departments for being thoughtful about teaching, and, in fact, we found them so. In speaking about change in their teaching and reasons for that change, the graduate students with whom we spoke identified aspects of classroom teaching that were also important to our faculty interviewees—such as active learning and student engagement. However, if our theory is true—that struggling with others' learning and, therefore, with teaching in one's discipline leads to an understanding of how best to teach the primary values of one's field—we would expect graduate students to be different in their thinking about teaching and learning than the faculty were. Graduate students were newer to that struggle than were the faculty we interviewed. In fact, we noted some differences.

Changes and Reasons for Change

In some ways, what we heard from graduate students about changes in their teaching and their reasons for those change were somewhat fuzzy versions of what we had heard from faculty—images that seemed slightly out of focus. As we had with the faculty members, we asked the graduate students to describe one or two changes they had made to their teaching and to talk about why they had made them. Some of the changes they mentioned were similar to those that faculty members noted. For example, three of the eight said that they had added active learning strategies to their sections, and two noted changes they had made to assignments.

However, sometimes the changes that the graduate students noted differed from those mentioned by faculty. For example, three graduate students said they had made their classes more "structured," a category of change that faculty members rarely mentioned. For the graduate students, "adding structure" meant being more intentional about how class time was divided. For example:

> The big shift I made from when I [first] TAed the course and now is that I set up that structure, so for every article the student had to figure out the main claim, the support, and the objections. The first day I modeled what I wanted the students to do on the board, and then I'd stand up there and have them tell me. By the middle of the quarter I didn't even have to put the questions up there.

The reasons for the changes the graduate students noted also shared some similarities with those of faculty. For example, two indicated that they hoped to advance students' learning, one of the primary reasons for change given by faculty in UW GIFTS (chapter 5). Graduate students also noted that they wanted to engage undergraduates more deeply and that they had heard from the students that they wanted such changes.

But the primary motivation for change was not always the same as the motivators faculty described. While faculty members spoke of advancing students' learning and careful observation of the students both in class and in the work they produced for the class, the graduate students often had other reasons for change. For example, a motivator for one graduate student to add small group work to his class was the need to fill up class time and the sense that small groups were what students wanted. In her words:

> Now I have two-hour sections, and I can't do Socratic method for the whole time. I think that method came very naturally to me, and I hated small group work as a student, and I've consistently gotten criticism from a small group of students, saying

they wished there was more small group work. I'm bringing in extra people to help me with that but I still hate it. I realize though that different students learn in different ways. Now I'm realizing that you can structure that and make it better.

In speaking about a change in assignments, to give a second example, one student said that he would switch to using multiple-choice exams, because it was too difficult to grade open-ended, short-essay-type exams. As he put it:

I think one of the first things I realized is that I had this high-minded ideal that multiple-choice exams [did not lead] to conceptual thinking, and they would just study the concepts, cram, and forget them the next day. So if I really wanted them to learn things and retain them, I needed open-ended, case-based work. I learned a few things about that. First it was incredibly hard to grade, especially since it was my first experience. I wanted to be a good guy so having any sort of curve was tough. [Second] I don't think my ideal concept—that open-ended translates into more retained information—is true. So the first thing I'm going to do is not to think that the exam will be the thing that helps them retain the information but everything else besides that. At the end of the day—there's a difference between aided and unaided recall, and all a multiple-choice exam is is aided recall. Inevitably, in open-ended exams, if you ask what color is the dog, they will write a million and a half things hoping the color of the dog will be in there.

Also, closer to their own undergraduate experiences than most faculty were, the graduate students sometimes made changes because they remembered liking or disliking activities or assignments as students. Along these lines, one student described adding small group work in his sections:

I brought in the first change—where they ask questions and then work together to answer them—because I loved classes like that. When you answer the questions, you bring in new material. They liked it a lot, and I got the highest evaluations I ever got.

In their discussions of change, the faculty members rarely mentioned what they had loved or hated doing as undergraduates, although that does not mean that those thoughts were not part of their decisions about change.

Certainly, there was overlap in the changes graduate students made to their classes and their reasons for making them, but there were important differences as well. Sometimes the graduate students made changes for reasons that differed from those of faculty. Sometimes the changes, themselves, were different, and sometimes, so were the reasons. Even when the changes were similar, there was a sense that change was tentative—just as we might expect from early practitioners in any field.

Big Directions of Change for Graduate Students

We asked our two focus groups if they had noted any big directions of change in their teaching thus far, and two threads of conversation echoed some of what we heard from faculty members in the UW GIFTS. First, students in both focus groups noted that they were moving away from classrooms centered on lecturing. As one graduate student said,

> I've definitely moved away from lecturing and towards getting the students to do the work themselves with me as a guide and a model.

Second, some of the graduate students in one of the focus groups spoke about feeling more comfortable being themselves in the classroom than they had at first. The following interchange illustrates this direction:

> Student A: I've learned that I don't need to be good at every-thing. I've tried to facilitate a debate, for example, and I was horrible at it, so I might bring you in to do that. I'm getting more comfortable with students getting a different skill set from me in my class and something else from someone else.
> Student B: I agree—I'm getting more comfortable with my own personality and style in teaching right now.

Students' comments about the big directions of change in their teaching suggest that they were moving in the same directions as faculty members were, but they were at an earlier point on that path.

Changes Shaped by the TA Role

Graduate students often described changes and reasons for changes that reflected their unique teaching situations as TAs, where their work was subordinate to the goals and direction of others. This relationship seemed most evident in graduate students' efforts to help students in their discussion sections do well on the faculty member's exams. As one graduate student said,

> I was trying to point out the thought processes in the exam, what are the logical steps in how you should be approaching them.

Helping undergraduates learn material well enough to be successful on course exams was made more challenging when the graduate student had not yet seen those exams. In the words of two graduate students:

> I wasn't very familiar with the topic, so when it came to the time for the midterm, I realized I hadn't been focusing in the right place.

> It's hard to know what the professor wants or where he's going until you see that first exam.

Using discussion sections to help students do well on class exams was not only a direction that graduate students took because of their subordinate roles to the faculty members teaching the class. It was also something that the students in their discussion sections wanted. Indeed, graduate students noted that students complained if they did not feel the discussion sections had prepared them well for the exams.

These comments show that the graduate students leading discussion sections had to satisfy the needs of the students in relation to the faculty member's goals for them. The TAs were only partially responsible for setting their own agendas for their students' learning and following them. In a way, the TA position put them outside the students-content-faculty triangle that we referred to in chapter 6. Furthermore, it sometimes put them outside that struggle with the meaning of learning in their disciplines and how best to cultivate it. Instead, they were often in the position of having to convey someone else's sense of the meaning of learning in the discipline, which they were sometimes uncertain about until the first exam. One of the graduate students illuminated this relationship by noting that when a faculty member did a great job of conveying the meaning of learning in the discipline, he felt useless. In his words:

> I worked with this professor whom I've worked with really well and the goals are really clear: "Here are these arguments for what we know about the solar system and here's how we know it." And you go out and apply that everywhere in the solar system. The third time I taught it with the different professor, the goal seemed to be to convey as much as you possibly could about the solar system until the term was over. What was kind of ironic is that the first quarter I got here, I TAed for the better professor, and because he had everything perfectly done, I felt that I had nothing to say. I felt like a babysitter.

However, this graduate student also made it clear that TAs are not just robots. He continued to describe his experience, noting that he learned to set goals for his own section by teaching with the bad faculty member—a practice he found useful later. As he put it: "In my sections, I would go in and try to make goals for each section, because there didn't seem to be any in the class. But now, I do that every time I teach." In addition, he described moving a little bit away from a focus on content in language that is reminiscent of the faculty path we tracked in chapter 6:

> I've changed drastically from my first quarter here to my second. Each time I changed it. The first time in the section I tried to go over the exact points that the professor did in class, just reiterate them. And that wasn't helpful. It was mostly because it was the first time I taught this topic, and I didn't know what I was doing. . . . The third time, I was able to distill the lecture down into what I thought were the most important topics based on the exams I'd seen. I tried to minimize telling them something and maximize getting them to ask questions to get me to tell them what I wanted to say. The other was interactive learning—getting them to write something down and talk about it among themselves to arrive at something.

In addition, graduate students noted that there was a difference between their roles as TAs and their roles as teachers of their own courses. For example, one of the graduate students told us that, as a TA, he could often count on figuring out in the moment what to do with his discussion section, but now that he was teaching his own classes at another college, it did not work to "show up for class and not really know" where he was going. Planning and organization became more important.

Graduate Student and Faculty Members: Teaching Training

In speaking about the training they had received to serve as teaching assistants and teach their own courses, graduate students described an uneven terrain. Our institution offers TAs training and orientation at a TA conference at the beginning of the fall quarter; some of the graduate students in our focus groups found that conference helpful to their teaching and others did not. Furthermore, some had received significant help in teaching training from their departments, as this student described:

> The first quarter of your first year as a doctoral student in [my field], you have to take this Friday teaching effectiveness class. It's taught by a faculty member. She and a couple of older doctoral students teach this course and it's mainly about presentation and syllabus development. It really showed that they were invested in us being good teachers, because generally speaking at most R1 doctoral programs in [this discipline], you hear that the focus is entirely on your research and your first job is not to be learning to be a teacher. As someone who likes teaching, I think that focus [in my department] is a good thing. Then throughout the time, [that faculty member] is a resource and older students are resources, and we talk about what we are doing. The fact that that's a requirement . . . helps you internalize how important being a good teacher is.

Others had not received much help from their departments, as this student said: "We didn't have any instruction; we just learned it informally."

A few graduate students mentioned faculty members making classroom visits as part of teaching training. One of the graduate students found such visits very helpful, as he noted:

We have the faculty come in and observe our courses over the quarter. And some of them have been extremely generous in their time after that, talking about what we were doing and what they used to do. I've gotten very specific feedback about what I've done in there. That one-on-one interaction with half a dozen faculty members has been very helpful.

Students in both focus groups noted that TAs both formally and informally mentored other TAs in their departments, and that such mentorship constituted the majority of the teaching training for most new TAs. As members of that group said:

Student A: I think that's where the real mentoring happens. When I came here there was a grad student here who helped me out and that helped me immeasurably. I do that for others now.
Student B: I agree. That happened to me too.
Student C: I agree too. So much came to me from informal conversations during weekly TA meetings with professors and other grad students in the classes we were teaching.
Student D: I would corner TAs, and it was essential that they were in my discipline and in my specific area, too.

This conversation suggests that, unlike the total lack of training that nearly two-thirds of the faculty in the UW GIFTS described (chapter 2), today's graduate students receive some training in teaching, albeit uneven, while they are students. Furthermore, our focus group conversations suggested that some departments do a better job of helping students improve their teaching than do others. Graduate students noted that they would like more training in teaching in their disciplines and more information about research on learning.

Evidence from UW GIFTS suggests that our graduate students will seek out teaching training once they are on the job. Although 63% of the UW GIFTS faculty participants reported having received no training in teaching as graduate students, close to 74% of the 53 interviewees we asked said that they had received some training in teaching after graduate school. Some identified teaching sessions at disciplinary conferences as providing them with training in teaching. Most of them identified university workshops, retreats, and talks as the training they had received. Some faculty members noted, as the graduate student did, that when institutions provide such training they send a message to faculty that teaching matters. As one faculty member put it:

> The week [of teaching training for new faculty] here at UW— the Faculty Fellows thing. That was great. That was really good. There were examples of many different effective teaching styles. Teachers got up and gave hints about teaching—things they used. Some I agreed with, and some I didn't. It gave me a lot of perspective. And I saw others who were trying to teach, and it's good to see a lot of people who are trying hard to teach. Our jobs and advancement don't depend on teaching, so you have to want to improve your teaching. That the program existed was evidence that the UW wants good teaching. Sometimes we feel that no one would care if you did a good job. (Faculty member in the sciences/math)

It is difficult to know exactly what role these workshops, talks, and retreats play in the changes faculty made to their teaching. When asked to rate (on a 4-point scale) the contributions of 17 potential sources of change to the change in their own teaching, faculty members in UW GIFTS gave "general workshops / talks on teaching / learning" a 2.10 rating, on average, designating such experiences as having played a "minor role" in change in their teaching. Furthermore, they gave "disciplinary workshops / talks on teaching / learning" an average score of 1.89—a score that faculty comments linked to the scarcity of such training opportunities. Yet a review of the content of some of the UW workshops and events and of UW GIFTS faculty reports on conferences and workshops in their disciplines shows that often these events focused on the same kinds of change that faculty members reported. For instance, most of these events presented an argument for the use of active learning strategies in the classroom, a major direction of change reported by many faculty members. Because of this discrepancy, it is difficult to understand the full effects of teaching training on faculty practice.

However, what is obvious from these results is that the majority of faculty members in our sample had sought out information about student learning in their postgraduate teaching years, and they had put into play some of the ideas that we can reasonably expect were communicated in those venues. In contrast, the same array of UW workshops, retreats, and talks on teaching that is available to faculty is not readily available to graduate students. Furthermore, it is possible that a focus on teaching in the disciplines—rather than on general teaching strategies—might be especially important for novice teachers who are still learning what learning means in their disciplines and how best to convey and recognize that meaning in the classroom.

Differences: Graduate Students and Faculty

The differences we saw between graduate students' changes and reasons for change in their teaching were expected. Some of their changes and their reasons for them were similar to those that faculty described; some were quite different. Even when similar, their descriptions of their changes and reasons were weaker versions of the faculty versions—indicators that graduate students were earlier on the path of change than were the more experienced faculty members. Also, the differences in changes and reasons for change may indicate the different kinds of training available to both groups. Faculty members have access to a number of teaching training opportunities that graduate students do not, and they report that they make use of those opportunities, even though they did not find them to be major contributors to change in their teaching.

Summary: Differences

As this chapter makes clear, there are some differences in the changes and reasons for changes that we noted in faculty groups. For example, our examination of change through the lenses of the three disciplines suggested differences in the disciplinary values that shaped change. Our consideration of the experiences of faculty of color suggested that, although in many ways their experiences are quite similar to those of white faculty, they also differ in ways that might affect change in teaching. Furthermore, conversations with graduate students show that, although they appear to be on the same teaching and learning path that faculty described, they are at a different place on that path. Also, there are barriers—such as their TA roles, their inexperience teaching in their chosen fields, and their access to teaching training—to their forward motion.

Although these differences are interesting, it is important to remember that our observation of them came from small samples of faculty and graduate students and further research is needed to determine the strength of these differences. Also, it is important to note that, with the possible exception of disciplinary differences, the similarities across groups were much greater than the differences among them. All of the faculty we tracked made changes in their teaching and most of that change was made in response to their connection to, interaction with, and observations of course content and the students in their classes.

10

Learning in the Act of Teaching

I have been impressed with the degree to which the emphasis on good
teaching has increased since I began as a faculty member. Not only are the
expectations for teaching performance higher, but the effort to provide
teachers resources and assistance has grown dramatically. I know a number
of faculty who struggled a bit when young but benefited enormously from
various types of input and assistance. I am quite astounded and gratified by
the fact that all of my colleagues in [my department] are not only outstand-
ing scholars, but they are very effective teachers who can inspire students.
Of course, that continues to increase the challenge for me to do my part,
but that is how it should be.
—Faculty member in the social sciences

We began the UW Growth in Faculty Teaching Study with three
questions. First, without external pressure to do so, do faculty
make changes to their teaching? Second, if faculty do make changes
to their teaching, what kinds of changes do they tend to make? Finally, what causes faculty to make those changes? In order to answer
these questions, we interviewed 55 faculty members of all ranks from
across campus, asking them to describe two courses, some of the changes
they had made to those classes, and why they had made them. We also
asked them to rate numerically the importance of 17 potential sources
of change to their teaching. In addition, we conducted two focus groups
with graduate students in order to compare their thoughts about change
with those of the faculty members we interviewed.

We found that all faculty members made changes to their teaching,
and all but one made substantive changes in their courses—changes
that often rippled out and touched many aspects of their classes and of
themselves. The changes they made varied and included shifts in the use
of technology, revisions in assignments, alterations in the ways exams

were administered, the integration of active learning strategies into the classroom experience, and complete restructuring of the whole class, to give a few examples.

The changes faculty members made to their teaching and the reasons they made them were more closely connected to the relationships faculty had with their course content and with their students than they were with techniques that many consider important to effective teaching. Even so, the changes that faculty described were consistent with much of the literature on "best practices." For example, UW GIFTS faculty reported high expectations for students' thinking and learning; the creation of classroom environments that fostered and required students' critical engagement with ideas and content; the use of active learning strategies and assignments as ways to both engage students' thinking and assess their learning; a sense of the importance of engaging students in disciplinary thinking; and the value of creating diverse learning experiences for students (Bain, 2004; Weimer, 2002; Barkley, 2010; Barr & Tagg, 1995, Angelo & Cross, 1993).

External influences on growth in teaching—for example, reading about best practices—played a role in change, but it was a small one. However, we note, here, that it would be difficult to be working in higher education today and *not* to have heard of "active learning" or "student engagement." Research about the learning benefits of active student engagement are included in most of the UW's faculty development activities, and many faculty members in our study had participated in one of our faculty development events or those offered by other institutions.

Even though they had participated in faculty development opportunities around teaching, it appeared that the path of change in teaching for most faculty members, although sometimes a long and challenging journey—was also an intimate one. Change emerged primarily from the interactions among faculty members, students, and the subjects of their classes. Faculty made changes because they noticed when students were not learning what they intended students to learn. They observed that *this* group of beginners did not understand how to write an effective argument in philosophy, for example, or *this* group of seniors needed more information about how to design a research study in biology. Indeed, about 85% of the reasons and sources for change that faculty described were "internal"—that is, changes that emerged from the faculty member's interaction with her students and course.

Similarly, for most faculty, the changes they made to their teaching also had to meet the test of effectiveness to be retained. In fact, sometimes the "best practices" that faculty members adopted did not improve learning, and faculty members described changing them once again.

As the faculty comments in this book illustrate, change appeared to begin when faculty members felt comfortable enough to step away from the need to demonstrate their own mastery of content to students and to enter the classroom as learners themselves. But from that point on, faculty paths differed quite a bit. Some were bumpy and uneven. Some were easily traveled. Some stopped suddenly and without reason. Faculty members in the UW GIFTS frequently described changes emerging from other changes, sometimes in an ongoing process that left the whole class transformed. Sometimes they described creating whole courses that they later felt they had to scrap, as this faculty member said:

> I didn't tinker with the class. I just dropped it all in the can. That's how I fixed it. (Faculty member in the social sciences)

For many, the process was a constant series of smaller changes, some of which worked and were retained and others that fell by the wayside. We heard about faculty members struggling with issues and ideas that kept them up at night and about engagement with intellectual and personal realities that were both humbling and rewarding.

Faculty members often noted that the changes they brought to their teaching required and fostered their own self-discovery and transformation. They also noted that the interaction between their own growth and their teaching was dynamic, with changes in their personal lives altering their course designs and challenging their approaches to teaching. Perhaps this close interaction between the teaching lives and personal lives of college faculty explains why the path of change does not seem to have an end. All faculty members reported that they were still making changes to their teaching—those who had been teaching for two years and those who had been teaching for more than 30—and presumably the lives of all faculty members continue to change as well.

Although we heard about fascinating, engaging classes in conversations with faculty members, results from the UW GIFTS do not argue that the faculty members in the study were effective teachers. We did not set out to measure, compare, or sift their students' learning or to evaluate their interviews in the light of their course evaluations. However, our results clearly show that all of the faculty members we interviewed were working hard to *become* effective teachers. They were doing what those of us involved in assessment of student learning would hope they were doing—carefully weighing their students' classroom responses and behaviors; carefully examining their students' coursework; challenging themselves to bring more of themselves into the classroom; thinking carefully about how to weave together the teaching of content and skills, such as critical thinking, in a discipline.

All of this careful focus that our faculty described giving to their teaching has been going on at the same time that grim prophets are ringing the death knell for higher education. They may note the "underachievement" of U.S. colleges (Bok, 2006) or the dismal future of higher education in the United States (U.S. Department of Education, 2006). Pundits are loudly warning the public about the dangers of tenure, collective bargaining, and faculty involvement in research (ignoring, of course, the reality that, without research, there would be nothing for teachers to teach). Furthermore, researchers are using standardized tests to argue that college students are not learning to think or write (Arum & Roksa, 2011), even though those tests are unlikely to measure what faculty members are actually teaching students about writing and thinking (Bazerman, 2000; Beyer et al., 2007; Bransford et al., 2000; Donald, 2002; Pace & Middendorf, 2004) and, therefore, cannot measure what students are learning in college. These collective concerns about higher education, their use as political drums, and the multiple policies and plans proposed to "fix" them often obscure the reality that the U.S. system of higher education is judged to be the best in the world (Times Higher Education, 2011).

Our study was conducted in exactly the kind of institution these critics would point to as a problem—a huge research university, where faculty often teach classes of up to 770 undergraduates and where there are few external demands or rewards for doing that job well. Furthermore, ours is an institution where undergraduates sometimes find themselves in the teaching hands of graduate students, rather than in those of tenured faculty members, and students, especially in their freshman and sophomore years, report they sometimes feel like a number.

As are all universities, large and small, we are far from perfect. But the UW GIFTS shows us that on this day today, faculty members of every race, gender, age, rank, and academic discipline are entering classes of every size and every level with ideas about what they hope students will learn and what they need to do to help them learn those things. They enter with new activities about how to improve student interaction in their classes, new video clips to help students apply concepts to situations outside academia, new writing assignments to help students build skills in reasoning in their disciplines, new ways of teaching old techniques, new ideas for generating creativity and innovation, new approaches to scholarship. They carry these changes into their classes because they care about their students' learning and because they want to do a good job. They enter these classrooms to transform students, and they end up also transforming their own work and themselves.

As our faculty members walk through those doors of classrooms all over the country, we call on those studying higher education and those working in faculty development, both inside and outside university structures, to pay closer attention to what these faculty members are actually doing in there. What is happening in those classrooms is the heart of the college experience, and as the UW GIFTS clearly demonstrates, it is complex, illuminating, inspiring.

APPENDICES

Appendix A:
UW GIFTS Interview
Questions for Faculty

Faculty member:

Department:

1. How long have you been a faculty member at this institution?

2. Have you taught at other places? If so, where?

3. Will you please describe two of the undergraduate classes you have taught more than once at the UW—maybe one you typically teach and the one you love to teach the best—and tell us first how long you've taught the class? (Name and number, size, TA-help, typical class status of students, content, assignments, technology).

4. Looking first at that first class and thinking about how you taught it the first time or two and how you teach it now, have you changed your teaching of that class in any way or not? Please describe some of the changes you've made and what motivated those changes?

5. What would you say were the effects of these changes on your students' learning and how could you tell?

6. What about that second class—any changes in the teaching you've done for that class over the years? Can you describe some of those changes and what motivated them?

7. What would you say were the effects of these changes on your students' learning and how could you tell?

8. Thinking about your undergraduate teaching career over the years, what would you say are the big directions of change in your teaching, if any, and what has caused you to move in those directions?

9. Have you made any mistakes in your teaching—in any of your classes—that you've had to fix? If so, can you tell us how you knew you'd made a mistake and what you did about it?

10. Thinking back to your graduate school years, did you receive any direct instruction in teaching while getting your PhD? If so, what kind?

11. Have you received any formal instruction in teaching since then—retreats, workshops, conferences, talks?

12. Are you still making changes to your teaching?

13. I'm going to read you a list of sources of change, and I'd like you to rate them from 1–4, with:

1 = played no role in the changes you've made to your teaching over the years

2 = played a minor role in the changes you've made

3 = played a moderately important role in the changes you've made

4 = played a significant role in the changes you've made to your teaching.

1. Monitoring your students' behaviors in class—listening, observing body language, taking their questions into account

2. Student performance on tests

3. Student performance on assignments (papers, projects, presentations, etc.)

4. Information that TAs or RAs gave you about your courses

5. Formal mentoring from another faculty member

6. Follow up: Set up by departments? How did it occur?

7. Informal feedback from another faculty member about your class

8. Your own observation and/or conversations with fellow faculty members about teaching

9. Course evaluations

10. Money/funding from inside or outside the UW that allowed you to make changes to your teaching

11. Workshops, retreats, presentations on teaching and learning in your discipline

12. General workshops, retreats, presentations on teaching and learning

13. Books on teaching and learning in your discipline

14. General books on teaching and learning
15. Educational technology—course websites, classroom technology
16. Class size
17. Your own maturity/growth (Explain)
18. Changes in students (Explain)
19. Other

14. Is there anything else you'd like to tell me about your teaching role at the UW?

Appendix B:
Focus Group Questions for Graduate Students

1. What department are you in, how long have you been a graduate student here, and what kinds of teaching experience have you had here?

2. Have you taught at other places? If so, where?

3. Will you please describe an undergraduate class you have taught or TAed for more than once at the UW.

4. Thinking about how you taught or TAed for that class the first time or two and how you teach it now, have you changed your teaching of that class in any way or not? Please describe some of the changes you've made and what motivated those changes?

5. What would you say were the effects of these changes on your students' learning and how could you tell?

6. Thinking about your teaching work over the years, what would you say are the big directions or themes of change in your teaching, if any? What has brought those changes about?

7. Have you made any mistakes in your teaching—in any of your classes—that you've had to fix? If so, can you tell us how you knew you'd made a mistake and what you did about it?

8. Have you received any direct instruction in teaching while getting your PhD? If so, what kind and how helpful has it been?

9. Is there anything else you'd like to tell us about your teaching role at the UW?

Appendix C:
Tables on Statistically Significant Differences

Table C1. Pairwise comparisons of faculty ranks for advancing learning as a reason for change

Ranks Compared	Number of Times "Advance Learning" Was Not Given as a Reason for Change	Number of Times "Advance Learning" was Given as a Reason for Change	p
Associate Professor	14 (58%)	10 (42%)	None
Assistant Professor	17 (55%)	14 (45%)	
Associate Professor	14 (58%)	10 (42%)	***
Lecturer	0 (0%)	9 (100%)	
Associate Professor	14 (58%)	10 (42%)	None
Professor	16 (59%)	11 (41%)	
Associate Professor	14 (58%)	10 (42%)	None
Senior Lecturer	9 (56%)	7 (44%)	
Assistant Professor	17 (55%)	14 (45%)	***
Lecturer	0 (0%)	9 (100%)	
Assistant Professor	17 (55%)	14 (45%)	None
Professor	16 (59%)	11 (41%)	
Assistant Professor	17 (55%)	14 (45%)	None
Senior Lecturer	9 (56%)	7 (44%)	
Lecturer	0 (0%)	9 (100%)	***
Professor	16 (59%)	11 (41%)	
Lecturer	0 (0%)	9 (100%)	***
Senior Lecturer	9 (56%)	7 (44%)	
Professor	16 (59%)	11 (41%)	None
Senior Lecturer	9 (56%)	7 (44%)	

$*p < 0.05$ $**p < 0.01$ $***p < 0.001$

Table C2. Pairwise comparisons of class size for advancing learning as a reason for change

Class Sizes Compared	Number of Times "Advance Learning" Was Not Given as a Reason for Change	Number of Times "Advance Learning" Was Given as a Reason for Change	p
Large	18 (46%)	21 (54%)	*
Medium	25 (74%)	9 (26%)	
Large	18 (46%)	21 (54%)	None
Small	13 (38%)	21 (62%)	
Medium	25 (74%)	9 (26%)	**
Small	13 (38%)	21 (62%)	

*$p < 0.05$ **$p < 0.01$ ***$p < 0.001$

Table C3. Pairwise comparisons of ethnicity for values and teaching philosophy as a reason for change

Groups Compared	Number of Times Values/Philosophy Was Not Given as a Reason for Change	Number of Times Values/Philosophy Was Given as a Reason for Change	p
White faculty members	84 (90%)	9 (10%)	***
Faculty members of color	7 (50%)	7 (50%)	

*$p < 0.05$ **$p < 0.01$ ***$p < 0.001$

NOTES

Chapter 1. GIFTS

1. All quotations that begin chapters are from UW GIFTS interviewees. Faculty members' real names are never used.

2. It is important to note that table 1.1 does not take into account the time faculty members spent on activities related to teaching, such as advising students, which the FSSE also tracked. Furthermore, the FSSE did not ask faculty members about other time-consuming aspects of their work lives, such as the time they spend teaching and working one-to-one with graduate students, the time they spend applying for grants—a regular part of the working lives of most faculty at R1s these days—or the time they spend doing departmental work and institutional work—part of all faculty members' work lives, regardless of the size or mission of their institutions. Adding these aspects of faculty work into the table might lead to a total number of hours of work per week that would surprise some people.

Chapter 2. How Was the Study Conducted?

1. Lecturers are on a different "track" than "tenure-track" professors, and they are evaluated only on teaching quality. Senior lecturers have worked at the UW longer than lecturers. The interviewees were selected before principal lectureships were made more widely available to senior lecturers.

2. When quoting faculty throughout the book, we have identified faculty members in forest resources and oceanography with the science/math disciplinary area and faculty members in informatics with social sciences.

Chapter 3. What Courses Did Faculty Describe?

1. This is the intellectual reality in which faculty and students in college operate, which raises questions about the validity of using standardized generic tests such as the Collegiate Learning Assessment, to measure learning, at any point in a student's academic path.
2. The numbers of students and teaching assistants per class often varied when faculty described classes they taught more than once; these numbers represent the averages of those reported.
3. Bloom's Taxonomy is a hierarchical system of classifying learning tasks or objectives, beginning with "easier" kinds of learning, such as "remembering" and "understanding" and moving into more complex learning tasks, such as application, synthesis, evaluation, or creation.

Chapter 5. Why Did Faculty Make Changes to Their Courses?

1. They also accounted for more than half (55.5%) of all the *changes* that faculty members described making in their courses.
2. Faculty Fellows is a week-long teaching training workshop for all newly hired UW faculty members.
3. Unlike the "observation" category that emerged as a prominent reason for change from faculty descriptions of their courses (table 5.1), in our list of 17 items, we separated observations into three types: observations of students' behavior, questions, and interactions in class; students' performance on assignments; and students' performance on exams and quizzes.
4. The UW course evaluation system is used in more than 12,000 UW courses annually, and at over 60 other postsecondary institutions in the United States.

Chapter 9. Were There Differences across Groups?

1. For a sometimes humorous account of a student's experience with racial microaggression in college, see Lull Mengesha's *The Only Black Student* (2009).
2. Women faculty in the UW GIFTS sometimes spoke of behaviors that we might have considered gender related, but we did not gather details on these interactions.
3. A UW study/tutoring center for underrepresented students.
4. The Center for Learning and Undergraduate Enrichment (CLUE) is a nightly UW study/tutoring center.

BIBLIOGRAPHY

Angelo, T. A. & Cross, K. P. (1993). *Classroom assessment techniques: A handbook for college teachers*. San Francisco: Jossey-Bass.

Ariely, D., Gneezy, U., Loewenstein, G., & Mazar, N. (2009). Large stakes and big mistakes. *The Review of Economic Studies* 76, 451–469. http://duke.edu/~dandan/Papers/largeStakes.pdf. Accessed on 6 November 2011.

Arum, R. & Roksa, J. (2011). *Academically adrift: Limited learning on college campuses*. Chicago: University of Chicago Press.

Austin, A. E. (2002). Creating a bridge to the future: Preparing new faculty to face changing expectations in a shifting context. *The Review of Higher Education* 26(2), 119–144.

Astin, A. W. (1993). *What matters in college: Four critical years revisited*. San Francisco: Jossey-Bass.

Baiocco, S. A. & DeWaters, J. N. (1998). *Successful college teaching: Problem-solving strategies of distinguished professors*. Needham Heights, MA: Allyn & Bacon.

Bain, K. (2004). *What the best college teachers do*. Cambridge, MA: Harvard University Press.

Barkley, E. F. (2010). *Student engagement techniques: A handbook for college faculty*. San Francisco: Jossey-Bass.

Barr, R. B. & Tagg, J. (1995). A new paradigm for undergraduate learning. *Change: The Magazine of Higher Learning* 27(6), 12–25.

Baxter Magolda, M. (1992). *Knowing and reasoning in college*. San Francisco: Jossey-Bass.

Bazerman, C. (2000). *Shaping written knowledge: The genre and activity of the experimental article in science*. Madison, WI: University of Wisconsin Press.

Beecher, T. & Trowler, P. R. (2001). *Academic tribes and territories: Intellectual enquiry and the culture of disciplines.* Suffolk, UK: St. Edmundsbury Press.

Berliner, D. C. (1991). Educational psychology and pedagogical expertise: New findings and new opportunities for thinking about training. *Educational Psychologist* 26(2), 145–155.

Beyer, C. H., Gillmore, G. M., & Fisher, A. T. (2007). *Inside the undergraduate experience: The University of Washington's Study of Undergraduate Learning.* San Francisco: Jossey-Bass.

Beyer, C. H. & Graham, J. B. (1990). The link between high school and first-term college writing. University of Washington, Office of Educational Assessment Report.

Beyer, C. H. & Graham, J. B. (1992). The freshman-sophomore writing study: 1989–91. University of Washington, Office of Educational Assessment Report.

Beyer, C. H. & Graham, J. B. (1994). The junior-senior writing study: 1991–93. University of Washington, Office of Educational Assessment Report.

Beyer, J. (2012). Women's engagement with male-dominated online communities. In Gajjala, R. & Oh, Y. J. (eds.), *Where have all the cyber-feminists gone?* New York: Peter Lang Publishing.

Biggs, J. (1999). What the student does: Teaching for enhanced learning. *Higher Education Research & Development* 18(1), 57–75.

Biglan, A. (1973). The characteristics of subject matter in different academic areas. *Journal of Applied Psychology* 57(3), 195–203.

Bloom, B. S. & Krathwohl, D. R. (1956). *Taxonomy of educational objectives: The classification of educational goals, by a committee of college and university examiners. Handbook 1: Cognitive domain.* New York: Longmans, Green.

Bok, D. (2006). Our underachieving colleges. Princeton, NJ: Princeton University Press.

Bonwell, C. C. & Sutherland, T. E. (1996). The active learning continuum: Choosing activities to engage students in the classroom. *New Directions for Teaching and Learning* 67, 3–16.

Boyer, E. (1990). *Scholarship reconsidered.* Princeton, NJ: Carnegie Foundation.

Bransford, J. D., Brown, A. L., & Cocking, R. R. (eds.) For the National Research Council. (2000). *How people learn: Brain, mind, experience, and school.* Washington, DC: National Academy Press.

Cham, J. (1997–2012). *Piled higher and deeper.* www.phdcomics.com.

Cranton, P. (2011). A transformative perspective on the Scholarship of Teaching and Learning. *Higher Education Research & Development* 30(1), 75–86.

Delucchi, M. & Korgen, K. (2002). "We're the customer—we pay the tuition": Student consumerism among undergraduate sociology majors. *Teaching Sociology* 30(1), 100–107.

Deresiewicz, W. (2011). Faulty towers: The crisis in higher education. *The Nation*, May 4, 2011.

Donald, J. G. (2002). *Learning to think: Disciplinary perspectives*. San Francisco: Jossey- Bass.

Elbow, P. (1997). High stakes and low stakes in assigning and responding to writing. *New Directions for Teaching and Learning* 69, 5–13.

Ewell, P. (1997). Organizing for learning. *AAHE Bulletin*.

Fairweather, J. S. & Rhoads, R. A. (1995). Teaching and the faculty role: Enhancing the commitment to instruction in American colleges and universities. *Educational Evaluation and Policy Analysis* 17(2), 179–194.

Gillmore, G. M. & Greenwald, A. G. (1998). Using statistical adjustment to reduce biases in student ratings. *American Psychologist* 54(7), 518–519.

Greenwald, A. G. & Gillmore, G. M. (1997). No pain, no gain? The importance of measuring course workload in student ratings. *Journal of Educational Psychology* 89(4), 743–751.

Hativa, N., Barak, R., & Simhi, E. (2001). Exemplary university teachers: Knowledge and beliefs regarding effective teaching, dimensions and strategies. *The Journal of Higher Education* 72(6), 699–729.

Hurtado, S., Millem, J., Clayton-Pedersen, A., & Allen, W. (1999). Enacting diverse learning environments: Improving the climate for racial/ethnic diversity in higher education. *ASHE-ERIC Higher Education Report* 26(8). Washington, DC: The George Washington University, Graduate School of Education and Human Development.

Hutchings, P. & Shulman, L. S. (1999). The scholarship of teaching: New elaborations, new developments. *Change: The Magazine of Higher Learning* 31(5), 10–15.

Indiana University Center for Postsecondary Research. (2010). Faculty survey of student engagement frequency report, all doctoral/research university. http://fsse.iub.edu/pdf/FSSE_IR_2010/FSSE10-GrandFreqs-(DRU-All-TS).pdf. Accessed on 10 May 2011.

Kane, R., Sandretto, S., & Heath, C. (2002). Telling half the story: A critical review of research on the teaching beliefs and practices of university academics. *Review of Educational Research* 72, 177–228.

Kohn, A. (1999). *Punished by rewards*. Boston: Houghton Mifflin.

Kramer, R. M. (1998). Paranoid cognition in social systems: Thinking and acting in the shadow of doubt. *Personality & Social Psychology Review* 2(4), 251–276.

Kuh, G. & Ikenberry, S. (2009). More than you think, less than we need: Learning outcomes assessment in American higher education, National Institute for Learning Outcomes Assessment. http://learningoutcomesassessment.org/documents/niloafullreportfinal2.pdf. Accessed on 1 February 2012.

Leslie, D. W. (2002). Resolving the dispute: Teaching is academe's core value. *The Journal of Higher Education* (73)1, 49–73.

Light, R. (2001). Making the most of college: Students speak their minds. Cambridge, MA: Harvard University Press.

Lilienfeld, S. O. (2010). Fear: Can't live with it, can't live without it. *Phi Kappa Phi Forum* 90(3), 16–18.

Lindlof, T. & Taylor, B. (2010). *Qualitative communication research methods* (3rd ed.).Thousand Oaks, CA: Sage Publications.

Lowery, J. W. (2004). Student affairs for a new generation. *New Directions for Student Services* 106, 87–99.

Mazur, E. (1997). *Peer instruction: A user's manual*. Upper Saddle River, NJ: Prentice Hall.

McAlpine, L., Weston, C., Berthiaume, D., & Fairbank-Roch, G. (2006). How do instructors explain their thinking when planning and teaching? *Higher Education* 51, 125–155.

McKee, A. (2003). *Textual analysis: A beginner's guide*. London: Sage Publications.

Menges, R. (2000). Shortcomings of research on evaluating and improving teaching in higher education. *New Directions for Teaching and Learning* 83, 5–11.

Menges, R. J. & Austin, A. E. (2001). Teaching in higher education. In Richardson, V. (ed.), *Handbook of research on teaching* (4th ed.). Washington, DC: American Educational Research Association, 1066–1101, 1122–1156.

Mengesha, L. (2009). *The only black student*. Seattle: Mengesha Publishing.

Merriam, S. B. (2001). *Qualitative research and case study applications in education*. San Francisco: Jossey-Bass.

Nathan, M. J. & Petrosino, A. (2002). Expert blind spot among pre-service mathematics and science teachers. Paper presented at the annual meeting of the International Conference of the Learning Sciences, Seattle, Washington, 23–26 October 2002.

Neumann, R., Parry, S., & Becher, T. (2002). Teaching and learning in their disciplinary contexts: A conceptual analysis. *Studies in Higher Education* 27, 405–417.

Norton, L., Richardson, J. T. E., Hartley, J., Newstead, S., & Mayes, J. (2005). Teachers' beliefs and intentions concerning teaching in higher education. *Higher Education* 50, 537–571.

Nyquist, J. D., Manning, L., Wulff, D. H., Austin, A. E., Sprague, J., Fraser, P. K., Calcagno, C., & Woodford, B. (1999). On the road to becoming a professor. *Change: The Magazine of Higher Learning* 31(3), 18–27.

Pace, D. & Middendorf, J. (eds.) (2004). *Decoding the disciplines: Helping students learn disciplinary ways of thinking*. San Francisco: Jossey-Bass.

Palmer, P. (1998). *The courage to teach*. San Francisco: Jossey-Bass.

Palmer, P. & Zajonc, A. (2010). *The heart of higher education*. San Francisco: Jossey-Bass.

Peterson, J., Beyer, C., Chang, S., & Giesbrecht, A. (2009). The University of Washington Senior Research Study. http://www.washington.edu/oea/pdfs/reports/OEAReport1001.pdf. Accessed on 15 November 2011.

Phillips, D. C. (1995). The good, the bad, and the ugly: The many faces of constructivism. *Educational Researcher* 24(7), 5–12.

Pierce, C. M., Carew, J. V., Pierce-Gonzalez, D., & Wills, D. (1977). An experiment in racism: TV commercials. *Education and Urban Society* 10(1), 61–87.

Pitre, E., Beyer, C., Lemire, S., & Snyder, C. (2006). University of Washington study of attrition and retention. http://www.washington.edu/oea/pdfs/reports/UWSTARReport.pdf. Accessed on 15 November 2011.

Seymour, E. & Hewitt, N. M. (1997). *Talking about leaving: Why undergraduates leave the sciences*. Boulder, CO: Westview Press.

R Development Core Team, R Foundation for Statistical Computing. (2011). R: A language and environment for statistical computing. http://www.R-project.org. Accessed on 26 October 2011.

Shenoy, G. F. (2011). Why assess student learning? What the "measuring stick" series revealed. *National Institute for Learning Outcomes Assessment Newsletter*, November. http://learningoutcomesassessment.org/NILOApieces.html. Accessed on 22 November 2011.

Shepard, L. (2000). The role of classroom assessment in teaching and learning. In Richardson, V. (ed.), *Handbook of research on teaching* (4th ed.). Washington, DC: American Educational Research Association, 1066–1101. Also available as a technical report online at http://datause.cse.ucla.edu/DOCS/las_rol_2000.pdf. Accessed on 15 November 2011.

Shulman, L. S. (1988). A union of insufficiencies: Strategies for teacher assessment in a period of educational reform. *Educational Leadership* 46(3), 36–42.

Solórzano, D., Ceja, M., & Yosso, T. (2000). Critical race theory, racial microaggressions, and campus racial climate: The experiences of African American college students. *The Journal of Negro Education* 69(1/2), 60–73.

Sue, D. W., Capodilupo, C. M., & Holder, A. M. B. (2008). Racial microaggressions in the life experience of Black Americans. *Professional Psychology: Research and Practice* 39(3), 329–336.

Tagg, J. (2012). Why does the faculty resist change? *Change: The Magazine of Higher Learning*, January/February. http://www.changemag.org. Accessed on 31 January 2012.

Taylor, E., Gillborn, D., & Ladson-Billings, G. (eds.) (2009). *Foundations of critical race theory in education*. New York: Routledge.

Taylor, E. & Antony, J. S. (2000). Stereotype threat reduction and wise schooling: Towards the successful socialization of African American doctoral students in education. *Journal of Negro Education* 69(3), 184–198.

Times Higher Education. (2011). http://www.timeshighereducation.co.uk/world-university-rankings/2010-2011/analysis-usa-top-universities.html. Accessed on 6 November 2011.

U.S. Department of Education. (2006). A test of leadership: Charting the future of U.S. higher education. Report of the commission appointed by Secretary of Education Margaret Spellings. http://www2.ed.gov/about/bdscomm/list/hiedfuture/reports/final-report.pdf. Accessed on 19 May 2011.

Weimer, M. (2002). *Learner-centered teaching: Five key changes to practice*. San Francisco: Jossey-Bass.

Welch, B. L. (1951). On the comparison of several mean values: an alternative approach. *Biometrika* 38, 330–336.

Wineburg, S. (1991). On the reading of historical texts: Notes on the breach between school and academy. *American Educational Research Journal* 28(3), 495–519.

Wineburg, S. (2001). Interview with Randy Bass. Visible Knowledge Project, Georgetown University, from http://crossroads.georgetown.edu/vkp/conversations/participants/html. Accessed on 12 October 2006.

INDEX